THE PESHARIM AND QUMRAN HISTORY

THE PESHARIM
and
QUMRAN HISTORY

Chaos or Consensus?

JAMES H. CHARLESWORTH

with appendixes by
Lidija Novakovic

WILLIAM B. EERDMANS PUBLISHING COMPANY
GRAND RAPIDS, MICHIGAN / CAMBRIDGE, U.K.

Wm. B. Eerdmans Publishing Co.
255 Jefferson Ave. S.E., Grand Rapids, Michigan 49503 /
P.O. Box 163, Cambridge CB3 9PU U.K.

Printed in the United States of America

07 06 05 04 03 02   7 6 5 4 3 2 1

Library of Congress Cataloging-in-Publication Data

The pesharim and Qumran history: chaos or consensus? /
James H. Charlesworth; with appendixes by Lidija Novakovic.
p.   cm.
Includes bibliographical references and index.
ISBN 0-8028-3988-6 (pbk.)
1. Dead Sea scrolls.   2. Bible. O.T. — Criticism, interpretation, etc., Jewish.
3. Qumran community.   4. Qumran community — Historiography.
I. Novakovic, Lidija.   II. Title.

BM487.C43   2002
296.1'55 — dc21

2002069679

www.eerdmans.com

Contents

Contents

Preface

The Pesharim, Other Commentaries, and Related Documents, volume 6B of the Princeton Theological Seminary Dead Sea Scrolls Project, brings together for the first time in one volume the texts and translations of all the pesharim together with other related Qumran commentaries.[1] These documents are separated into three categories. First are collected the "Pesharim." This category contains 17 pesharim (and one fragment) that were composed at Qumran. Second are assembled the "Other Commentaries." This second category collects together commentaries that are similar in genre to the pesharim but are not pesharim, even though the word פשר occasionally appears in them. The third category contains the "Related Documents." These works are neither pesharim nor strictly commentaries. While they do not contain the word פשר, they are related, sometimes loosely, to the genre of pesharim.

The Pesharim, Other Commentaries, and Related Documents illustrates the broad spectrum of Qumran exegeses and hermeneutics. The volume draws attention to other early Jewish compositions, or sections of them, that are quasi-commentaries, like the *Rule of the Community* (viz. 1QS 8.13-16), *Damascus Document, Temple Scroll, Genesis Apocryphon, Wicked and Holy* (in which פשר appears in 4Q180 frg. 1 lines 1,7). Also to be considered within the world of biblical commentaries and hermeneutics are the Targumim, and some of the Biblical Apocrypha and Pseudepigrapha found in the Qumran caves. One should not forget the

---

1. James H. Charlesworth et al., eds., *The Dead Sea Scrolls: The Pesharim, Other Commentaries, and Related Documents.* PTSDSSP 6B (Tübingen: Mohr [Siebeck]; Louisville: Westminster John Knox, 2002).

exegetical dimensions of the so-called parabiblical works, compositions now labeled "Re-written Bible," and expansions of biblical books. Finally, there is only a fine line that separates these compositions from the textual fluidity of books preserved, sometimes in later edited forms, in the *Biblia Hebraica*.

The volume also clarifies that not all Qumran commentaries are pesharim, and that there is a variety within them. For example, the *Nahum Pesher* has numerous references to known historical persons, but *Psalm Pesher 1* does not contain a clear reference to historical luminaries.

The present monograph focuses on one storm-center of controversy in publications devoted to Qumran commentaries, generally, and the pesharim, specifically. An apparent chaos has been caused by scholars arguing over the proper means to obtain historical information from the pesharim. The central question is, thus: how and in what ways, if at all, can one obtain reliable historical data from the pesharim?

The focused study in this monograph will be useful to specialists in Second Temple Judaism by providing a better understanding of the beginnings and methods of Jewish biblical interpretation and the history preserved in the pesharim. It will be important to New Testament specialists in providing insights into the hermeneutics and exegesis that antedate the Jewish compositions preserved in the New Testament. Both the Qumranic pesharim and the New Testament books employ a similar method. The authors of the pesharim and the authors of the New Testament books shared a similar means of interpreting the same Scriptures. These were interpreted, the authors claimed, through special revelation and with the help of "the Holy Spirit." The authors belonged to different Jewish communities with different agendas, but they were both (especially Jesus' group) shaped by messianology. Clearly, the Qumran sect and Jesus' sect were shaped by a shared penchant to think that they were living in the last days when God's promises would be fulfilled in and for them. Both the Qumran pesharim and the New Testament documents are to be perceived as Jewish works, and the methodology for interpreting Torah should be labeled as fulfillment interpretation (or as fulfillment hermeneutics); that is, the words of Scripture are perceived as fulfilled in the life of each community.

Two appendixes to this monograph contain data that I hope will be helpful in studying the pesharim. Biblical excerpts followed by Qumran interpretations define the pesharim. These lemmata frequently preserve readings of books in the *Biblia Hebraica* that are dissimilar to those in the so-called Masoretic Text. Do these divergent readings help us comprehend Qumran's boldness in shaping texts? Do the variants help us discern the provenience of possible text types and also the evolution and fluidity of the biblical texts that became canonized? Such questions can be more adequately answered thanks to the list of variants compared with known text types compiled by Professor Lidija Novakovic.

The critical texts and translations used in this monograph are taken from the Princeton Theological Seminary Dead Sea Scrolls Project, volume 6B. It is entitled *The Pesharim, Other Commentaries, and Related Documents.* I am grateful to Mohr Siebeck Verlag and Westminster/John Knox Press for permission to use these texts and translations.

I am deeply indebted to Frank Cross, David Noel Freedman, J. Ross Wagner, and Doron Mendels for reading earlier drafts of this publication and helping me to improve it. John Strugnell and I discussed this work over several weeks; his insights and suggestions are deeply appreciated. Philip R. Davies and George J. Brooke also read a draft of this publication and made significant helpful insights. Listening to their insights helped me avoid idiosyncracies and aim for a balanced presentation that carefully represented their own opinions, which sometimes differ markedly from my own. Casey D. Elledge and Cory P. Hall helped me polish the English presentation and discussed some problems with me. I am grateful to Lidija Novakovic for publishing some of her research in this monograph.

JHC
Princeton
July 2001

Abbreviations

ABD	*Anchor Bible Dictionary,* ed. David Noel Freedman
ABRL	Anchor Bible Reference Library
ANRW	*Aufstieg und Niedergang der römischen Welt,* ed. Hildegard Temporini and Wolfgang Haase
BAR	*Biblical Archaeology Review*
BASOR	*Bulletin of the American Schools of Oriental Research*
BETL	Bibliotheca ephemeridum theologicarum lovaniensium
BHT	Beiträge zur historischen Theologie
BJS	Brown Judaic Studies
BRev	*Bible Review*
BZNW	Beihefte zur Zeitschrift für die neutestamentliche Wissenschaft
CBQ	*Catholic Biblical Quarterly*
CBQMS	Catholic Biblical Quarterly Monograph Series
ConBNT	Coniectanea biblica: New Testament Series
CRINT	Compendia rerum iudaicarum ad Novum Testamentum
DJD	Discoveries in the Judaean Desert
DSD	*Dead Sea Discoveries*
ErIsr	*Eretz-Israel*
ExpTim	*Expository Times*
FB	Forschung zur Bibel
GKC	*Gesenius' Hebrew Grammar,* ed. E. Kautsch, trans. A. E. Cowley, 2nd ed.
HAL	*The Hebrew and Aramaic Lexicon of the Old Testament,* ed. Ludwig Koehler and Walter Baumgartner
Herm	Hermeneia
HSS	Harvard Semitic Studies
HTR	*Harvard Theological Review*
IEJ	*Israel Exploration Journal*

Abbreviations

JBL	*Journal of Biblical Literature*
JJS	*Journal of Jewish Studies*
JSOTSup	Journal for the Study of the Old Testament: Supplement Series
JSP	*Journal for the Study of the Pseudepigrapha*
JSPSup	Journal for the Study of the Pseudepigrapha: Supplement Series
NEA	*Near Eastern Archaeology*
NEAEHL	*The New Encyclopedia of Archaeological Excavations in the Holy Land,* ed. Ephraim Stern
NJPS	*Tanakh: The Holy Scriptures: The New Jewish Publication Society Translation*
NTOA	Novum Testamentum et Orbis Antiquus
OTL	Old Testament Library
OTP	*The Old Testament Pseudepigrapha,* ed. James H. Charlesworth
PEFQS	*Palestine Exploration Fund Quarterly Statement*
PTSDSSP	Princeton Theological Seminary Dead Sea Scrolls Project
RB	*Revue biblique*
RevQ	*Revue de Qumran*
RGG	*Religion in Geschichte und Gegenwart,* ed. Kurt Galling
RHPR	*Revue d'Histoire et de Philosophie Religieuses*
SBLDS	Society of Biblical Literature Dissertation Series
SBLMS	Society of Biblical Literature Monograph Series
SBLTT	Society of Biblical Literature Texts and Translations
SBT	Studies in Biblical Theology
SDSSRL	Studies in the Dead Sea Scrolls and Related Literature
Sem	*Semitica*
SFSHJ	South Florida Studies in the History of Judaism
SJLA	Studies in Judaism in Late Antiquity
SSN	Studia Semitica Neerlandica
ST	*Studia theologica*
STDJ	Studies on the Texts of the Desert of Judah
SUNT	Studien zur Umwelt des Neuen Testaments
TSAJ	Texte und Studien zum antiken Judentum
TUGAL	Texte und Untersuchungen zur Geschichte der altchristlichen Literatur
VT	*Vetus Testamentum*
WO	*Die Welt des Orients*
WUNT	Wissenschaftliche Untersuchungen zum Neuen Testament
ZRGG	*Zeitschrift für Religions- und Geistesgeschichte*

Illustrations

The Hermeneutics of the Pesharim

Over two thousand years ago, a group of highly trained scholars gathered west of the Dead Sea. They were the Sons of Zadok, King David's high priest and the one who placed the crown on Solomon. They knew they were special. Their passion was to search the Scriptures for hidden secrets. They knew that God had spoken to them. They had the key that would unlock the mysteries of Scripture. The key had been given to them by God's elect one, the Righteous Teacher. Their compositions have been discovered. Among the Dead Sea Scrolls are their creations: the pesharim.

As one enters the world of the Qumran pesharim, one enters not only the world of Second Temple Judaism but also the Mediterranean world controlled by Rome. As Warwick Ball states in *Rome in the East,*

> The original home of the Carthaginians was not North Africa, but the Phoenician homelands of the Levant. The eventual annexation of Palestine, therefore, was vital to Rome once it had established its foothold on the north Levantine coast.[1]

The truth of Ball's insight came home to me as I sat in a Beirut restaurant, enjoying a special meal, seeing the sunset over the Mediterranean, and thinking about what I had seen that day at Tyre and Sidon. I thought about the colony the Phoenicians had established at Carthage and how disparate aspects of ancient history seemed to come together like some intriguing pieces of a jigsaw puzzle.

1. Warwick Ball, *Rome in the East: The Transformation of an Empire* (New York: Routledge, 2000), 49.

1

The cliffs of Qumran, looking west from the Dead Sea; the Qumran caves are south of these cliffs. Tanks from the Six-Day War are in the foreground, reminiscent of the War Scroll.

Photo by James H. Charlesworth

The Romans are mirrored in the pesharim. There they appear as the Kittim, as we shall see. So, in a real sense, studying the pesharim is to explore world history. In them generals and battles are reflected, but before we can explore the possible history in the pesharim we must obtain a pellucid view of their genre and why they were composed.

The pesharim are the creations of one Community, the Qumran Yaḥad. They are primarily and foremost hermeneutical compositions. They have two foci: the sacred text of the Torah (God's word) and the commentary (pesher) that both follows the *lemma* (scriptural citation) and is adumbrated in the *lemma*. These two are united in that both are perceived and understood as God's word directed only to the Qumranites, their own history, and their own special place in the economy of salvation. The interpretation, pesher, proceeds by viewing the *lemma* with an eye on the special history of the Righteous Teacher and the origins of the renewed covenant. One main intention is to explain in terms of cosmology and chronology why the Righteous Teacher and his followers suffered and lived in exile in the wilderness, far from the former *axis mundi*, God's dwelling in Zion, the Temple.

The guidance of the Holy Spirit helps the Qumran exegete obtain the precise hermeneutic, which is defined by the belief that God's chosen "holy ones" — the Qumranites — are living in the latter days. The present time — when the pesharim were being composed — is the culmination of God's time. Now, according to the Qumran collective mind, all of God's mysteries are being understood, but only by those in the Community, and all of God's promises are being fulfilled, especially the elevation of and rewards for his elect.

The present monograph is possible because of the publication of the critical texts and translations of all the pesharim. The *Pesharim, Other Commentaries, and Related Documents* conveniently focuses attention on the texts and translations of all the biblical Qumran commentaries.[2]

Chaos Regarding History Camouflaged as Hermeneutics?

We many now focus on the central question of the present work: How, and in what ways, if at all, can one obtain reliable historical data from the pesharim?

The *Pesharim, Other Commentaries, and Related Documents* has been prepared so as to assist the scholar to avoid fanciful suggestions about historical episodes mirrored in the commentary. Perhaps four cautions or suggestions might prove helpful at this time. First, the lengthy restorations of texts as in earlier editions are avoided. The extensive, unfounded, restorations often led to speculative historical restorations that were without foundation. The restorations of *lacunae* in the pesharim were too often extensive. This was especially the case in the sections on the "interpretation." Often the pesher sections were apparently restored, without guides and anchors like portions of remaining letters, because the *lemmata* (biblical quotations) that preceded them were easy to restore. Most restorations, as J. T. Milik warned about proposed corrections to other Qumran texts in the late 1960s,[3] are frequently disproved by subsequent discoveries. Thus,

2. James H. Charlesworth et al., eds., *The Pesharim, Other Commentaries, and Related Documents.*
3. J. T. Milik: "Parmi les variantes on trouvera quelquefois des leçons de mss de 4 Q

for critical work that is based on accurate restorations, the editors of the new edition have kept restorations of the pesher section to controlled limits. The restorations in the new critical edition are thus *pro forma* and attempted only when we have a base text (the document is preserved at this point elsewhere [*lemmata*, intertext, etc.]), formulae,[4] known *termini technici*, or when a word is anchored by the remains of ink (before, after, above, or below) the lacuna.

Second, the mutilated extent of the preserved portions of each pesher or commentary now becomes graphically clear in the new printed texts. We should not speculate too much on what has been lost, as if it is the only relevant part of the original for our present concerns. For example, only unguided speculation is possible if we seek to recover what may have been reported about the Righteous Teacher in the truncated portions of *Psalm Pesher 3* (4Q173 = 4QpPs[b], Frg. 1 and Frg. 2), esp. Frg. 2 (in total): "[. . .] The interpretation of the mat[ter . . .] the Right[eous Te]acher."

Third, the extant interpretations are often characterized by a pastiche of scriptural allusions that are elusive. There are frequently no guidelines to offer anything but areas for speculations for some sobriquets; namely, among the latter are Gilead, Ephraim, Manasseh, and infrequently also the house of Judah.[5]

Finally, a study of all the texts in the new critical edition of the pesharim should lead to caution and to the question why only a few of them seem to preserve historical allusions. Only two pesharim offer significant historical data; they are the pesharim on Habakkuk and Nahum. Were historical allusions in other, much more mutilated, pesharim present in sections now lost? And are other commentaries pesharim, but that clarification is now lost?

In the first two decades of work on the Qumran Scrolls, numerous scholars tended to treat the pesharim as if they were not first and foremost biblical commentaries. These scholars mined the pesharim for historical information without allowing sufficiently for the hermeneutical nature of the documents. There was an early tendency to treat the pesharim as if they were

---

qui sont identiques à celles de 1 QS mais qui je cite pour montrer l'inutilité des corrections proposées par différents savants"; review of P. Wernberg-Møller, *The Manual of Discipline translated and annotated.* STDJ 1 (Grand Rapids: Wm. B. Eerdmans, 1957), *RB* 67 (1960): 411.

4. See C. D. Elledge, "A Graphic Index of Citation and Commentary Formulae in the Dead Sea Scrolls," in Charlesworth et al., *The Pesharim, Other Commentaries, and Related Documents.*

5. For "the house of Judah," see 4QFlor Frg. 4.4. For "Ephraim and Judah," see 4QTest 27. For "the offspring of Judah," see 4QCat 12.

examples of Hellenistic historiography or Jewish historical compositions. In several senses, the pesharim are *sui generis* and certainly distinct from other contemporaneous Jewish works that may be perceived as historical works. The pesharim are paradigmatically different from Jewish histories like 1 Maccabees and Josephus's *War* and *Antiquities*. They are also distinct from the more impressionistic histories of 2 Maccabees and the creative histories like Eupolemus, Pseudo-Eupolemus, and Cleodemus Malchus.

This flawed methodology led to a backlash during the past 20 years. A second group of scholars thus focused their publications on cautioning against looking for history in Qumran commentaries. In essence, they called for a moratorium on the search for history in the pesharim. This recent trend has led to a better methodology for ascertaining history in nonhistorical works; and such refined methods can learn from the methodology developed to help search for Jesus' own words and actions within the confessional and kerygmatically shaped gospels. Indeed, it is clear to most scholars that history can be found in works that are not categorized as "historical documents."

A third group of scholars has charted a middle course in searching for history in the pesharim. The present monograph attempts to examine these primary texts and to discern if some reliable history can be obtained from them. It also seeks to discern if we might be able to perceive chaos or some consensus among the leading Qumran experts.

At the outset, it must be emphasized that any historical data obtained from the pesharim will not present us with objective historical data. We will be seeing history as perceived from within the Qumran Community. The pesharim are the creations of the Qumranites, who believed they were living in "the latter days" and that the prophets, guided by the Holy Spirit, prophesied not about their own time but about the latter days and especially about the Qumranites' place in the "economy of salvation." That is, the Qumranites perceived secular history through ancient prophecies now revealed pristinely by God through the Righteous Teacher.

Qumran Hermeneutics

The previously mentioned misperceptions among many scholars indicate that it is pertinent to clarify the literary genre of the pesharim. First, we need to proceed with the perception that the pesharim are Qumranic commentaries on texts, and that to the Qumranites these sacred works preserve God's word on target for them.

Second, the pesharim are hermeneutically focused. They are biblical commentaries in the sense of *fulfillment hermeneutics*. They reveal primarily the way the Qumranites viewed their recent past by finding meaning for their own lives and special history by pouring over the words from God preserved by the prophets, his servants. They read Habakkuk, Nahum, and other prophets and biblical books by focusing on divine promises, predictions, and prophecies, and then affirming that they had been fulfilled in the life and history of their own special Community.

To understand Qumran exegesis and hermeneutics one should consult the context of Jewish exegesis. This is reviewed in an authoritative manner, with special attention to *Florilegium*, by George J. Brooke in his *Exegesis at Qumran: 4QFlorilegium in Its Jewish Context.*[6] Still valuable are the survey and insights found in many earlier publications, especially Daniel Patte's *Early Jewish Hermeneutic in Palestine.*[7] More recent work is summarized and new insights developed in David Instone Brewer's *Techniques and Assumptions in Jewish Exegesis Before 70 CE.*[8] The Jewish imagination created new genres and compositions, including not only the pesharim but also works like Pseudo-Philo's *Liber Antiquitatum Biblicarum.* Bruce N. Fisk draws attention to the "imaginative work of early Jewish biblical exegesis" found in this document.[9]

The Sociology of Qumran Hermeneutics

After 50 years of Qumran research it is now certain that the pesharim were composed at Qumran. Sociological forces impregnate the mind and thought of the Qumranite as he composes a pesher. A more erudite interpretation of the pesharim depends upon a better grasp of the social world of Qumran; the latter now is in need of sociological explorations.[10] Only a few asides must suffice for the present monograph — as I step outside my primary area of expertise. Initially, it is fundamental to stress that sociology must not be imposed on Qumran texts. The only appropriate method is to bring to bear upon Qumran phenomena the sensitivities and insights obtained by leading sociologists.

6. JSOTSup 29 (Sheffield: JSOT, 1985).
7. SBLDS 22 (Missoula: Scholars, 1975).
8. TSAJ 30 (Tübingen: Mohr [Siebeck], 1992).
9. *Do You Not Remember? Scripture, Story and Exegesis in the Rewritten Bible of Pseudo-Philo.* JSPSup 37 (Sheffield: Sheffield Academic, 2001).
10. Surprisingly absent in Qumranology is the influence of sociology. Exceptions are found in the works by Shemaryahu Talmon. See the quotations from his publications in the following pages.

When the attentive reader studies the world of the pesharim, he or she may begin to imagine and perceive a distinct and learned Community (the Yaḥad). In the pesharim are mirrored dedicated religious people seeking meaning and understanding by pondering and discussing Hebrew manuscripts. They share the same common use of special language. Many know and can speak Hebrew, and some erudite priests are familiar with Paleo-Hebrew, which is at least 500 years old.

The Qumranites' language is shaped by the sociology of knowledge. While Plato clearly elevated place over time, the Qumranites generally stressed the importance of time over place. They expended an abundance of time contemplating the meaning of Scripture and shaping their theology by reflections on the meaning of time. They believed they were in the wilderness as a place of preparation for the fulfillment of God's time. God's word to them became meaningful, because it was intended to be fulfilled in the latter days, their own time. The Qumranites were caught in the interstices of time: They lived in the not-yet of the present-future.

This liminality shaped their hermeneutics, especially after the death of their master, the Righteous Teacher.[11] Their hermeneutic was enhanced by the strong social barriers that separated them from all others. The world was divided cosmologically between two warring cosmic angels, the Angel of Light and the Angel of Darkness. Humanity was bifurcated into two opposite camps: the Sons of Light and the Sons of Darkness. Dangers existed outside Qumran's high barriers. Purity and salvation were only within the Community. Inside there is the community of love; outside there is only the hated others. As Mary Douglas stated in her influential *Purity and Danger*, "Holiness means keeping distinct the categories of creation.... To be holy is to be whole, to be one; holiness is unity, integrity, perfection of the individual and of the kind."[12]

Liturgy instilled in the Qumranite a perpetual sense of community and of this enmity against outsiders.[13] Ritual had shaped and defined the

---

11. Note the insight of Victor Turner: "In the interstitial, interfacial realm of liminality, both in initiation rites and the pilgrimage process, the dead are conceived of as transformative agencies and as mediating between various domains normally classified as distinct." Do such reflections help us to perceive how important the death and continuing memory of the Righteous Teacher are for the shaping of the hermeneutic and Endtime perspective of the pesharim? See Turner, *Process, Performance, and Pilgrimage: A Study in Comparative Symbology* (New Delhi: Concept, 1979), 42.

12. (New York: Praeger, 1966), 53-54.

13. As Richard K. Fenn states, "to take part in any liturgy is to signify to oneself and others that one is constituting a community and oneself as a member of that community"; *Liturgies & Trials* (New York: Pilgrim, 1982), 28.

life of priests and Levites before they lived at Qumran. At Qumran it indicated both a refusal to continue with usual social routines and, as millenarianists, preparation for new birth.[14] During the renewal of the covenant, perhaps at the Day of Atonement (Yom Hakippurim), the hatred of others was voiced collectively in a ritual enactment of entering the renewed covenant in the latter days. Note the opening of the *Rule of the Community*:

> When they cross over into the covenant the priests and the Levites shall praise the God of salvation and all his true works, and all those who cross over into the covenant shall say after them: "Amen, amen." . . . Then the priests shall bless all the men of God's lot. . . . Then the Levites shall curse all the men of Belial's lot. . . . (1QS 1.18–2.5)[15]

When studying the pesharim, the serious person readily perceives in them the overpowering influence of the Righteous Teacher. Numerous pesharim focus on him in an attempt to explain and comprehend his sufferings in the history of salvation. Note, especially, the interpretation of Habakkuk 1:13 in *Pesher Habakkuk* 5:

> Its interpretation concerns the House of Absalom and the men of their counsel, who were quiet at the rebuke of the Righteous Teacher and did not support him against the Man of the Lie (VACAT) who rejected the Torah in the midst of all their counsel. (1QpHab 5.9-12)[16]

In the perspectives of sociologists, the Righteous Teacher is the "Big Man" who strides within the Community, casting his shadow over exegesis and hermeneutics. He is clearly the charismatic — and in the very sense defined by Max Weber:

> The holder of charisma seizes the task that is adequate for him and demands obedience and a following by virtue of his mission. His success determines whether he finds them. His charismatic claim breaks down if

---

14. Maurice Bloch suggests that all millenarianists "herald a rebirth" and refuse "to continue with earthly life. When matters are beyond practical remedy, the remedy is to hasten the end of the practical"; *Prey into Hunter: The Politics of Religious Experience* (Cambridge: Cambridge University Press, 1992), 90-91.

15. Trans. by Charlesworth in *Rule of the Community and Related Documents.* PTSDSSP 1 (Tübingen: Mohr [Siebeck]; Louisville: Westminster John Knox, 1994), 9.

16. Trans. by Maurya P. Horgan in Charlesworth et al., *The Pesharim, Other Commentaries, and Related Documents.*

his mission is not recognized by those to whom he feels he has been sent. If they recognize him, he is their master — so long as he knows how to maintain recognition through 'proving' himself. But he does not derive his 'right' from their will, in the manner of an election. Rather, the reverse holds: it is the *duty* of those to whom he addresses his mission to recognize him as their charismatically qualified leader.[17]

These sociological reflections surely help us understand the hermeneutic of the pesharim. Note how a Qumranite, long after the death of the Righteous Teacher, continued to follow him and affirm his charisma, as he interpreted Habakkuk 2:4b in the *Pesher Habakkuk:*

> Its interpretation concerns all those who observe Torah in the House of Judah, whom God will save from the house of judgment on account of their tribulation and their fidelity to the Righteous Teacher. (1QpHab 8.1-3)[18]

Suffering and asceticism are continuous with all human attempts at culture or society. Emile Durkheim showed that "society itself is possible only at" the price of sacrificing our natural appetites. If an asceticism is "inherent in all social life," and if it "is an integral part of all human culture,"[19] then scholars reveal their ignorance of social phenomena and expose their own foolishness when they claim that the Qumran Community could not have been occupied by a group of priests who were ascetics.

The pesharim reveal the extent to which the Qumranites revered the Righteous Teacher and saluted him as their "charismatically qualified leader." He alone was the bearer of charisma; he alone had been led by the Holy Spirit to build in the wilderness "the House of Holiness." He had demanded a following, and to those who followed him from the Temple into the wilderness he revealed the meaning of Scripture. He clarified God's will for them. They were the elect of the renewed covenant, "the Holy Ones." The Qumranites knew, and explained through the hermeneutics of the pesher that they knew, that the Righteous Teacher is he who "has been sent." He "is their master." Note the paradigmatically important interpretation of Habakkuk 2:2b in the *Pesher Habakkuk:*

17. "The Sociology of Charismatic Authority," in *From Max Weber: Essays in Sociology,* trans. and ed. by Hans H. Gerth and C. Wright Mills (Oxford: Oxford University Press, 1946), 246-47.

18. Trans. by M. P. Horgan in Charlesworth et al., *The Pesharim, Other Commentaries, and Related Documents.*

19. *Elementary Forms of the Religious Life,* trans. by Joseph Ward Swain (New York: Macmillan, 1915), 316.

and God told Habakkuk to write down the things that are going to come upon the last generation, but the fulfillment of the period he did not make known to him. (VACAT) And when it says, **so that he can run who reads it,** its interpretation concerns the Righteous Teacher, to whom God made known all the mysteries of the words of his servants the prophets. (1QpHab 7.1-5)[20]

Shemaryahu Talmon, who alone brings to the forefront in Qumranology the importance of sociological studies, focuses on the role of the Righteous Teacher and his task of shaping the Qumran Community. Here are his words, which are singularly important for perceiving the social world in which the pesharim crystallized and were written:

> The Teacher was born out of intense emotional stress, triggered by the profound disappointment that the unrealized hope for an imminent onset of the millennium had evoked in the initial nucleus of Covenanters when the precalculated date passed uneventfully. Thus, emerging in a second stage of the group's history, and not being its initiator, he cannot be defined as a "founding prophet" (in the typology introduced by Max Weber), nor has the occasionally proposed identification with Jesus Christ any basis. Rather, he must be seen as an inspired interpreter whose latent inspiration revealed itself in his response to his fellows' despair. It fell to him to find the means for bridging the gap between the unduly protracted *now* and the disappointingly delayed *then.* This he apparently did by transforming the loose group-cohesion of the founding members into a structured socioreligious system. Under his guidance, their utopian millenarism, which originally had anarchistic overtones, crystallized into a structured order. Before long the basically antiestablishment millenarians formed a socioreligious establishment of their own which was soon to surpass in rigidity and normative exactitude the system of the mother community from which they had separated.[21]

Talmon's reconstruction of Qumran origins is in harmony with the research that is the focus of this monograph. In interpreting the pesharim it is imperative to grasp Talmon's point about the Righteous Teacher being the "inspired interpreter."

---

20. Trans. by M. P. Horgan in Charlesworth et al., *The Pesharim, Other Commentaries, and Related Documents.*

21. Shemaryahu Talmon, *The World of Qumran from Within* (Leiden: Brill, 1989), 284-85.

The *Rule of the Community* (1QS 3), the section that contains the definitive Qumran teaching on dualism and the reason for evil

Photo courtesy of Kodansha, Ltd., Tokyo

The language of the Qumranites was distinctly and uniquely developed. Characteristic of the language of Qumran theology and hermeneutics is anonymity,[22] which functions as a literary device.[23] There is every reason to conclude that the *Rule of the Community,* the *Thanksgiving Hymns,* and *More Works of the Torah* (4QMMT) and other sections of early Qumran documents were composed by the Righteous Teacher or significantly shaped by his teachings. Studying these works leads to the conclusion, or at least assumption, that he chose to emphasize anonymity and metaphor.

Using imagination sparked by historical data, one can guess that the Righteous Teacher might have chosen anonymity and metaphor (cf. esp. 1QH 16) to articulate the illusion that he saw refracted in all the self-centered egos that he had encountered and knew were born to die.[24] His self-awareness was shaped by two main factors: his archenemy the Wicked Priest and his abode in the wilderness as the place of preparation. Perhaps this rare poetic genius knew that a perspicacious person avoids images that attempt too clearly to present phenomena that can be refracted only in mirrored images of words.[25] These insights deserve pondering; for — as will become obvious in the following pages — now it is clear that we do not know, and will probably never discover, the name of the leader of the Qumran Community. He remains the great metaphor of Qumran, the elusive and anonymous one.

Why are such comments propitious in comprehending the hermeneutics of the pesharim? While the Righteous Teacher did not compose the pesharim, the trajectory of Qumran theology reveals that he probably created the pesher method and taught it to his disciples.[26] Those who composed the pesharim, probably after his death, remembered him in a singular fashion. He alone was the right Teacher. He alone had received God's full disclosure of all the mysteries in the words of the prophets. He alone had been chosen to plant the final planting of God's vineyard, the elect and "holy ones" (cf. 1QH 16).

22. Josephus also never mentions the leader of the Essenes.

23. For further reflections, see James H. Charlesworth, *The Beloved Disciple* (Valley Forge: Trinity, 1995), xiv-xvi, 145-46, 384-85.

24. See the penetrating insights that need historical grounding in Joseph Campbell, *The Hero with a Thousand Faces.* Bollingen Series 17 (Princeton: Princeton University Press, 1949, 2nd ed. 1968), 46.

25. I am indebted to Friedrich Nietzsche for these reflections; see *Basic Writings of Nietzsche,* trans. and ed. by Walter Kaufmann (New York: Modern Library, 1966, 1992), 240-41.

26. This insight is developed in the following research on Qumran history.

The careful reader of the pesharim will discern how the Qumranite defined himself. He lived in one Community (the Yaḥad), and all in it held everything in common, including a common storehouse. They shared a common focus, dedication, and especially a common perspective on history that they developed in the pesharim.

To comprehend the life of the Qumranites we must turn to the other works they composed and which contain concepts and ideas that defined them. We learn most about their life from the *Rule of the Community*. From this document, which evolved within and reflects the evolution of Qumran thought, we learn that the Community always defined the Qumranite. It was a worshipping Community. It followed the same seven-day week as other Jews; but there is a major difference between Qumran and so-called mainstream Judaism. Qumran aligned all social life according to a quasi-solar calendar[27] in which ancient prayers were recited and new ones composed, especially those that conclude the *Rule of the Community* and those that define the *Thanksgiving Hymns*, the hymnbook of the Community. Since prayer often originates in magic, as Weber claimed,[28] and since magic is related to the forming of sects and the psychology of charismatic movements as Daniel Lawrence O'Keefe has shown,[29] something more may be apparent. It now becomes more clear that the Qumran prayers are linked to otherwise ostensibly unrelated compositions, like the *Horoscopes* (4Q186), the collection of incantations in 11Q11 that mention a "demon" (שד), and the apotropaic prayers in 4Q510-511.[30]

The Qumranite was always self-defined as one of the Many, one of the Sons of Light within the Community of the renewed covenant. The Qumran dualism developed out of Iranian thought and biblically conceived divisions and separations;[31] it was cosmic but focused on humans, separating them into the predetermined Sons of Light or Sons of Darkness (see esp. 1QS 3-4). As Durkheim showed, even though he could not know

27. I note a failure of sociologists to concentrate on the paradigmatic importance of time in societies. See, however, the fascinating reflections by Elias Zerubavel in *The Seven Day Circle: The History and Meaning of the Week* (Chicago: University of Chicago Press, 1989).

28. Max Weber, *The Sociology of Religion*, trans. by Ephraim Fischoff (Boston: Beacon, 1922, 4th rev. ed. 1956), 26.

29. *Stolen Lightning: The Social Theory of Magic* (New York: Vintage, 1983).

30. Other works known and influential at Qumran are shaped by demonology, including the *Books of Enoch*, the *Genesis Apocryphon*, and Tobit.

31. Durkheim, *The Elementary Forms of the Religious Life*. See esp. the sociological reflections by Janina Chasseguet-Smirgel in *Creativity and Perversion* (New York: W. W. Norton, 1984).

about Qumran phenomena, a classification system is produced by social relations.[32]

The Qumranites had gone into the wilderness, they claim, because they had heard the Voice calling them. The Voice pointed them to Scripture. In it they would find their way and their meaning. The Qumranites had separated

> themselves from the session of the men of deceit in order to depart into the wilderness to prepare there the Way of the Lord (?); as it is written: "In the wilderness prepare the way of the Lord, make level in the desert a highway for our God." This (alludes to) the study of Torah wh[ic]h he commanded through Moses to do, according to everything which has been revealed (from) time to time, and according to that which the prophets have revealed by his Holy Spirit. (1QS 8.13-16)[33]

The social consciousness and the self-understanding of the Qumranites were shaped by the study of Torah. The crucial text for their perception of why they are in the wilderness and desert is Isaiah 40:3. In the view of sociologists, the Qumranites had escaped from the established institutions they had once experienced, including the pollution from crowds, an institution especially in antiquity.[34]

The Pesharim as Fulfillment Hermeneutics

By intimating the importance of a sociologically sensitive reading of the pesharim, we come to comprehend more fully and deeply how Scripture and its interpretation define Qumran thought. The pesharim allow us, as it were, to peer into a mirror that reflects both history and the spirituality of the Qumranites. This concept of a two-way mirror may help us conceptualize some of the importance of the Qumran pesharim.

In light of these introductory reflections, we come to a crucial ques-

32. See also, Mary Douglas, *Natural Symbols: Explorations in Cosmology,* 2nd ed. (New York: Vintage Books, 1973).

33. Trans. by Charlesworth in PTSDSSP 1:37.

34. See esp. Gustav Le Bon, *The Crowd: A Study of the Popular Mind,* trans. by R. K. Merton (New York: Viking, 1960); Elias Canetti, *Crowds and Power,* trans. by Carol Stewart (New York: Seabury, 1978); and Richard K. Fenn, "Crowds, Time, and the Essence of Society," in *Secularization, Rationalization, and Sectarianism: Essays in Honour of Bryan R. Wilson,* ed. by Eileen Barker, James A. Beckford, and Karel Dobbelaere (Oxford: Clarendon, 1993), 287-304.

tion: What defines and characterizes the Qumran pesharim? Granted they are biblical commentaries, but how are they really different from other Jewish commentaries on Scripture? The answer lies in two Qumran perceptions.

First, the men at Qumran claimed to know that they were living in biblical history and time that had been made sacred by the acts of God in earlier history and time. History and time had a meaning, and that meaning had been understood only obliquely and imperfectly by the ancient prophets, God's servants. Thus, God's purposes had never before been so clearly and perfectly comprehended as at Qumran and in the mind-set of those who perpetually studied Scripture and created something new, the pesharim.

Was there an adequate answer to the questions aroused by suffering, especially by the Righteous Teacher and his group? For the Qumranites, the answer was found in their conviction that God had chosen them and predestined them to be "the Sons of Light." Their task was to serve God in bringing into history and time the fulfillment of *all* the promises encapsulated in Scripture. They were to suffer "in the wilderness," preparing the Way of the Lord; a perception that was grounded in their hermeneutical understanding of Isaiah 40:3. According to the Qumranites, the day of judgment — a concept inherited from the prophets — would vindicate their suffering and reveal that they that had been predestined to be the "Sons of Light." At that time they alone would be rewarded by God.

Second, God has chosen only one man, the Righteous Teacher, to inaugurate the final drama in the history of salvation (see esp. 1QH^a 16). This priest was the specially chosen descendant of Aaron (as we shall see). God had revealed to him *all* the secrets preserved in the sacred words recorded in Scripture by God's servants, the prophets (1QpHab 7). This person, the Righteous Teacher, knew he had been chosen by God. This priest, and scribe, then helped the Qumranites comprehend how, and in what ways, God's Word in the words of Scripture had been directed only to their time, and only to them. Fulfillment hermeneutics was possible because "the Holy Spirit" dwelt within "the House of Holiness," in which "the Most Holy of Holy Ones" dwelt. In fact, angels visited them at Qumran in their "House of Holiness."

For the Qumranites, the "House of Holiness" was not only on the earth; it was also open to revelation and to heaven itself. The Qumran Scrolls often give me the impression that the Qumranites often believed they were living in an antechamber of God's throne room.

Like the later books in the Hebrew Scriptures (the Old Testament), the pesharim recast and refract some of the earlier compositions in Scrip-

ture, but the pesharim were not deemed part of Scripture. For the Qumranites, they rather were necessary to complete Scripture. For us, they are
the first commentaries on Scripture.

What type of biblical commentaries, then, are the pesharim? They
are the first examples of *fulfillment interpretation;* that is, *fulfillment hermeneutics.* The Righteous Teacher taught his followers to think that only in
their own special history and only in their own lives, now and in the near
future (which was beginning to break into the present), can one perceive
how God is fulfilling his promises for Israel, which, of course, has been re-
defined.

Two appendixes by Professor Lidija Novakovic complete this monograph and help the scholar study the new texts and translations of the
pesharim and related commentaries. Each contains data that will be helpful in placing these commentaries within the world of Second Temple Judaism.

The first appendix provides an index of biblical quotations in the
pesharim and other commentaries collected in PTSDSSP vol. 6B. This index reveals how important Genesis, the Psalms, Isaiah, Hosea, Nahum, and
Habakkuk were for Qumran hermeneutics.

The second appendix lists the text-critical variants to be found in the
pesharim and related commentaries. In a convenient fashion, this index
presents variants that will raise many questions and guide more careful research and reflection on the origins of the biblical texts. Novakovic's list
presents the readings in the *lemmata* and aligns them with text witnesses
of the so-called Masoretic Text and of biblical texts found in the Dead Sea
Scrolls broadly defined (i.e., Qumran caves, Masada, and at Muraba'at).

Some interesting variants appear in Novakovic's list and raise arresting questions. For example, why does Ps 37:13 in *Psalm Pesher 1* (4Q171)
witness to the Tetragrammaton in Paleo-Hebrew characters? The MT pre-
serves אֲדוֹנָי? Is the latter reading the result of an error in transmission? If
the MT is the result of copying, then the error is easily explained. The
Tetragrammaton would have been heard out loud as "Adonai," the perpetual qere of YHWH (יְהוָה).

Finally, having clarified that the pesharim are Jewish compositions
shaped by exegesis and hermeneutics, we may now proceed to seek how
and in what ways, if at all, one may discern some historical information in
them. While I shall use the verb "mine," I do not want to suggest that one
can merely enter the pesharim as if they are mines into which one can de-
scend with questions and from which one can ascend with historical gems.
The context and the hermeneutical interpretation will always shape the
gem and be a part of it.

The Pesharim and Qumran History:
Chaos or Consensus?

The pesharim are Qumranic compositions that are interpretations of Scripture. They are primarily important for a perception of exegesis and hermeneutics in Second Temple Judaism. Yet, the pesharim have been the center of debate because of the divergent assessments of historical information found, or mirrored, in them. This monograph thus attempts to examine the pesharim to see if historical episodes are reflected in them, and also to see if it is possible to discern a consensus regarding the most likely reconstruction of Qumran history in light of the critical edition of the pesharim.[1]

Introduction

I shall attempt to provide a synopsis of the history of the Community (יחד)[2] in which the pesharim were composed. It is the same Community in which other documents were composed, at least *More Works of the Torah* (4QMMT), the *Rule of the Community,* the *Thanksgiving Hymns,* the *War Scroll,* the *Blessings,* and the *Rule of the Congregation.*[3] There are no

---

1. It seems necessary to restrict the notes to the more recent and most important publications. I am grateful to BIBAL Press for allowing me to pre-print much of my monograph on Qumran history. All translations are my own, unless otherwise noted.

2. Shemaryahu Talmon has shown that this noun has a biblical base; see his "The Qumran יחד — A Biblical Noun," in *The World of Qumran from Within,* 53-60.

3. For criteria and Qumran *termini technici,* see Hartmut Stegemann, "Die Bedeutung der Qumranfunde für die Erforschung der Apokalyptik," in *Apocalypticism in the*

Qumran Caves 4A and 4B in which most of the Dead Sea Scrolls were
discovered. Cave 4B is directly behind the large cave.

Photo by James H. Charlesworth

valid reasons to doubt that some of the pesharim — though most were
written late in the life of the Community — preserve, *mutatis mutandis,*
some relatively reliable historical memories. Devorah Dimant states suc-
cinctly what I think is the *consensus communis:*

---

*Mediterranean World and the Near East: Proceedings of the International Colloquium on
Apocalypticism at Uppsala, August 12-17, 1979,* ed. David Hellholm, 2nd ed. (Tübingen:
Mohr [Siebeck], 1989), esp. 511; Devorah Dimant, "The Qumran Manuscripts: Contents
and Significance," in *Time to Prepare the Way in the Wilderness,* ed. Dimant and Lawrence H.
Schiffman. STDJ 16 (Leiden: Brill, 1995), 23-58; and Carol A. Newsom, "'Sectually Explicit'
Literature from Qumran," in *The Hebrew Bible and Its Interpreters,* ed. Baruch Halpern, Wil-
liam H. Propp, and David Noel Freedman. Biblical and Judaic Studies from the University of
California, San Diego 1 (Winona Lake: Eisenbrauns, 1990), 167-87; Henry W. L. Rietz,
"Compositions of the Qumran Community," in *Collapsing of the Heavens and the Earth:
Conceptions of Time in the Sectarian Dead Sea Scrolls* (diss., Princeton, 2000), 25-27. Finally,
see James H. Charlesworth, "Scrolls Composed at Qumran," *The Dead Sea Scrolls: Rule of the
Community,* Photographic Multi-Language Edition, ed. Charlesworth with Henry W. L.
Rietz (Philadelphia: American Interfaith Institute/World Alliance of Interfaith Organiza-
tions, 1996), 17.

The commentaries are identified as belonging to the Qumran community by virtue of their terminology, subject matter, and ideology. These commentaries are the only Qumran texts so far published that refer to historical persons and events, and they constitute the main evidence for dating the Qumran community and understanding its history.[4]

Sources for Qumran History

The sources for reconstructing Qumran history are literary and archaeological. Among the former, the most important are 1 Maccabees, Josephus's works, the Qumran scrolls themselves (esp. 1QS and 4QS, CD, and the pesharim), and some historical summaries in the apocryphal books. Among the primary archaeological data are the *realia* found at Qumran and in the 11 Qumran caves. In addition, we need to include the insights obtained from over 50 years of archaeological work at other Hasmonean and Herodian sites, especially along the western littoral of the Dead Sea, at Jericho, Caesarea Maritima,[5] Masada, and Jerusalem.

We must examine the pesharim also in view of the vast corpus of Qumran Hebrew and Aramaic texts, the numerous texts found in other areas near the Dead Sea (esp. on Masada),[6] the study of pre-70 C.E. Jewish inscriptions on monuments[7] and coins,[8] and early Mishnaic Hebrew. It is

---

4. Devorah Dimant, "Pesharim, Qumran," *ABD* 5:244-51; quotation, 245.

5. See esp. Lee I. Levine, *Caesarea Under Roman Rule.* SJLA 7 (Leiden: Brill, 1975).

6. The most important recent publication of the Masada manuscripts is Shemaryahu Talmon's *Hebrew Fragments from Masada.* Masada 6 (Jerusalem: Israel Exploration Society, 1999).

7. See, *inter alia,* Robert C. Gregg and Dan Urman, *Jews, Pagans, and Christians in the Golan Heights: Greek and Other Inscriptions of the Roman and Byzantine Eras.* SFSHJ 140 (Atlanta: Scholars, 1996).

8. For the numismatic evidence, see the publications cited in the following discussion on Jonathan Alexander Jannaeus. For the "inscriptions," see esp. the Samaria (Daliyeh) Papyri that are self-dated to as late as 335 B.C.E. (see DJD 24 and 28), the inscriptions on the Punic Tophet Stelae that date from the 5th to the 1st centuries, "the Place of the Trumpeting" inscription (actually the place of blowing the shofar from the Temple Mount [see Josephus *War* 5.582]) which was chiseled between 20 B.C.E. and 70 C.E., the Hebrew and Aramaic scripts found in tombs from Giv'at ha-Mivtar from the 2nd century B.C.E. to ca. 70 C.E. (esp. the inscription on the Ossuary of "Simon the Temple Builder" which is in Herodian script), the Pontius Pilate inscription in Latin from Caesarea Maritima, the marble Uzziah Plaque with a Herodian script, and the inscriptions on the ossuaries of presumably the family of Qayapa' (Caiaphas) that are in Herodian script (esp. *yhwsp br qp'*). For a handy introduction to most of these inscriptions, see P. Kyle McCarter, Jr., *Ancient Inscriptions: Voices from the Biblical World* (Washington: Biblical Archaeology Society, 1996).

clear that Qumran Hebrew — even with all the variety among texts composed at Qumran such as 4QMMT, 1QS, and CD — is to a certain extent *sui generis*.[9] It is a link between Biblical Hebrew and Mishnaic Hebrew (with much Aramaic influence), but it is also shaped by Qumranology and isolation — thus, it is somewhat like an "antilanguage."[10]

If we focus on the internationally celebrated scholars in Qumran research, and allow for the fact that a consensus does not mean unanimous opinion but the judgment of a large percentage of specialists, then we can talk about a consensus regarding Qumran history.[11] Certainly, the Princeton Theological Seminary Dead Sea Scrolls Project's editorial board of advisors (Frank M. Cross, David Noel Freedman, James A. Sanders, and

9. See the proceedings of a third international symposium on the Hebrew of the Qumran scrolls in T. Muraoka and J. F. Elwolde, eds., *Diggers at the Well*. STDJ 36 (Leiden: Brill, 2000).

10. See the challenging and insightful comments by William M. Schniedewind in "Qumran Hebrew as an Antilanguage," *JBL* 118 (1999): 235-52.

11. Obviously, not all scholars would agree with this judgment. Some scholars hear discordant voices; see esp. Philip R. Davies, "Qumran and the Quest for the Historical Judaism," in *The Scrolls and the Scriptures: Qumran Fifty Years After,* ed. Stanley E. Porter and Craig A. Evans. JSPSup 26 (Sheffield: Sheffield Academic, 1997), 24-42. I certainly agree with Lester L. Grabbe that we must continue to use the requisite qualifications and nuances, that Qumran and Essene are not "interchangeable terms" (even if there should be no doubt that Qumran was the conservative branch of the Essenes), and that progress comes when we question a staid or orthodox consensus. I must disagree with Grabbe, however, when he states that "Seekers-After-Smooth-Things" are not the Pharisees because Josephus does not clarify that those whom Jannaeus crucified were "Pharisees." While Josephus does not make that identification obvious when he describes the event, he does suggest such an identification when he presents Alexander's advice to his wife, Alexandra (probably the former wife of Aristobulus). Alexander told Queen Alexandra to give some power "to the Pharisees" (τοῖς Φαρισαίοις ἐξουσίαν τινὰ παρασχεῖν) because they were admired by and very influential with the Jewish masses, and because *he had severely mistreated them* (ὑβρισθέντας ὑπ' αὐτοῦ) and *they had suffered "many calamities"* (πολλὰ πεπονθότες [LSJM 1346-47]) at *his hands* (see *Ant.* 13.401-4). The Greek πολλὰ translated as "many calamities" reflects the uncontrolled passion of Jannaeus. See my following discussion on Jannaeus and 4QpNah. For Grabbe's reflections, see "The Current State of the Dead Sea Scrolls: Are There More Answers than Questions?" in Porter and Evans, *The Scrolls and the Scriptures,* 54-67. I certainly agree with Grabbe that too many experts miss how uncertain are all historical reconstructions and that the Qumran manuscripts reveal cumulatively that we should reflect on how much we will never know about pre-70 C.E. Judaism. There is documentary support for my conclusion that Josephus does imply that the Pharisees were among those crucified by Jannaeus. It is a *baraita* in the Babylonian Talmud (*b Kiddushin* 66a) which as Daniel R. Schwartz shows "derives from quite an ancient source"; thus, "the Pharisees led the opposition" to Jannaeus. See Schwartz, "On Pharisaic Opposition to the Hasmonean Monarchy," in *Studies in the Jewish Background of Christianity.* WUNT 60 (Tübingen: Mohr [Siebeck], 1992), 44-56, esp. 46-48.

Shemaryahu Talmon)[12] and those working as subeditors in the PTSDSSP tend to agree on the basic issues regarding the history of the Qumran Community.[13] While we all concur with Sanders that "the observer is a part of the observed" and that "objectivity is but subjectivity under constraint,"[14] we have also been pointing to a Qumran consensus. Having stated that, I do want to stress that it is not a consensus of leading scholars that makes a historical judgment valid. It is the knowledge, relevant data amassed, wise insight, precise methodology, careful exegesis of all relevant passages, and solid argumentation that make a position sound.

Qumranology may appear to be chaos, but a deeper look seems to suggest an impressive consensus. The Qumran scrolls are not medieval works or post–70 c.e. writings. They are not to be assigned to the Zealots or to "Christians."[15] Early Judaism is not defined by a normativity, as represented by later Pharisaism and Rabbinics.[16] The Qumran scrolls are not

12. Talmon, on the one hand, points to agreements with the *communis opinio*, and on the other hand, warns of missing the point that in many ways Qumran is *sui generis*. In need of further discussion is his claim that men retreated to Qumran, "the spearhead of the 'Community,'" for only a specified number of years and were celibate, in preparation for an impeding final battle, "only during" a "circumscribed span of time" (332). Talmon rightly warns that we must strive to think and to live within the Qumran Community and to see Qumran "from within." See Talmon, "The Essential 'Community of the Renewed Covenant': How Should Qumran Studies Proceed?" in *Geschichte — Tradition — Reflexion: Festschrift für Martin Hengel zum 70. Geburtstag*, ed. Hubert Cancik, Hermann Lichtenberger, and Peter Schäfer (Tübingen: Mohr [Siebeck], 1996), 1:323-52.

13. Within the broad lines of consensus there is abundant but respectful dissension. And scholarly debates, within accepted contours (such as whether the Hasmonean Jonathan or Simon is the Wicked Priest), are certainly welcome and healthy.

14. James A. Sanders, "The Judaean Desert Scrolls and the History of the Text of the Hebrew Bible," in *Caves of Enlightenment*, ed. James H. Charlesworth (North Richland Hills: BIBAL, 1998), 1-17; see esp. 17.

15. It is now clear that the jar found in Cave VII with the letters ROMA [in Latin script], which led some to think of a connection between "Christians" in Rome and Qumran, was not made in Italy. It shares the chemistry of the pottery made at Qumran. See the neutron activation analysis (NAA) of this jar, and others, in Jan Gunneweg and Marta Balla, "How Neutron Activation Analysis Can Assist Research into the Provenance of the Pottery at Qumran," in *Historical Perspectives: From the Hasmoneans to Bar Kokhba in Light of the Dead Sea Scrolls*, ed. David Goodblatt, Avital Pinnick, and Daniel R. Schwartz. STDJ 37 (Leiden: Brill, 2001), 179-85.

16. Qumran scroll experts unitedly have distanced themselves from George Foot Moore's construct of a "Normative Judaism." More representative of Jewish variegated groups and sects is something like "Mainstream Judaism" or "Majority Judaism." See Moore, *Judaism in the First Centuries of the Christian Era*, 3 vols. (Cambridge, Mass.: Harvard University Press, 1927-1937). Only to a certain extent is it appropriate to state that Moore's work resurfaces *redivivus* in E. P. Sanders' brilliant study (which is too dependent on the

to be branded as inferior products of some putative heterodox Judaism. They are a not insignificant dimension of Second Temple Judaism (or Early Judaism) left behind by a fringe and irrelevant Jewish group. They prove to us, perhaps most importantly, that "Early Judaism was pluralistic, that is, the Judaism that existed prior to the end of the first century CE when surviving Pharisaism evolved into what we call Rabbinic Judaism, existed in a variety of modes."[17]

The Qumran scrolls — including those that were not composed at Qumran — date palaeographically from the 3rd century B.C.E. to ca. 68 C.E. Many of them represent the life of a community — the Qumran Community. It began as a priestly movement that protested the corruption of the temple cult, the wrong means of interpreting Torah, and the ordering of life and liturgy by following a wrong calendar. The Wicked Priest is a Hasmonean high priest who persecuted the anonymous Righteous Teacher. The pesharim are reliable and essential witnesses to early Jewish history, especially in the 2nd and 1st centuries B.C.E. John Strugnell, who has offered special counsel and guidance to me as editor of the PTSDSSP, rightly states that it is better to recognize "the main outlines of Qumran-ological 'orthodoxy'" than to abandon such widely accepted conclusions and perceptions for "more recent heresiarchs."[18]

The vast majority of Qumran experts working in Israel, Europe, Canada, and the United States tend to agree with some assessment of a consensus,[19] since we have been working on, and discussing with each other, these issues,[20] in some cases much longer than 30 years.[21] Thus, the

tractates of the later Mishnah) *Judaism: Practice & Belief, 63 BCE–66 CE* (Philadelphia: Trinity, 1992). For an introduction that gives pride of place to Jewish apocryphal works that antedate Bar Kokhba and the Qumran scrolls in reconstructing Early Judaism, see Mark A. Elliott, *The Survivors of Israel: A Reconsideration of the Theology of Pre-Christian Judaism* (Grand Rapids: Wm. B. Eerdmans, 2000).

17. James A. Sanders, "The Impact of the Judaean Desert Scrolls on Biblical Studies: Scripture in the First Century," in *The Bible and the Dead Sea Scrolls*, ed. James H. Charlesworth (North Richland Hills: BIBAL, 2000), 1:38-39.

18. John Strugnell, "Qumranology Then and Now," *NEA* 63 (2000): 175.

19. Regarding the broad areas of agreement, see Florentino García Martínez, "The History of the Qumran Community in the Light of Recently Available Texts," in *Qumran between the Old and New Testaments*, ed. Frederick H. Cryer and Thomas L. Thompson. JSOTSup 290 (Sheffield: Sheffield Academic, 1998), 194-216.

20. The pioneering work on the so-called Zadokite document (CD) by, *inter alios*, R. H. Charles, Albert-Marie Denis, Louis Ginzberg, Eduard Meyer, Chaim Rabin, and H. H. Rowley, and on the calendar by J. Dominique Barthélemy and Annie Jaubert should not be ignored; they intermittently offered valuable insights. For helpful bibliographical references to the older publications, see esp. Gerhard Delling, *Bibliographie zur jüdisch-hellenistischen und intertestamentarischen Literatur: 1900-1970*, 2nd ed. TUGAL 106 (Berlin: Akademie-

following is a brief synopsis of what I perceive to be a consensus on Qumran history; it has developed among most scholars who have been contributing to Qumran research — some of them since the early 1950s. When it becomes necessary to express my own insights I have chosen to employ the first person pronoun singular.

Here then is a synopsis of my attempt to reconstruct Qumran history.[22] It should be obvious that all attempts at historical reconstruction depend on what little we know and what seems to be only probable, perhaps possible, and sometimes only conceivable. Surely, no one needs to be shown, but only reminded, that all historical reconstructions are dependent on numerous factors. The most important are the following: (1) whatever has survived for review (including literary sources and *realia*), (2) a judgment on what is deemed most important among such data (in the present case, the pesharim, esp. 1QpHab and 4QpNah), and (3) historiography (the science of allowing the sources to speak with some clarity about history by immersing oneself within the physical topography and cultural ethos represented by the texts, and without misleading subjective agendas).

It is clear to most specialists, and certainly to me, that all scientific methods must be employed in any attempt at reconstructing Qumran history. Thus, palaeography and archaeology are now recognized to be reliable and precise scientific methods.[23] Along with historiography and soci-

---

Verlag, 1975), and Bastiaan Jongeling, *A Classified Bibliography of the Finds in the Desert of Judah 1958-1969.* STDJ 7 (Leiden: Brill, 1971). For help with more recent publications, see Florentino García Martínez and Donald W. Parry, *A Bibliography of the Finds in the Desert of Judah 1970-95.* STDJ 19 (Leiden: Brill, 1996).

21. Some experts have been involved in Qumran research since the late 1940s, others since 1980, and a few since 1990. I include, in particular and in alphabetical order, the following Qumran specialists: Baumgarten, Benoit, Broshi, Collins, Cross, de Vaux, Dimant, Duhaime, Duncan, Fitzmyer, Flusser, Freedman, Horgan, Lichtenberger, McCarter, Milgrom, Milik, Newsom, Pfann, Qimron, Sanders, Schuller, Schwartz, Segal, Strawn, Strugnell, Stuckenbruck, Talmon, Tov, Ulrich, VanderKam, Vermes, White Crawford, Yarbro Collins, Yardeni, and Zuckerman.

22. See also Hermann Lichtenberger, "Qumran," *Theologische Realenzyklopädie* 28 (Berlin: de Gruyter, 1997), 45-79, esp. "Die Geschichte der Gemeinschaft von Qumran," 65-68.

23. This is denied only by those who have not studied and learned how to work in such fields. Foremost among the palaeographers is Frank M. Cross; he taught Joseph Naveh who taught Ada Yardeni. For Cross's more recent studies on palaeography, see "Palaeography and the Dead Sea Scrolls," in *The Dead Sea Scrolls after Fifty Years,* ed. Peter W. Flint and James C. VanderKam (Leiden: Brill, 1998), 1:379-402 and pl. 9-14; and "Palaeography," in *Encyclopedia of the Dead Sea Scrolls,* ed. Lawrence H. Schiffman and James C. VanderKam (Oxford: Oxford University Press, 2000), 2:629-34.

ology, and especially the careful sifting of the texts composed at Qumran for historical data, they help bridge the gap from mere conceivable hypotheses to reliable probability in historical reconstruction.[24] Finally, in discerning history within the Qumran pesharim, we must assess what is available in light of previous work on other documents. In particular, we need to recall what has been known from all the Qumran scrolls and Qumran pseudepigraphical works,[25] all the Jewish works in the biblical Apocrypha (esp. 1 Maccabees and Tobit) and Pseudepigrapha (esp. *Jubilees* and the *Books of Enoch*), and Josephus's writings.

At the outset, it seems prudent to stress two perceptions. On the one hand, Qumran lore and thought developed over more than one century; hence, we should not seek to find a systematic Qumran perception. Over the centuries the Qumranites developed ideas and symbols that are probably different from those Jews who first went into the desert around the middle of the 2nd century B.C.E.[26] The members of the Qumran Community, then, did not develop a systematic and closed system of thought. There is no reason to doubt that a Qumranite at the same time probably held what modern thinkers would judge to be conflicting ideas (the Mishnah reveals how attractive and desirable were different conceptions and halakot).

On the other hand, this emphasis on variety of thought at Qumran needs to be balanced with a perception of what seems to be central at Qumran. Obviously, the *Rule of the Community* contains not only what developed at Qumran but also what was fundamental and basic. For example, the Qumran dualism, clearly developed in 1QS 3 and 4, seems to be central to this collection of rules and shaped other documents, especially the *War Scroll* and most likely *Horoscopes* (4Q186; cf. also 4Q561 and 4Q534).[27] This

---

24. Helpful are the summaries, insights, and sources collected by and found in Louis H. Feldman and Meyer Reinhold, eds., *Jewish Life and Thought Among Greeks and Romans: Primary Readings* (Minneapolis: Fortress, 1996).

25. See the list of documents in the PTSDSS Project at the back of each volume.

26. The Qumran drama took place in an extraordinary geographical setting. It was international because of the world leaders involved in it (from the Seleucids to the Flavian dynasty); it was parochial because the center of Qumran's problems was the cult in Jerusalem. See Denis Baly, "The Geography of Palestine and the Levant in Relation to Its History," in *The Cambridge History of Judaism*, ed. W. D. Davies and Louis Finkelstein (Cambridge: Cambridge University Press, 1984), 1:1-24.

27. See, e.g., Devorah Dimant, "Dualism at Qumran," in Charlesworth, *Caves of Enlightenment*, 55-73. Dimant can talk about dualism as "one coherent system of central importance to the Qumran Community" (59). While I am in full agreement with Dimant on the uniqueness of Qumran dualism, I am more convinced that it was of "central importance" and demur that it was "one coherent system."

dualism developed early in the Community and may well be related to what was taught by the Righteous Teacher.[28]

Synopsis of Qumran History

Too often scholars have talked about Qumran history as if there were no developments. The origins of the Qumranites — or their precursors — seem to appear sometime between 200 and 150 B.C.E. The Righteous Teacher seems to have led a collection of priests and Levites from the Temple into the inhospitable wilderness ca. 150.[29] They remained in the wilderness — a place of preparation, not punishment[30] — and eventually resided in the remains of an Israelite fort. The foundation stones of the fort are still visible just beneath the northern portion of the eastern wall of Khirbet Qumran.[31]

28. I personally think a case can be made that the Righteous Teacher developed the Qumran dualistic paradigm, but this hypothesis cannot be proved nor disproved. If he did, then 1QS would probably reflect some editing of his teaching. Some of my ideas on this issue were developed and published by my student, Dale C. Allison, Jr., in "The Authorship of IQS III,13–IV,14," *RevQ* 10 (1979-1980): 257-68. See also Jean L.-Duhaime, "La rédaction de *1QM* 13 et l'évolution du dualisme à Qumrân," *RB* 84 (1977): 210-38; and Philip R. Davies, "Dualism and Eschatology in the Qumran War Scroll," *VT* 28 (1978): 28-36; "Dualism and Eschatology in 1QM: A Rejoinder," *VT* 30 (1980): 93-97.

29. Jürgen Zangenberg explains the wilderness as a place where history and nature have conspired to provide tragic drama and awful theatre. See Zangenberg's "Wildnis unter Palmen? Khirbet Qumran im regionalen Kontext des Toten Meer," in *Jericho und Qumran,* ed. B. Mayer. Eichstätter Studien N.F. 45 (Regensburg: Friedrich Pustet, 2000), 129-64. Both Hartmut Stegemann and George Brooke inform me they are convinced that the Righteous Teacher never went to Qumran.

30. See esp. Shemaryahu Talmon, "The Desert Motif in the Bible and in Qumran Literature," in *Literary Studies in the Hebrew Bible* (Leiden: Brill, 1993), 216-54. Esp. see 247 and 253: "the desert initially was for the Qumran Covenanters a place of refuge from persecution. . . . Ultimately the desert became the locale of a period of purification and preparation for the achievement of a new goal."

31. It is somewhat misleading to state that Khirbet Qumran "first attracted attention after the discovery of the Dead Sea Scrolls in 1947." See Robert A. Kugler in *Dictionary of New Testament Background,* ed. Craig A. Evans and Stanley E. Porter (Downers Grove: InterVarsity, 2000), 883. It is mentioned in early archaeological surveys, and I remember professors at the University of Edinburgh describing how they examined what was thought to be a Roman fort in the 1930s. E.g., see Charles S. Clermont-Ganneau, "The Jerusalem Researches: Letters from M. Clermont-Ganneau, III," *PEFQS* (1874), 80-111; *Archaeological Researches in Palestine During the Years 1873-1874,* 2 vols., trans. A. Stewart (London: Palestine Exploration Fund, 1896-99); see esp. vol. 2. The Palestine Exploration Fund in London contains these letters and much of the raw data has not been carefully perused. I am grateful to the curator and staff for most cordial and helpful assistance.

The entrance to the Qumran Community; this is the only section
of the ruin that seems to have been well constructed.

Photo by James H. Charlesworth

The Community continued, probably with some interruptions, until it was
burned by Roman troops in 68 C.E.

In 1957 J. T. Milik rightly insisted on "the growth that is to be observed in tenets and organization, a growth which is rapid in the first gen-
erations but which slows down towards the end."[32] He organized Qumran
history into four phases: Strict Essenism, Essenism with Pharisaic Nuances, Essenes During Herod's Reign, and Essenism with Zealot Tendencies. In 1980 I stressed that there were at least four transitional phases
in Qumran history.[33] There is now a consensus that we should speak about
Qumran history in terms of periods and developments.

32. J. T. Milik, *Ten Years of Discovery in the Wilderness of Judea*, trans. John Strugnell.
SBT 26 (Naperville: Allenson, 1959; French ed. 1957]), 80.

33. James H. Charlesworth, "The Origin and Subsequent History of the Authors of
the Dead Sea Scrolls: Four Transitional Phases Among the Qumran Essenes," *RevQ* 10
(1980): 213-33.

Phase I (Archaeological Period Ia)

Sometime before 150 B.C.E. centuries of tension within the many priestly groups in the Jerusalem Temple came to a climax.[34] The debates seemed to circulate around four issues: the legitimacy of the priesthood, the appropriate calendar (e.g., *Genesis A* [4Q252]), the proper legal means for keeping the Temple pure and observing Torah (4QMMT), and the technical means for interpreting Scripture (1QS 6.6-8; 8.2, 15-16; and the pesharim, esp. 1QpHab 2.8-10; cf. CD 6.3-11). For example, the attitude of the Qumranites to the Temple as defiled is reflected in an interpretation of Torah that shifts the payment of the Temple tax from once a year to once in a lifetime (*Ordinances* [4Q159]; see also 5Q *Second Commentary on Malachi*). Of course, many of these proto-Qumran concerns continued within the Community and shaped Qumran theology.

The Qumran group originated, according to the *Damascus Document*, "390 years" after the fall of Jerusalem in 586 B.C.E. (CD MS A 1.5-6).[35] That would mean, roughly, sometime ca. 196 B.C.E. Hence, if we take this mathematical figure as indicative of the earliest beginnings of what became the Qumran group, we are led to surmise that they originated sometime in the first half of the 2nd century B.C.E. Most likely, these precursors of the Qumran group originated in Jerusalem and in the Temple cult.[36] The *Damascus Document* also states that "20 years" transpired be-

---

34. This crisis within the Jerusalem priesthood has been highlighted by Paul D. Hanson in numerous publications; see esp. his *The Dawn of Apocalyptic*, rev. ed. (Philadelphia: Fortress, 1979). While Hanson sees the origin of Jewish apocalypticism in these priestly social crises, John J. Collins points to differences between late prophecy and the early apocalypses (esp. in regard to personal immortality). See esp. Collins, "Early Jewish Apocalypticism," *ABD* 1:282-88.

35. In my judgment, it is clear that CD represents the life and concepts of Jews similar to those at Qumran, but living elsewhere in ancient Palestine. Later in this essay I will discuss the Essenes and the Qumranites; one can state (in light of that discussion) that 1QS represents the life of celibate Essenes living at Qumran, and CD represents Essenes who were not so strict, had commerce with other Jews, and were married. It is far from clear how non-Qumran Essenes related to Qumran Essenes; it is conceivable that some Qumranites shunned those living outside Qumran as contaminated and impure (some extreme Qumranites may have judged them not to be Sons of Light). I should state also that I disagree with those who think that the *Songs of the Sabbath Sacrifices* was not composed at Qumran; it quotes a passage from 1QS that probably had been memorized (i.e., the claim that the God of Knowledge is the source of all creation; 1QS 3.15).

36. It is conceivable, as Jerome Murphy-O'Connor argues, that the origins of the precursors of Qumran were those who returned from Babylon. See Murphy-O'Connor, "La genèse littéraire de la *Règle de la Communauté*," *RB* 76 (1969): 528-49; review of Georg Klinzing's *Die Umdeutung des Kultus in der Qumran Gemeinde und im Neuen Testament, RB*

fore the group received the leadership of a person referred to in the Qumran scrolls as "the Righteous Teacher" (CD MS A. 1.10). Most scholars do not want to ignore such data but do not accept them as accurate and definitive. John J. Collins presents a judgment with which I concur: "While this information is neither as clear nor as exact as we would wish, it does reflect the Community's own recollection of its history. To overrule this evidence, we would need to find passages in the scrolls which *require* (and not merely *permit*) a different calculation."[37]

How to Translate מורה הצדק?

In the Qumran sectarian writings we confront a term: מורה הצדק.[38] How should we translate this *terminus technicus* at Qumran?[39] "The Teacher of Righteousness" was once the dominant English equivalent in Qumran research; and this rendering was defended by many, especially I. Rabinowitz and Per Wallendorff.[40] The source for the present rendering would be not only the early custom for translating the construct chain in Qumran studies,[41] but also possibly CD 6.10-11: "until the rise of one who will teach righteousness in the end of days."[42] It is possible that CD 6.8-11 is the "essential

---

79 (1972): 435-40; "The Essenes and Their History," *RB* 81 (1974:) 215-44; and "Community, Rule of the (1QS)," *ABD* 1:1110-12.

37. John J. Collins, "The Origin of the Qumran Community: A Review of the Evidence," in *To Touch the Text: Biblical and Related Studies in Honor of Joseph A. Fitzmyer,* ed. Maurya P. Horgan and Paul J. Kobelski (New York: Crossroad, 1989), 159-78; quotation, 170.

38. The form is always with an anarthrous *nomen regens* and a *nomen rectum* with an article, except in CD 1.1 and 20.32: מורה צדק.

39. The form appears in 1 Sam 20:36, but it denotes the arrows which Jonathan "shoots" to warn his friend David; it is clearly a Hiphil active participle.

40. Isaac Rabinowitz, "The Guides of Righteousness," *VT* 8 (1958): 391-404; Per Wallendorff, *Rättfärdighetens Lärare: En Exegetisk Undersökning* (Helsingfors: Aarhuus Stiftsbogtrykkerie, 1964), 27-28.

41. John C. Kesterson points out "the structural variety of this syntactic unit in *1QS*"; "The Indication of the Genitive Relationship in *1QS*," *RevQ* 13 [Mémorial Jean Carmignac] (1988): 513-24.

42. Translation by Joseph M. Baumgarten and Daniel R. Schwartz, in *The Dead Sea Scrolls: Damascus Document, War Scroll, and Related Documents,* ed. James H. Charlesworth. PTSDSSP 2 (Louisville: Westminster John Knox, 1995), 23. Jerome Murphy-O'Connor claims that CD 6.10-11 explains why this construct chain is translated "Teacher of Righteousness." See his comment in *ABD* 6:341. Some scholars, understandably, think that CD 6.11 refers "to the present experiences of the Qumran group," and thus denotes the Righteous Teacher. See Håkan Ulfgard, "The Teacher of Righteousness, the History of the Qumran Community, and Our Understanding of the Jesus Movement: Texts, Theories and Trajectories," in Cryer and Thompson, *Qumran between the Old and New Testaments,* 324-45; quotation, 325.

clue to the problem of the rôle of" the Righteous Teacher,[43] but it is far from clear that the מורה הצדק is the subject of this passage and that the construct chain should be translated "the Teacher of Righteousness." The compiler or the *Damascus Document* addressed his work only to "all those who know righteousness" (CD 1.1); presumably that is because they know and practice righteousness because they have the Right Teacher.[44] Conceivably, the passage points to another person who will arise in the future after the death of this person.[45] If that is what is intended, then it is also conceivable that the one who will return might be viewed in terms of the life of the מורה הצדק; but even so, if the one to come "will teach righteousness" it is not clear that this statement should be retroverted so as to describe the career of the מורה הצדק. The passage in CD may, or may not, refer to the מורה הצדק.[46] In any case, CD 6 does not prove that the construct chain should be translated "the Teacher of Righteousness"; and that is our only concern at this point.

As we would expect for proper grammar, we find in the Qumran scrolls only the anarthrous form of the *nomen regens:*[47] usually מורה הצדק but also מורה הצדקה in 1QpHab 2.2 (cf. מורה צדק in CD 1.11 and 20.32).[48] The Hebrew מורה הצדק can be translated either "the Teacher of

43. See Philip R. Davies, "The Teacher of Righteousness and the 'End of Days,'" *Sects and Scrolls: Essays on Qumran and Related Topics.* SFSHJ 134 (Atlanta: Scholars, 1996), 89-94; see esp. 90.

44. One could conceivably claim that his intended audience knows righteousness because the Teacher taught them righteousness; but that is an interpretation that seems forced and is not supported by exegesis.

45. Ben Zion Wacholder is even of the opinion not only that CD 6.8-11 refers to a future person but that all references to the Righteous Teacher denote a future, imminent, person; "Who Is the Teacher of Righteousness?" *BRev* 15/2 (1999): 26-29. Paolo Sacchi recently intrepreted CD 6 as follows: "The Law is like a well which must be continually deepened until the arrival of a final" Righteous Teacher; *The History of the Second Temple Period.* JSOTSup 285 (Sheffield: Sheffield Academic, 2000), 325.

46. The issue relates not only to the date of the *Damascus Document,* but to the date of the "Admonition." If CD 6 antedates the rise of the Righteous Teacher, it probably was interpreted by some Jews to refer to him. If it postdates his death, it might have been interpreted by some Jews as referring to another future figure. For bibliographical data and pertinent insights on the dating of this section of CD (esp. the work by Murphy-O'Connor and Davies), see Joseph M. Baumgarten, "Damascus Document," in Schiffman and VanderKam, *Encyclopedia of the Dead Sea Scrolls* 1:166-70. Baumgarten rightly dates the document known as CD (in something like a final form) before the beginning of the 1st century B.C.E. and after the death of the Righteous Teacher ca. 110 B.C.E. Some components of the work thus antedate 110.

47. Håkan Bengtsson incorrectly copied the *nomen regens* with a definite article; *What's in a Name? A Study of Sobriquets in the Pesharim* (Uppsala: University, 2000), 191.

48. See James H. Charlesworth et al., eds., *Graphic Concordance to the Dead Sea Scrolls.* PTSDSSP (Louisville: Westminster John Knox, 1991), 140, 390.

Righteousness" or "the Righteous Teacher." The Hebrew literally means "the teacher of the righteousness," but that is improper English. English "the teacher of righteousness" imprecisely represents the Hebrew. What is the best way to translate this construct chain, and — most importantly — what does it mean?

The second noun in the construct chain, the *nomen rectum,* can be either an objective genitive, giving "the Teacher of Right" (which would contrast with "the Man of the Lie" who is also "the Spreader of the Lie"),[49] or a subjective genitive, "the Righteous Teacher" or "the Right Teacher." The latter grammatical meaning is not only characteristic of Qumran Hebrew, as William H. Brownlee observed,[50] but also clarifies the rightness and truthfulness of the Teacher. This technical term also connotes that this Qumran leader is the only rightful teacher. As Schiffman states, the construct chain denotes the "correct teacher."[51] This Qumran leader is presented and conceived in contrast to "the Wicked Priest," as seems clear from 1QpHab 1.13-14; thus, the translation "the Righteous Teacher" seems preferable. This rendering emphasizes that the anonymous one is the Right Teacher and it also implies that he teaches righteousness; both meanings are present but the former is paramount.[52] The means of translating מורה הצדק as "the Righteous Teacher" was thus wisely chosen by the advisors and subeditors consulted when the consistency chart was developed for the PTSDSS Project in the mid-1980s.

Who Was the Righteous Teacher?

Although there are no fewer than 19 references to him by this sobriquet or as the "Teacher" in the Qumran scrolls,[53] this Qumran leader remains a shadowy figure. He is anonymous and elusive. The term probably does not refer to a generic function in the Community. The pesharim and the auto-

---

49. See Bengtsson, *What's in a Name?* 108.

50. William H. Brownlee, *The Midrash Pesher of Habakkuk.* SBLMS 24 (Missoula: Scholars, 1979), 46.

51. Lawrence H. Schiffman, *Reclaiming the Dead Sea Scrolls* (Philadelphia: Jewish Publication Society, 1994), 117.

52. See also the discussions by Gert Jeremias, *Der Lehrer der Gerechtigkeit.* SUNT 2 (Göttingen: Vandenhoeck & Ruprecht, 1963), 308-16; Ulfgard, "The Teacher of Righteousness," 310-46; and Wallendorff, *Rättfärdighetens Lärare,* 27-28. Wallendorff argued that the Righteous Teacher "was tied to a certain era in the life of the sect and was not expected at all after that. His literary contribution remains unverified and hidden by lively writing activity in the sect" (175). He observed that from "fourteen analyzed text passages it appears that no literary trait is mentioned in connection to the" Righteous Teacher (174).

53. See Charlesworth et al., *Graphic Concordance,* 361, 390.

biographical sections of the *Thanksgiving Hymns* indicate that he is a distinct person.[54] He was probably charismatic and dynamic. He clearly had a brilliant intellect and was a priest who rose to some prominence within the priestly circles in the Jerusalem cult. He probably descended from Aaron and Zadok, and was thus accounted among the Sons of Aaron and especially the Zadokites. He seems to have attracted the following of many of the legitimate Zadokite priests, but we do not know what percentage of the Zadokites followed him. Many of the Levites also attached themselves to his group, but it is unwise to assume most of them followed him into the wilderness. He may have served as high priest during the so-called intersacerdotium (159-152 B.C.E.)[55] and before the Hasmonean Jonathan accepted the high priesthood and title of "my Friend" (φίλον ἐμὸν) from Alexander Balas.[56] After Alcimus, and between 159 and 152, there was no "officially appointed" high priest officiating in the Temple, but a high priest was frequently demanded for tasks within the Temple cult, especially during the "Days of Awe," which included *Yom Hakippurim*. Presumably, some priest — or consecutively priests — served, if only intermittently, during the period from 159 to 152.

Eventually, his small group lost against the powerful Hasmoneans, who claimed the high priesthood forever "until a trustworthy prophet should arise" (1 Macc. 14:41). This admission reveals that the Hasmoneans could not appeal to Scripture, tradition, or prophets to establish themselves. Thus, despite the tendencies of Chronicles to offer a synthesis of divergent traditions in Israel,[57] and of 1 Maccabees to support the legitimacy of the Maccabees and Hasmoneans, it is apparent that the Hasmonean line of priests is not legitimate and it certainly did not derive from Zadok.

The Righteous Teacher, a Zadokite, and his small group "separated" from the Temple cult. Many Qumran experts conclude that they then left the Temple and went into the wilderness. The key text is 1QS 8.13-15: "they shall separate themselves (יבדלו)[58] from the session of the men of

54. Murphy-O'Connor rightly reports that this is a consensus; see *ABD* 6:340-41 and the modern publications he lists.

55. See Josephus *Ant.* 20.237: διεδέξατο δ' αὐτὸν οὐδείς, ἀλλὰ διετέλεσεν ἡ πόλις ἐνιαυτοὺς ἑπτὰ χωρὶς ἀρχιερέως οὖσα. This hypothesis was advanced by Hartmut Stegemann; see *Die Entstehung der Qumrangemeinde* (Bonn: Rheinische Friedrich-Wilhelms-Universität, 1971); and esp. *Die Essener, Qumran, Johannes der Täufer und Jesus* (Freiburg: Herder, 1993).

56. See esp. 1 Macc. 10:15-20; Josephus *Ant.* 13.43-46.

57. See Rainer Albertz, *A History of Israelite Religion in the Old Testament Period*, trans. John Bowden. OTL (Louisville: Westminster John Knox, 1994), esp. 2:547.

58. Niphal imperfect.

deceit (הנשי העול)[59] in order to depart into the wilderness to prepare there the Way of the Lord (?); as it is written: 'In the wilderness prepare the way of the Lord, make level in the desert a highway for our God'" (the intertext is Isa. 40:3).[60] In fact, "separated" is a term that clearly defines the Righteous Teacher's group in *More Works of the Torah:* "we have separated (פרשנו[ש]) ourselves from the multitude of the people" (4QMMT C 7 [Composite Text]).[61]

Numerous scholars have sought to identify the Righteous Teacher.[62] Working primarily from the Qumran pesharim, they have nominated a wide variety of men as the Righteous Teacher, offering candidates who span four centuries, from the early 2nd century B.C.E. through the First Jewish Revolt of 66-70 (74) C.E. to even the 2nd century C.E.[63] Candidates as the Righteous Teacher include Zadok (ca. 200 B.C.E.),[64] Onias III (170 B.C.E.),[65] Mattathias and Judas Maccabeus (ca. 167-162 B.C.E.),[66] Simon III (159-152 B.C.E.),[67]

---

59. MS D of the *Rule of the Community* rightly reads אנשי העול. This *terminus technicus* refers to the wicked priests officiating in Jerusalem.

60. See James H. Charlesworth, "Intertextuality: Isaiah 40:3 and the Serek Ha-Yahad," in *The Quest for Context and Meaning: Studies in Biblical Intertextuality in Honor of James A. Sanders,* ed. Craig A. Evans and Shemaryahu Talmon (Leiden: Brill, 1997), 197-224. See also James M. Scott, "Korah and Qumran," in *The Bible at Qumran: Text, Shape, and Interpretation,* ed. Peter W. Flint. SDSSRL (Grand Rapids: Wm. B. Eerdmans, 2001), 182-202.

61. Diacritics not shown; from Elisha Qimron and John Strugnell, *Qumran Cave 4.V.* DJD 10 (Oxford: Clarendon, 1994), 58-59.

62. See the short sketch of this research by Håkan Ulfgard, "Rättfärdighetens Lärare och Qumranförsamlingens historia: En kort skiss över problematiken," in *Dødehavsteksterne og Bibelen,* ed. Niels Hyldahl and Thomas L. Thompson (Copenhagen: Copenhagen University and Museum Tusculanums, 1996), 129-57.

63. See Emil Schürer, *The History of the Jewish People in the Age of Jesus Christ,* rev. ed. 3/1, ed. Geza Vermes et al. (Edinburgh: T. & T. Clark, 1986), 436; and esp. Bengtsson, *What's in a Name?* 185-89.

64. Ben Zion Wacholder, *The Dawn of Qumran: The Sectarian Torah and the Teacher of Righteousness* (Cincinnati: Hebrew Union College Press, 1983), 99 [the Righteous Teacher "seems to be a paronomasia on the name Zadok"].

65. Bo Reicke, "Die Taʿāmire-Schriften und die Damaskus-Fragmente," *ST* 2 (1949): 45-70; H. H. Rowley, *Zadokite Fragments and the Dead Sea Scrolls* (New York: Macmillan, 1952), 67-68; also "The Historical Background of the Dead Sea Scrolls," *ExpTim* 63 (1952): 378-84; and M.-A. Michel, *Le Maître de Justice d'après les Documents de la Mer Morte, la littérature apocryphe et rabbinique* (Avignon: Maison Aubanel Père, 1954), 321-22.

66. Rabinowitz, *VT* 8 (1958): 391-404, esp. 403. Rabinowitz prefers to translate מורה הצדק as "guide of righteousness."

67. Émile Puech, "Le grand prêtre Simon (III) fils d'Onias III, le Maître de Justice?" in *Antikes Judentum und frühes Christentum: Festschrift für Hartmut Stegemann,* ed. Bernd Kollmann, Wolfgang Reinbold, and Annette Steudel. BZNW 97 (Berlin: Walter de Gruyter, 1999), 137-58, esp. 157.

Eleazar the Pharisee (ca. 134-104),[68] Judas [or Judah] the Essene (100 B.C.E.),[69] and Onias the Righteous [Honi Ha-Meaggel ("the Circlemaker")] (ca. 65 B.C.E.).[70] Even John the Baptizer,[71] Jesus of Nazareth,[72] James the Just,[73] Menahem (the son of Judas the Galilean (ca. 66-68 C.E.),[74] and Yose ben Yoezer (ca. 2nd cent. C.E.)[75] have been suggested as the Righteous Teacher.[76] In the judgment of most experts, the latter five cannot be candidates, since Qumran archaeology and palaeography[77] prove that the texts mentioning "the Righteous Teacher" — especially the pesharim — were written decades before the careers of John the Baptist and the others.[78]

68. William H. Brownlee, "The Historical Allusions of the Dead Sea Habakkuk Midrash," *BASOR* 126 (1952): 10-20. In his later publications Brownlee was more concerned with the function of the Righteous Teacher than with his identity. He still held to the possibility that the Pharisee who challenged John Hyrcanus may be the Righteous Teacher. See Brownlee, *The Midrash Pesher of Habakkuk*, 46-50, esp. 96.

69. Brownlee, *BASOR* 126 (1952): 18-19; A. S. van der Woude, *Die Messianische Vorstellungen der Gemeinde von Qumrân*. SSN 3 (Assen: Van Gorcum, 1957), 239; Jean Carmignac, "Qui était le Docteur de Justice?" *RevQ* 10 (1980): 235-46, 585-86.

70. Roger Goossens, 'Onias le Juste, le Messie de la Nouvelle Alliance," *La Nouvelle Clio 1-2* (1949-1950): 336-53.

71. B. E. Thiering, *Redating the Teacher of Righteousness* (Sydney: Theological Explorations, 1979), 212; *Jesus & the Riddle of the Dead Sea Scrolls* (San Francisco: HarperSanFrancisco, 1992), 66-72.

72. J. L. Teicher, "Jesus in the Habakkuk Scroll," *JJS* 3 (1952): 53-55.

73. Robert H. Eisenman, *The Dead Sea Scrolls and the First Christians* (Shaftesbury: Element, 1996); and *James the Brother of Jesus: The Key to Unlocking the Secrets of Early Christianity and the Dead Sea Scrolls* (New York: Viking, 1997).

74. H. E. del Medico, *Deux manuscrits Hébreux de la Mer Morte* (Paris: Librairie Orientaliste Paul Geuthner S.A., 1951), 132-37; *L'Énigme des manuscrits de la Mer Morte* (Paris: Librairie Plon, 1957), 181-88, 342-57; G. R. Driver, *The Judaean Scrolls* (Oxford: Blackwell, 1965), 267-81.

75. E. Stauffer, "Der gekreuzigte Thoralehrer," *ZRGG* (1956), 250-53.

76. John C. Trever is convinced that the author-compiler of Daniel is the Righteous Teacher (whom he calls, following Brownlee, "the Right Teacher"). See Trever, "The Qumran Teacher — Another Candidate?" in *Early Jewish and Christian Exegesis: Studies in Memory of William Hugh Brownlee*, ed. Craig A. Evans and William F. Stinespring (Atlanta: Scholars, 1987), 101-21.

77. Phillip R. Callaway summarizes the evidence concisely; the persons mentioned in CD 1 and 4QpNah, e.g., must antedate 75 B.C.E.; *The History of the Qumran Community*. JSPSup 3 (Sheffield: JSOT, 1988), 61.

78. It is unlikely that Joel 2:23 explains the meaning of the Righteous Teacher at Qumran. The phrase in Joel is ambiguous, and we do not have a pesher on Joel. Perhaps Joel was not a major text at Qumran. See Hans Walter Wolff, *Joel und Amos*. Herm (Philadelphia: Fortress, 1977), 64. I doubt that the *Testaments of the Twelve Patriarchs* (viz. *T.Benj.* 9:2) explains the title, as Chaim Rabin claimed in "The 'Teacher of Righteousness' in the 'Testaments of the Twelve Patriarchs'?" *JJS* 3 (1952): 127-28.

Most scholars rightly conclude that we do not know the name of the Qumran leader who is habitually called "the Righteous Teacher."[79] As is the case in history, many of the most important people sometimes remain anonymous.[80] We can discern, however, the Teacher's time period. His main opponent is "the Wicked Priest." The latter is most likely either Jonathan (152-143/2) or Simon (143/2-135/4). It is obvious that some Qumranites knew the name of the Righteous Teacher, but it is unwise to think that they refused to mention his name out of reverence.[81] More likely, the main reasons for our failure to identify the name of the Righteous Teacher are the selective quality of our sources, the cryptic nature of the Qumran scrolls, and — most importantly — the paucity of proper names and penchant for anonymity in them.

It is clear the Righteous Teacher was the most important person in the history of the Qumranites.[82] He was a distinct person and not just a generic name for a succession of teachers at Qumran;[83] his passion for believing that God had sent him to plant the final planting for God's glory shapes many of the *Thanksgiving Hymns*.[84] The Teacher spoke with abso-

79. Murphy-O'Connor thinks he may be the high priest who must have succeeded Alcimus; see *RB* 81 (1974): 215-44. Gert Jeremias, Cross, and most Qumran experts wisely refrain from trying to identify the Righteous Teacher.

80. Some leading specialists conclude that the most important person in American history is the anonymous one who brought smallpox to America and wiped out the native "Indians." We do not know with certainty the names of the ones who brought Christianity, for example, to Alexandria and Rome (although myths always fill such gaps).

81. This was the suggestion of A. Dupont-Sommer, *Observations sur le Commentaire d'Habacuc découvert près de la Mer Morte* (Paris: Librairie Andrien-Maisonneuve, 1950), 14-15.

82. See Wallendorff, *Rättfärdighetens Lärare;* see the English summary, 173-75.

83. T. H. Gaster incorrectly thought that "the Righteous Teacher" denoted a succession of teachers, and thus preferred the translation of *môrēh haṣ-ṣedeq* as "the teacher who expounds the Law aright"; *The Dead Sea Scriptures in English Translation* (Garden City: Doubleday, 1956), 5. It is a pity that Gaster never published the notes to his translation. I also disagree with Schiffman, who thinks that the Righteous Teacher "may have designated not only one but a series of figures who occupied the role of sectarian leader over a period of time"; *Reclaiming the Dead Sea Scrolls,* 117. For me, the unique authority of the Righteous Teacher, clarified in 1QpHab 7, and evidence of his paradigmatic role, especially evident in 1QH, suggest that there was one and only one Righteous Teacher. His later followers, in contrast to CD 1, thought that he was their founder.

84. See James H. Charlesworth, "An Allegorical and Autobiographical Poem by the *Moreh haṣ-Ṣedeq* (1QH 8:4-11)," in *"Sha'arei Talmon,"* ed. Michael Fishbane and Emanuel Tov (Winona Lake: Eisenbrauns, 1992), 295-307. According to the new and correct arrangements of columns in 1QH this column is 1QH 16. Gert Jeremias developed the method for discerning the hymns of the Righteous Teacher within the *Thanksgiving Hymns;* see Jeremias, *Der Lehrer der Gerechtigkeit.* Michael C. Douglas also claims that portions of the *Hodayot* go

lute authority.[85] He seems to have identified himself with the Servant of Isaiah 53, but sufferings were incidental to his mission.[86] He was primarily a teacher, as indicated by the *terminus technicus* מורה הצדק. While we do not know his name, we do know his sobriquet.[87]

The person known only as "the Righteous Teacher" is conspicuously absent in most of the Qumran sectarian scrolls. It is rather surprising that he is mentioned neither in the historically important *More Works of the Torah* (4QMMT) nor in the paradigmatically important *Rule of the Community*.[88] No Qumran text was composed to describe or celebrate him. This fact clarifies a contrast between him and Jesus of Nazareth,[89] since the Gospels were composed to proclaim Jesus as Messiah and Son of God.[90] Unlike Jesus, the Righteous Teacher did not found a Jewish movement;[91]

---

back to the Righteous Teacher but presents criteria that differ from Jeremias; "The Teacher Hymn Hypothesis Revisited: New Data for an Old Crux," *DSD* 6 (1999): 239-66.

85. See Paul Schulz, *Der Autoritätsanspruch des Lehrers der Gerechtigkeit in Qumran* (Meisenheim am Glan: Anton Hain, 1974).

86. See John J. Collins, "Teacher and Servant," *RHPR* 80 (2000): 37-50.

87. See Bengtsson, *What's in a Name?* 180-216.

88. Schiffman opines that the Righteous Teacher does not appear in 4QMMT because it was not written by him (modesty would also explain the absence of his name) but by "the collective leadership of the sect in those initial years"; *Reclaiming the Dead Sea Scrolls,* 87. He is convinced that the leadership of the Righteous Teacher postdates this so-called *"Halakhic Letter"* (90). Schiffman rightly does not attempt to identify the Righteous Teacher (121). I agree with Philip R. Davies that to talk about "halakah at Qumran" is "seriously misleading"; "Halakhah at Qumran," *A Tribute to Geza Vermes,* ed. Davies and Richard T. White. JSOTSup 100 (Sheffield: JSOT, 1990), 49. We should not confuse Qumran legal rules with later rabbinic *halakot;* and we need terms that enable us to make such essential distinctions.

89. Regarding the Righteous Teacher and Jesus, see the following recent publications: Hartmut Stegemann, "The 'Teacher of Righteousness' and Jesus: Two Types of Religious Leadership in Judaism at the Turn of the Era," in *Jewish Civilization in the Hellenistic-Roman Period,* ed. Shemaryahu Talmon. JSPSup 10 (Sheffield: Sheffield Academic, 1991), 196-213; Samuel Byrskog, *Jesus the Only Teacher: Didactic Authority and Transmission in Ancient Israel, Ancient Judaism and the Matthean Community.* ConBNT 24 (Stockholm: Almquist & Wiksell, 1994); James H. Charlesworth, "The Righteous Teacher and the Historical Jesus," in *Earthing Christologies,* ed. Charlesworth and Walter P. Weaver (Valley Forge: Trinity, 1995), 46-61.

90. It is simply an error to think that the followers of the Righteous Teacher thought he was "a messiah." Thus, one should be aware of the exaggerations continued by Michael O. Wise, esp. in "Dead Sea Scrolls: General Information," in Evans and Porter, *Dictionary of New Testament Background,* 252-66, esp. 264; and also in *The First Messiah: Investigating the Savior Before Christ* (San Francisco: HarperSanFrancisco, 1999).

91. See the insightful comments by Davies, *Sects and Scrolls,* 90-91. Davies contends, and I think correctly, that according to CD Col. 1, the Righteous Teacher "is described as being sent to an existing community which (retrospectively, of course) sees itself as having been 'blindly groping for the way' before his arrival" (90).

he was heir to a dissident priestly group who traced their lineage back to Aaron with special attention on Zadok (CD 1.9-11 and 3.20–4.4 [with a quotation from Ezek. 44:15]).[92] He became a catalyst for a reforming and strict movement within Judaism that was eventually exiled (or exiled itself) from the Temple and resided at Qumran "in the wilderness." As Frank M. Cross states, it is unwise to attempt a systematic reconstruction of the life of the Righteous Teacher; the data clarify that such is impossible.[93]

Who Was the "Man of Lies"?

There was a split in this movement and it seems to have occurred before the group settled at Qumran. A "Man of Lies" apparently led the larger part of the early group. His group included possibly not only those who had questioned the leadership of the Righteous Teacher but also some of those who had shown initial allegiance to him. According to the pesharim, the Man of Lies led those who, in the minds of those later at Qumran, "turned back" and "departed from the Way." While scholars can only speculate about the time and meaning of such ambiguous phrases and terms, it seems possible that the "renewed (or new) covenant" is a concept that antedates the leadership of the Righteous Teacher.[94] I have no doubt that the early portions of the *Books of Enoch* and *Jubilees* not only antedate the establishment of a community at Qumran but also embody pre-Qumran thought.[95] The palaeographical dating of the *Books of Enoch* proves that the early portions of this corpus antedate 200 B.C.E.

Who Was the "Wicked Priest"?

The opponent of the Righteous Teacher is also anonymous. He is merely called "the Wicked Priest." The high priest in charge of the Jerusalem cult, he could thus be either Jonathan or Simon — both of whom were

---

92. At Qumran, and probably much later than CD, the Righteous Teacher was considered the founder of the Community, as we know from 4QpPs 3.15-16.

93. *The Ancient Library of Qumran*, 3rd ed. (Sheffield: Sheffield Academic, 1995), 117.

94. See John J. Collins, "Essenes," *ABD* 2:625.

95. A succinct summary of the consensus is given by James C. VanderKam, one of the experts who has focused on studying *1 Enoch* and *Jubilees*, in *The Dead Sea Scrolls Today* (Grand Rapids: Wm. B. Eerdmans, 1994), 36-41. However, Doron Mendels, one of the leading experts on Hellenistic historiography, contends that *Jubilees* was composed ca. 125 B.C.E. (R. H. Charles's conclusion); see Mendels, *The Rise and Fall of Jewish Nationalism* (repr. Grand Rapids: Wm. B. Eerdmans, 1997), 44.

Hasmoneans (and not Zadokites). The consensus today is that Jonathan seems more likely to be the Wicked Priest. If he was the first one to be so labeled, it is likely that this sobriquet was later used to designate whoever was the Hasmonean high priest presently controlling the Temple cult and who thereby continued to be the adversary of the Righteous Teacher's group. Thus the "Wicked Priest" could have been Jonathan, then Simon, and finally others of the Hasmonean line. Accordingly, with many experts like Strugnell, I consider it wise to think about the code name "the Wicked Priest" not as a static constant but as a floating reutilization of an epithet that appeared early in Qumran history.[96]

The Exodus of the Righteous Teacher

Thus, some scholars find it conceivable (but it is by no means certain) that sometime during the middle of the 2nd century B.C.E. the Righteous Teacher led a group out of the Temple and Jerusalem and southeastward into the wilderness.[97] There is no way we can discern the size of his group. There is no evidence to cause us to think his initial group was large; perhaps it numbered only 20 to 50 Zadokite priests and Levites. The importance of a movement does not reside in its initial numbers, but in the passion and charisma of its leader and the tenacity of his followers. The passion derives from the leader, but the charisma is a sociological feature that primarily depends on the group that follows him. Thus, truth and some longevity reside not in numbers of followers but in the clarity, vision,

---

96. Strugnell, *NEA* 63 (2000): 175. I differ with Strugnell (whom I admire greatly; after all, he taught me Qumran grammar, philology, and palaeography) when he thinks that "the Righteous Teacher" is an epithet that was reused. There is clear evidence, however, that the Qumranites admired him and thought he was incomparable (cf. 1QpHab 7), and autobiographical passages in the *Thanksgiving Hymns* point to one distinct personality. There were certainly other teachers and officers at Qumran like "the Examiner," "the Master" and "the Overseer." There is certainly no inconsistency in concluding that there were many priests whom the Qumranites identified successively as "the Wicked Priest," but that there was only one Righteous Teacher. That conclusion is sound historiographically (since logic does not shape history), and it derives from an exegesis of the relevant passages in the pesharim and elsewhere.

97. Jodi Magness contends that Qumran was first inhabited in the early portions of the 1st century B.C.E.; "Qumran Archaeology: Past Perspectives and Future Prospects," in Flint and VanderKam, *The Dead Sea Scrolls after Fifty Years,* 1:47-77, esp. 64-65. Magness is well informed and her position makes sense if one looks only at the archaeological evidence; much of the pottery and coins do not lead to conclusive evidence that de Vaux's Period Ia existed. The evidence of the Qumran scrolls and the renovations of earlier phases tend to shift the probability to de Vaux's dating.

and passion of the instigator (originator or founder) and in the continuing charisma that galvanized him to his group.

If the Righteous Teacher did lead his exiled group into the wilderness, what would they have found there? They would have found an abandoned Israelite fort that had been destroyed when the kingdom of Judah fell in the beginning of the 6th century B.C.E. (a *lammelek* jar handle, an ostracon with Palaeo-Hebrew letters, and a layer of ash were recovered by Roland de Vaux's team).[98] From this Iron Age II period the Righteous Teacher's band also found a round cistern and remains of a rectangular building with a long eastern wall.

What renovations did this first Qumran group make to the site? They added a channel to provide water more adequately for the extant (Iron Age) cistern, a decantation basin to remove sand, and two additional rectangular cisterns. Rooms were added in the north of the complex. The exiled priests constructed two pottery kilns on the southeast of the complex. This first phase of Qumran occupation was modest, leaving few archaeological remains; and the subsequent massive renovations and expansions obliterated many of the traces of this first phase. What is clear in it is an inordinate concern for water, not for normal living purposes but for ritual purification.[99]

The Righteous Teacher died probably sometime before 100 B.C.E.[100] He was not crucified. It is possible that he may have been severely wounded by the Wicked Priest (as we known from the pesharim and most likely also from some of the hymns in the *Thanksgiving Hymns*). His followers did not consider him the Messiah or expect him to return as the Messiah. He was also probably not celebrated as the prophet who was to precede the Messiah, yet he was the centripetal force that galvanized the Yaḥad, defined its purpose, and led the group into the wilderness from the house of God, the Temple. He may have been the one who developed the

---

98. Roland de Vaux, *Archaeology and the Dead Sea Scrolls* (London: Oxford University Press, 1973), 2-3. See also de Vaux, "Qumran, Khirbet and 'Ein Feshka," *NEAEHL* 4:1235-41 and Magen Broshi's appendix, 1241.

99. I discern a consensus here among scholars. For recent research, see Bryant G. Wood, "To Dip or Sprinkle? The Qumran Cisterns in Perspective," *BASOR* 256 (1984): 45-60; Patricia Hidiroglou, "L'Eau et les bains à Qumrân," *Revue des études juives* 159 (2000): 19-47; "Aqueducts, Basins, and Cisterns: The Water Systems at Qumran," *NEA* 63 (2000): 138-39. Hidiroglou opens the way for a deeper, more phenomenological study of the importance and meaning of water at Qumran.

100. Joseph A. Fitzmyer rightly points out that CD 19.33–20.1 and CD 20.13-15 refer to the death of the Righteous Teacher; "The Gathering In of the Community's Teacher," *MAARAV* 8 (1992): 223-28; repr. in Joseph A. Fitzmyer, *The Dead Sea Scrolls and Christian Origins*. SDSSRL (Grand Rapids: Wm. B. Eerdmans, 2000), 261-65.

Roland de Vaux before Qumran Cave 1

Photo courtesy of Brian Nolan and James H. Charlesworth

concept, preserved in 1QS 8.12-14,[101] that they — the Qumranites — were in the wilderness because they had heard the Voice calling them into the wilderness: "In the wilderness, prepare the Way of YHWH" (Isa 40:3). Perhaps the Righteous Teacher created the pesher method of interpreting Scripture. If so, then Timothy H. Lim judges rightly that the Righteous Teacher, with the claim of "divine sanction, inaugurated this sectarian form of biblical interpretation, and his followers carried it forward by composing exegetical works that modern scholarship now describes as pesharim."[102]

101. I think Murphy-O'Connor is correct in concluding that 1QS 8 and 9 preserve what substantially derives from the Righteous Teacher. See "Teacher of Righteousness," *ABD* 6:340-41; *RB* 76 (1969): 528-49; and *RB* 81 (1974): 215-44. Also, we should not forget the portions of the *Thanksgiving Hymns* that seem to preserve autobiographical and metaphorical compositions by the Righteous Teacher.

102. See Timothy H. Lim, "The Qumran Scrolls, Multilingualism, and Biblical Interpretation," in *Religion in the Dead Sea Scrolls,* ed. John J. Collins and Robert A. Kugler.

Joseph A. Fitzmyer has conclusively shown that CD 19.35 and 20.14 figuratively denote the death of the Righteous Teacher.[103] His death must have been a shock to the members of the Community, but no texts have survived that clarify how the Qumranites were affected by his death ca. 110 B.C.E. (cf. CD 20.13-17).[104] Surely, some of his followers had expected during his lifetime to return to the Temple and be recognized as the only legitimate priests. There is no reason to have any doubts that his death, with no evidence of God's promises to and through him being fulfilled, precipitated a difficult stage in the history of the Qumranites.

During this first phase, and the subsequent one, the main tasks of the Qumranites were to observe the proper means of interpreting Torah, to prepare the Way of YHWH in the wilderness by studying Torah, to copy ancient manuscripts, to compose new collections of rules and hymns, and to praise God for their being created among "the Sons of Light." Recent study has removed doubts that Room 30 at Qumran was a scriptorium in which members of the Yaḥad copied or composed manuscripts.[105] It is possible that the Qumranites were settled at Qumran by the time of John Hyrcanus (135/4-104). Yet, it is not clear from archaeological work when the Qumranites first settled there.[106]

During this first phase of Qumran history numerous *termini technici* appeared in the Qumran compositions; these terms developed and helped shape the theological and sociological contours of the Qumran Community. Among such terms, some of which were inherited but received new meanings, the following are most significant:[107]

SDSSRL (Grand Rapids: Wm. B. Eerdmans, 2000), 57-73; quotation, 60. Also, see Lim, *Holy Scripture in the Qumran Commentaries and Pauline Letters* (Oxford: Oxford University Press, 1997), for a study of the authorial adaptations to the lemmata.

103. Fitzmyer, "The Gathering In of the Community's Teacher."

104. I am grateful to Philip R. Davies for discussions at this point.

105. In addition to de Vaux's archaeological reports, observe the publication of de Vaux's notes and the photographs of Room 30 in Jean-Baptiste Humbert and Alain Chambon, *Fouilles de Khirbet Qumrân et de Aïn Feshkha.* NTOA 1 (Fribourg: Éditions universitaires, 1994), photographs 110-26. See also Roland de Vaux, *Die Ausgrabungen von Qumran und En Feschcha,* ed. F. Rohrhirsch and B. Hofmeir. NTOA 1A (Fribourg: Universitätsverlag Freiburg Schweiz, 1996). See esp. Ronny Reich, "A Note on the Function of Room 30 (the "Scriptorium") at Khirbet Qumran," *JJS* 46 (1995): 157-60.

106. See esp. de Vaux, *Archaeology and the Dead Sea Scrolls;* Ernest-Marie Laperrousaz, *Qoumrân, L'Établissement essénien des bords de la Mer Morte: Histoire et archéologie du site* (Paris: Picard, 1976); "Archéologie du Khirbet Qumran et de la région," *Supplément au Dictionnaire de la Bible,* fasc. 51 (Paris: Letouzey, 1978), cols. 744-89; Jerome Murphy-O'Connor, "Qumran, Khirbet," *ABD* 5:590-94; Humbert and Chambon, *Fouilles de Khirbet Qumrân;* and de Vaux, *Die Ausgrabungen von Qumran.*

107. For the Hebrew terms, see "Consistency Chart," *The Dead Sea Scrolls* 6B, xiv-xv.

Belial (as a term for the evil angel)
the Examiner
Holy Ones, Most Holy Ones
Holy Spirit (or Spirit of Holiness)
House of Holiness (as a sanctuary)
Yaḥad (or Community)
the Overseer
Man of the Lie
the Many
the Master
Messiah(s) of Aaron and Israel
Perfect Ones
Poor Ones
the Righteous Teacher (the Right Teacher)
Sons of Darkness
Sons of the Dawn
Sons of Light
Sons of Zadok
Spirit of Truth
the Man of the Lie and the Spouter of the Lie
the Wicked Priest
pesher

Many of these terms appear in the pesharim. Obviously, the various formulae with the term "pesher" define many of the biblical commentaries composed at Qumran. These formulae defined the Qumranites. They are Qumran creations like the Hodayot formula, "I thank you, O Lord, because," which is the standard formula for introducing praise in the *Thanksgiving Hymns*.[108] The Qumranites' interpretation of Scripture defined and shaped their ideology and categorized their Community.[109]

---

108. In order to distinguish Qumran interpretation and expansion of Scripture from the rabbinic ones, I avoid the term "Midrash," even though מדרש is found in the commentaries (cf. 4QFlor frgs. 1-2, 21, col. 1.14). I agree with Horgan that this *terminus technicus*, which is not found in the pesharim, is "neither a useful nor an informative term by which to characterize the pesharim"; Horgan, in James C. Charlesworth et al., *The Pesharim, Other Commentaries, and Related Documents*, 252. See also the similar judgment of Isaac Rabinowitz, "*Pēsher/Pittārōn:* Its Biblical Meaning and Its Significance in the Qumran Literature," *RevQ* 8 (1972-74): 219-32, esp. 231.

109. Brooke compares "Qumran exegesis with Christian eisegesis." For me, both of these are examples of Jewish eisegesis; "Biblical Interpretation in the Qumran Scrolls and

41

Typical of Qumran sociology are high social barriers and exclusiveness. Inside the group are the predestined and elect Sons of Light; outside it are the damned Sons of Darkness. Clearly, only in the Qumran group, and in the group defined by the *Damascus Document,* are located the faithful of Israel who live in the latter days. Archaeology and the study of the evolution of 1QS indicate that the first phase of Qumran probably runs from ca. 150 B.C.E. to ca. 102 or 100 B.C.E.

Reactions to Archaeological Period Ia

Some scholars are convinced we should rethink Archaeological Period Ia. Some suggest moving the date of occupation at Qumran from 150 B.C.E. to a later period. Two critics are most prominent.

First, Jean-Baptiste Humbert contends that the early phases at Qumran were not sectarian.[110] He contends that during the early years, and even up until 57 (when Gabinus allegedly destroyed Qumran)[111] or even 31 B.C.E. (when Herod gained control over the Qumran area), Qumran was defined by agricultural activities.

This position seems unlikely for numerous reasons. First, the archaeological evidence does not suggest an agricultural center at Qumran, and the abundant *realia* associated with agricultural activity were not found at Khirbet Qumran. Second, the installations at Qumran indicate the religious dimensions of those who lived there; this is clear because of the abundant provisions made for water purification, and the large area set aside for communal dining with more than 1000 dishes (cf. Josephus's account of the Essenes' common room for meals; *War* 2.30). Third, if Qumran were in Galilee or in Jericho, one could imagine it being a center for agriculture; but the Qumran area is one of the most inhospitable places on earth: in a wilderness beside a killing "Dead Sea." Fourth, even if the first Hellenistic buildings at Qumran might remind one of a rural or agricultural estate, there is no reason to dismiss the possibility that priests could copy what they had seen and use the concept for religious purposes. Fifth, Qumran is poorly built; most of the stones are uncut. It contrasts markedly from the fine Hasmonean and Herodian structures found, for example, at Jericho and Ramat Hanadiv.[112]

---

the New Testament," in *The Dead Sea Scrolls Fifty Years after Their Discovery,* ed. Lawrence H. Schiffman, Emanuel Tov, and James C. VanderKam (Jerusalem: Israel Exploration Society, 2000), 63.

110. "L'espace sacré à Qumrân," *RB* 101 (1994): 161-214.

111. There is no evidence to support this hypothesis.

112. Yizhar Hirschfeld, *Ramat Hanadiv Excavations: Final Report of the 1984-1988*

The Great Hall in which the Qumranites assembled for meals
and then later, after it was cleaned, for worship
(and perhaps the reading of some pesharim)

Photo by James H. Charlesworth

Second, Jodi Magness is convinced "that de Vaux's Period Ia" does not exist.[113] She points out that de Vaux failed to find coins from Period Ia and that "none of the pottery that de Vaux published from Qumran has to antedate the first century CE." She thus concludes that "the settlement at Qumran was apparently established much later than de Vaux thought, probably some time in the first half of the first century BCE." She rightly judges, however, that Qumran "settlement was sectarian from the beginning of its establishment."

It is obvious why these criticisms appear. De Vaux pointed out that the renovation of the earliest Hellenistic phase of Qumran removed evidence of Period Ia. This certainly makes sense. Also, those living at Qumran would have removed, intentionally or unintentionally, *realia* from the first occupation. Those who want the Wicked Priest and Righteous Teacher to be someone later in history obviously are biased against the possibility of Period Ia. The coins are another matter. If John Hyrcanus was the first one to mint Jewish coins, then one cannot find Jewish coins before his time. Finally, the sequence of pottery chronology does not change from Period Ia to Ib. To claim that none of the pottery found at Qumran must date before 100 B.C.E. is not insightful or helpful. Any evidence of a Phase Ia proves there was such a phase at Qumran; and it seems to be demanded if Jonathan or Simon was the Wicked Priest, as most scholars have concluded since the 1950s.

Phase II (Archaeological Period Ib)

According to de Vaux, the installations and buildings at Qumran "acquired what was virtually their definitive form" in Archaeological Period Ib.[114] What was the nature of this expansion? The most important additions are

---

Seasons (Jerusalem: Israel Exploration Society, 2000). The 768-page report contains the work of many archaeologists, and concludes with 16 color plates.

113. Jodi Magness, "Qumran Archaeology"; quotations, 64-65. See *The Archaeology of Qumran and the Dead Sea Scrolls.* SDSSRL (Grand Rapids: Wm. B. Eerdmans, 2002); also "The Archaeology of Qumran Reassessed," *American School of Classical Studies at Athens Newsletter* 45 (Winter 2001): 16. Most of her views are harmonious with those presented in this monograph. Although she dates the occupation of Qumran from "the late second century B.C. to 68 A.D.," she judges it to be Essene. While many of the Essenes lived "in towns and villages around Palestine" and married, "there were also isolated communities consisting mostly or entirely of adult celibate men." Qumran reveals "a communal social structure." It was certainly not "a villa or a manor house."

114. *Archaeology and the Dead Sea Scrolls,* 5; the review that follows is dependent on de Vaux, my teacher, with references to follow to more recent excavations and insights.

the following: a northern entrance and massive tower, a western entrance leading up to the Buqeiʿa and to Jerusalem, an eastern entrance near the potter's kiln, and the construction of a complex of rooms, some with a second story and stone steps,[115] to the south and east of the tower. One room (loc. 4) has stone benches *in situ,* two recesses, and a plastered basin that could be filled with water from an outside corridor. It was probably an assembly room (perhaps for the secret sessions of the Community). Immediately to the east of this stone-benched room is a rectangular room running north and south (loc. 30). It had a second story, and on the floor de Vaux's team found plastered benches and inkwells. This is the room identified as the scriptorium by de Vaux (a claim hotly debated lately but still most probable).[116]

While the purpose of most of these rooms is unclear, the lack of doors and windows along with the isolated nature of the tower indicates that "the builders were especially preoccupied with considerations of defence."[117] A large rectangular room was built in the south (loc. 77), just outside of the old Israelite wall. It is probably the refectory, since stacks of dishes for eating were found in a room to the south and contiguous with it (loc. 86 and 89). A wall, running almost perfectly north and south, was added on the east,[118] and a potter's workshop near it.

An aqueduct extended up to the base of the cliffs, the walls of the earliest and round cistern were increased, and four more large cisterns were added (most with steps) to bring the total number of cisterns (probably mikvaʾot) to seven (not counting the four basins). A bath was established on the northwest (loc. 138), and decantation basins to filter the water were added to the cisterns. Five of the cisterns received an extensive series of steps (loc. 117, 118, 49 with 48, 56 with 57, and 71), and small channels in the south allowed excess water to flow southward onto the marl terrace (loc. 92, 94, 143). Virtually everyone, especially those who study the ruins, agrees with de Vaux that the "highly developed and carefully constructed water system is the most striking characteristic of

---

115. This description derives from decades of studying the ruins.

116. See n. 105 above.

117. De Vaux, *Archaeology and the Dead Sea Scrolls,* 6.

118. When I surveyed this area and placed a compass on the eastern wall, I was surprised that it was constructed almost due north. Some speculations regarding the importance of this cosmic alignment are justified. The cosmic alignment of the wall could help gauge the seasons and esp. the rising of the sun toward the west. To what extent were the morning and evening prayers clarified by architecture, and to what degree did the astronomical books of Enoch help shape the buildings of Qumran (and the direction of the tombs)?

A main aqueduct at Khirbet Qumran and the remains of columns

Photo by James H. Charlesworth

Khirbet Qumran."[119] There should be little doubt, despite some unin-
formed claims, that this excessive preoccupation with water and cisterns
(mikva'ot) with steps suggests some connection with Jewish rites for purification, which increased during the history of Qumran.[120]

The consensus has been that Qumran was designed not "as a community residence but rather for the carrying on of certain communal activities."[121] The first basis for this judgment is the lack of living quarters,
although some may have been on the second floor or in the western wing
that has some well-crafted plastered rooms. Some living quarters have now
been located just north of Khirbet Qumran in the marl terrace.[122] The second reason that Qumran seems to be a communal center and not a residence is the numerous workshops, with the excessive amount of attention
to installations for water (some "cisterns" are clearly mikva'ot or ritual
baths). The third basis is the large assembly room (loc. 77); nearby (in loc.
86 and 89) over 1000 eating vessels (21 small jars, 38 dishes, 11 jugs, 210

119. De Vaux, *Archaeology and the Dead Sea Scrolls,* 10; see pl. 39.

120. See the publications cited in n. 99 above.

121. De Vaux, *Archaeology and the Dead Sea Scrolls,* 10.

122. I am grateful to Magen Broshi and Hanan Eshel for allowing me to participate in
their excavations. See Broshi and Eshel, "Residential Caves at Qumran," *DSD* 6 (1999): 328-
48; "Daily Life at Qumran," *NEA* 63 (2000): 136-37.

plates, 708 bowls, and 75 beakers) were found. Thus loc. 77 is probably a common refectory.

When did the expansion of Qumran occur? Cumulatively, the archaeological evidence suggests that Qumran was expanded sometime near the end of the 2nd century B.C.E. Most of the coins can be dated. Three of the silver coins are related to Antiochus VII Sidetes (138-129 B.C.E.), and one silver coin seems to belong to Demetrius II Nicator (129-125). Additional coins were unearthed, notably one of the rare coins of John Hyrcanus (135/4-104), one coin of Aristobulus I (104-103), and, most significantly, 143 coins of Alexander Jannaeus (103-76). Additional coins were found that date to the time of King Herod. There can be little doubt that the site was occupied by the time of Alexander Jannaeus and probably by the time of John Hyrcanus; but coins alone do not clarify when Qumran was first occupied or when it was expanded.

Why was Qumran expanded, and by whom? These are clearly interrelated questions. The *realia* obtained from an archaeological excavation can never provide such answers. All archaeological discoveries need to be evaluated in light of other data, especially reliable historical information and the general consensus regarding historical and sociological reconstructions at pertinent times. Since Qumran was expanded, and since an influx of religious Jews would have caused such expansion, it is wise to look for political and religious disturbances sometime about, and probably after, 100 B.C.E. to explain the renovations of Archaeological Period Ib.

Perhaps the Jews who flooded into Qumran were Pharisees or Pharisaic sympathizers.[123] According to Josephus (*Ant.* 13.380), Alexander Jannaeus crucified about 800 of them in (an error by Josephus) or perhaps just outside the walls of Jerusalem (see the discussion of this event in the following section on the pesharim).[124] If Pharisees, or precursors of the

---

123. If this scenario seems attractive, then we need to explore how these alleged Pharisees would fit in with, or cause some alteration, of the Qumranic opposition to "Pharisaic practices." The latter are now better known, thanks to the publication of the 4Q fragments of CD; see Joseph M. Baumgarten and Davis in Charlesworth, *Damascus Document;* and Baumgarten in Schiffman and VanderKam, *Encyclopedia of the Dead Sea Scrolls,* 1:167-69.

124. There is reason to question the historicity of Josephus regarding Jannaeus. Joseph G. Klausner concluded that "it may be said with certainty that he did not commit the acts of cruelty which Josephus ascribes to him"; "Judah Aristobulus and Jannaeus Alexander," in *The Hellenistic Age,* ed. Abraham Schalit (Jerusalem: Massada, 1972), 234. Josephus was biased; those who hated Jannaeus composed some of his sources. Despite Josephus's exaggerations, it is clear that Jannaeus cruelly punished the Pharisees. That fact becomes clearer, thanks to the pesharim. Also, the references to Jannaeus as one who slew the Rabbis should not be ignored (*Soṭah* 47a and *Sanh.* 107b [unedited edition]). I am grateful to Klausner for drawing my attention to these rabbinic texts.

The cistern in which the Qumranites were immersed and purified.
They entered on the left, descended into the water, and ascended
on the right. The crack is from the earthquake of 31 B.C.E.
Photo by James H. Charlesworth

Pharisees,[125] joined the Qumran Community, then either there were in it more lenient legal rules than we often assume or these so-called Pharisaic Jews modified their own legal rules to accept the Qumran rules.

It is reasonable to conclude that the second phase of Qumran history would include the years from ca. 102 to ca. 40 or 31 B.C.E. It seems relatively certain that virtually all the pesharim and related commentaries were composed during this period (and, as we shall see, Jannaeus seems to be alluded to in the pesharim and in other documents found in the Qumran caves). Yet, one must proceed with caution, and with careful nuance, in placing a Qumran composition in relation to an archaeological period. These texts do not date themselves and are not characteristically dated by external sources. What seems evident is the conclusion that the Qumran sectarian documents were composed, and in almost all cases received final editing, before the end of Phase II.[126] This widely affirmed consensus results from five decades of intensive research and an assessment of the archaeological discoveries made in and around Qumran. Such work is aided by reflections on the palaeographical dating of manuscripts,[127] which has been confirmed by carbon dating [AMS C-14].[128]

125. See Louis Finkelstein, "Pharisaic Leadership After the Great Synagogue (175 B.C.E.-135 C.E.," in Davies and Finkelstein, *The Cambridge History of Judaism,* 2:245-277.

126. Geza Vermes rightly refers to the editing of documents at Qumran as "as it were Essene by naturalisation"; *ErIsr* 20 (1989): 184-91; see esp. 185.

127. See esp. the photographs, drawings, and insights summarized in Ada Yardeni, *The Book of Hebrew Script: History, Palaeography, Script Styles, Calligraphy, & Design* (Jerusalem: Carta, 1991), esp. 47-66, 129-91.

128. For example, my dating of the Joshua fragment to the turn of the era was later confirmed by Professors Douglas J. Donahue and A. J. T. Jull of the NSF-Arizona AMS Facility (University of Arizona; the same laboratory as used by Emanuel Tov et al.). They reported that the probability distribution of 2 ranges at 95 percent accuracy, from "118 BC to 73 AD." This was reported in a private letter to me, 10 November 1999. See James H. Charlesworth, "XJoshua," in Charlesworth et al., *Miscellaneous Texts from the Judaean Desert.* DJD 38 (Oxford: Clarendon, 2000): 231-39. See the following major publications on the confirmation of palaeography by AMS C-14: A. J. T. Jull, D. Donahue, M. Broshi, and E. Tov, "Radiocarbon Dating of Scrolls and Linen Fragments from the Judean Desert," *Radiocarbon* 37 (1995): 11-19; "Radiocarbon Dating of Scrolls and Linen Fragments from the Judean Desert," *'Atiqot* 28 (1996): 85-91; G. Bonani, Broshi, I. Carmi, S. Ivy, J. Strugnell, and W. Wölfi, "Radiocarbon Dating of Fourteen Dead Sea Scrolls," *'Atiqot* 20 (1991): 27-32; Bonani, Ivy, Wölfi, Broshi, Carmi, and Strugnell, "Radiocarbon Dating of Fourteen Dead Sea Scrolls," *Radiocarbon* 34 (1992): 843-49. Also see Frank M. Cross, in Charlesworth, ed., PTSDSSP 1:57. Greg Doudna has advanced the surprising hypothesis that "almost all scribal copies of Qumran texts come from a single generation," that can be dated to the first century B.C.E.; "Dating the Scrolls on the Basis of Radiocarbon Analysis," in Flint and VanderKam, *The Dead Sea Scrolls after Fifty Years,* 1:430-65. Doudna dates the Qumran scrolls before the 1st century C.E. There are many reasons to doubt his conclusion that all the Qumran scrolls were composed within one gener-

Phase III (Archaeological Period of Abandonment)

Archaeological excavations at Qumran indicate that there may have been an exodus from Qumran from ca. 40 or 31 B.C.E. to sometime after 4 B.C.E.[129] The excavator of Qumran, Roland de Vaux, thought that the exodus was caused by the devastating earthquake of 31 B.C.E. While it is clear that de Vaux found evidence of an earthquake in the ruins, and additional evidence of an earthquake has been unearthed in the last decade, yet an earthquake can leave its mark on an abandoned site. I think it is more likely that the Qumranites left the site during the devastating invasion by the Parthians in 40 B.C.E. Since de Vaux's work the additional evidence of Parthian destruction, especially on the western shores of the Dead Sea from Qumran to Ein Gedi, has been impressive.[130] A section of *1 Enoch* refers to some Parthian invasion. The possibilities run from the 1st century B.C.E. to ca. 270 C.E.[131] More and more Enoch specialists are affirming that the passage probably refers to the Parthian conquest in ca. 40 B.C.E.:

> In those days, the angels will assemble and thrust themselves to the east at the Parthians and Medes. They will shake up the kings (so that) a spirit of unrest shall come upon them, and stir them up from their thrones; . . . And they will go up and trample upon the land of my elect ones, and the land of my elect ones will be before them like a threshing floor or a highway. But the city of my righteous ones will become an obstacle to their horses. (*1 En.* 56:5-7)[132]

This section of *1 Enoch* (*1 En.* 37–71) has now been dated to the 1st century B.C.E.[133] Yet, we must be very cautious in using this section of *1 Enoch*

---

ation. Despite the overwhelming confirmation of the science of palaeography, there is a disclaimer; see G. A. Rodley and B. E. Thiering, "Use of Radiocarbon Dating in Assessing Christian Connections to the Dead Sea Scrolls," *Radiocarbon* 41 (1999): 169-82.

129. See de Vaux, *Archaeology and the Dead Sea Scrolls*. See also the discussion and publications cited by Charlesworth in *RevQ* 10 (1980): 213-33.

130. See the excavation reports published by Yizhar Hirschfeld.

131. J. T. Milik dated the Book of Parables (*1 En.* 37–71) to "around the year A.D. 270" because he thought the invasion of ca. 270 was preserved in it. Although a date in the 1st century B.C.E. for the Book of Parables is not convincing to all scholars, virtually none follows Milik. See Milik, *The Books of Enoch: Aramaic Fragments of Qumrân Cave 4* (Oxford: Clarendon, 1976), 95-96.

132. E. Isaac, "1 (Ethiopic Apocalypse of) Enoch," in *OTP* 1:39. Some specialists on Enoch (esp. Milik and Michael A. Knibb) think this passage refers to a much later Parthian invasion.

133. See esp. James H. Charlesworth, "The Date of the Parables of Enoch (1 En 37–

to perceive Qumran history. It has not been identified among the Qumran Aramaic fragments of *1 Enoch,* and it was probably not a part of Qumran's Enoch corpus. Before the death of Herod the Great, this section of Enoch most likely belonged to the Enoch communities that seem to be located in Galilee or somewhere north of Qumran.

To what location did the Qumranites flee in 40 or later? Perhaps the Qumranites fled to Jerusalem.[134] It is *prima facie* likely that in the face of the Parthian invasion of 40 B.C.E. the Qumranites fled to cities — especially Jerusalem — for refuge. Some friendly relations between the Qumranites (since they are most likely Essenes [see the following]) and King Herod seem evident, if we follow Josephus (*Ant.* 15.372-78). Indeed, bonds between the Qumranites and Herod seem clear. On the one hand, Menahem the Essene allegedly saluted Herod as "king of the Jews"[135] — before the fact and when Herod's future looked bleak. On the other hand, and more importantly, the Herods and the Qumranites shared a mutual hatred of the Hasmoneans. The return to Qumran coincides also with Herod's death in or about 4 B.C.E. Many experts see this as further evidence of some positive support of the Qumranites by Herod the Great.

To be taken seriously, however, is Magness's suggestion that an abandonment of Qumran from 40 to 4 seems rather extensive.[136] She contends — I think correctly — that "it does not make sense that an earthquake would have caused the inhabitants to abandon the site for thirty years."[137] She notes that 1231 coins were recovered from Qumran; among these are 561 silver Tyrian tetradrachmas that were found beneath Period II and above Period Ib. The coins found in this hoard, preserved in three pots, date up to 9 or 8 B.C.E. She rejects de Vaux's argument that the hoard dates from the reoccupation in Period II, and contends that "common sense" places it with the end of Period Ib. That could mean that Qumran was burned not in 40 (the Parthian invasion) or 31 (the earthquake) but about the time of the end of the reign of Herod the Great (40-4). Magness sug-

---

71)," *Henoch* 20 (1998): 93-98. Leading Enoch experts, including G. W. E. Nickelsburg and Paolo Sacchi, also date *1 En.* 37–71 to the late 1st century B.C.E. (see citations in the article).

134. They probably did not flee to Jericho, since Josephus (if he can be trusted here) reports that Jews fled Jericho before Herod's invasion and before Vespasian's incursion. I tend to trust Josephus here, since Herodian Jericho did not have walls, as we know from decades of archaeological work there, and would be impossible to defend; moreover, the wilderness offered many hiding places.

135. See Josephus *Ant.* 15.373.

136. Jodi Magness, "The Chronology of the Settlement at Qumran in the Herodian Period," *DSD* 2 (1995): 58-65; "A Reassessment of the Excavations of Qumran," in Schiffman, Tov, and VanderKam, *The Dead Sea Scrolls Fifty Years after Their Discovery,* 708-19.

137. Magness, "Qumran Archaeology," 57.

gests that the Qumranites repaired the damage caused by the earthquake of 31 and remained at the site "without interruption until 9/8 BCE or some time thereafter." She postulates a conflagration ca. 9 or 8, and then an abandonment of the site until the reign of Herod Archelaus "in 4 BCE or shortly thereafter."[138]

Magness has challenged the consensus, but I think the abandonment was extensive, from 40 to 4, because of Herod the Great's support of the Essenes (one should not ignore the literary evidence). There were disturbances after his death, but that is in 4 not 9/8 B.C.E., and there is no evidence of burning at Qumran at that time. Finally, the failure of the one that hid the hoard to return and recover it seems easier to explain if it is associated with the *final* abandonment of the site, either by one who hid it ca. 40 and never returned or by a later Qumranite who never returned.

Phase IV (Archaeological Period II)

Some Qumranites returned to the site sometime about the time of the death of King Herod. They seem to have comprised a smaller group, since some areas of Qumran seem not to have been cleaned or renovated for occupation.[139] We know little about this time in the life of the Community, since no new composition comparable to the *Temple Scroll*, the *Thanksgiving Hymns*, the *War Scroll*, or the *Rule of the Community* was composed during this time. Daily work seems to be devoted to copying the most important scrolls, praying, studying, worshipping, and performing the necessary chores. The latter would include the agricultural tasks at the nearby Ein Feshka.

In June 68 C.E. the Roman soldiers, under the leadership, but not necessary direction, of Vespasian burned Qumran.[140] The archaeological evidence is impressive, especially the numismatic sequence of Jewish coins up to 68[141] and the Roman arrowheads within and above a layer of conflagration.[142] This archaeological evidence neatly coincides with Josephus's report that in June 68 Vespasian's soldiers subdued Jericho and its environs (see *Wars* 4.440-85).

What did the Qumranites do just before the invasion by Vespasian's

---

138. See Magness's publications on this point: *DSD* 2 (1995): 58-65; "Two Notes on the Archaeology of Qumran," *BASOR* 312 (1998): 37-44; and "Qumran Archaeology," 1:58-59.

139. De Vaux, *Archaeology and the Dead Sea Scrolls*, 120.

140. See Stegemann, *Die Essener*, 86-93.

141. See Charlesworth, *RevQ* 10 (1980): 228.

142. De Vaux, *Archaeology and the Dead Sea Scrolls*, 24-41.

troops in 68? Since there were different ideas in the Community from the beginning and usually even in the mind of a Qumranite, there probably was no unified response to this Roman threat. Perhaps the only organized response was the hiding of some scrolls. Conceivably, some Qumranites marched straight into the Roman ranks, taking the *War Scroll* literally and thinking that angels would fight with them. Perhaps, with that in mind, some even carried a copy of the *War Scroll* into battle.

Other Qumranites probably fled to Jerusalem and died in the conflagration of 70 C.E.; they may have joined Essenes who most likely were living in the southwestern section of Jerusalem.[143] The evidence of an early Herodian gate, which seems to be the Essene gate mentioned by Josephus (*War* 4.144-45),[144] and two mikva'ot nearby indicate to many experts that Essenes were conceivably living in the southwestern section of Jerusalem before the destruction of 70.[145]

Most likely some Qumranites fled away from the Romans and southward. This suggestion, which is supported by many[146] but not all Qumran experts, explains the presence of the *Angelic Liturgy* and other texts associated with Qumran on Masada, which fell in 74 C.E.[147]

143. I am grateful for decades of conversations with Bargil Pixner, who knows more about this section of Old Jerusalem than anyone. I am also grateful to him for hours spent in and near the Essene Gate, the mikva'ot nearby, and for the opportunity to "clean" around near a large Herodian mikva. See Pixner, "Die Essener-Quartier in Jerusalem," in his *Wege des Messias und Stätten der Urkirche: Jesus und das Judenchristentum im Licht neuer archäologischer Erkenntnisse*, ed. Rainer Riesner (Basel: Brunnen, 1991), 180-207.

144. For a color photograph, see James H. Charlesworth, *The Millennium Guide for Pilgrims to the Holy Land* (North Richland Hills: BIBAL, 2000), the photograph section following p. 40; also see the comments and photographs, 148-50.

145. See Rainer Riesner, "Jesus, the Primitive Community, and the Essene Quarter of Jerusalem," in *Jesus and the Dead Sea Scrolls*, ed. James H. Charlesworth. ABRL (New York: Doubleday, 1992, repr. with corrections 1995), 198-234. The development of a typology of mikva'ot is still in its infancy. See the photograph of one of the alleged Essene mikva'ot near the "Essene Gate," in Charlesworth, *The Millennium Guide*, 32. Regarding the Qumran ritual baths and those in the mansions of the Upper City of Jerusalem, Ronny Reich has shown, in a brilliantly illuminating way, that the Qumran purification facilities are mikva'ot that are similar to those in Jerusalem and dissimilar to those in Jericho. His work is a major corrective to de Vaux, who wrote before the typological study of mikva'ot. See Reich, "*Miqwa'ot* at Khirbet Qumran and the Jerusalem Connection," in Schiffman, Tov, and VanderKam, *The Dead Sea Scrolls Fifty Years after Their Discovery*, 728-31. The major discoveries of Herodian installations in the Upper City (by Nahman Avigad), near the Temple Mount (by Benjamin Mazar), and at Jericho (by Ehud Netzer) are definitive and help us correct and supplement, not replace, de Vaux's conclusion.

146. E.g., see Carsten Peter Thiede, *The Dead Sea Scrolls and the Jewish Origins of Christianity* (New York: Palgrave, 2001), 39.

147. I agree with Emanuel Tov that some of the nonbiblical texts found at Masada

There is now evidence to suggest that some Qumranites may have fled eastward before Vespasian and the Roman troops began their campaign again after the winter of 67 and 68. This hypothesis seems implied for three reasons. First, the presence of a dualism similar to Qumran's is found in Syrian asceticism, and some terms are reminiscent of Qumran; this scenario was noted long ago by Arthur Vööbus.[148] Second, what look suspiciously like Qumran *termini technici* appear in so-called gnostic texts "along the silkroad" and these terms do not look like influences from Parthian dualism.[149] Third, as Chaim Rabin pointed out in the 1950s, one needs to explain the appearance of concepts and terms similar to those found in the Qumran scrolls in the Qur'an, notably the "intense preoccupation with the end of the world."[150] Thus, we should not think that all Qumranites died in 68. That conclusion becomes even more obvious when we realize that the Qumranites were most likely the conservative branch of the Essenes,[151] and those living elsewhere would not have perished in the fires at Qumran. Yet, while some Qumranites and Essenes may have survived the War of 66-74,[152] it seems likely that the Qumranites and the Essenes as a sect ceased to exist in 70.

---

may have been taken from Qumran to Masada. See Tov, "A Qumran Origin for the Masada Non-Biblical Texts?" *DSD* 7 (2000): 57-73.

148. *Celibacy: A Requirement for Admission to Baptism in the Early Syrian Church* (Stockholm: Estonian Theological Society in Exile, 1951).

149. In particular, note the dualistic contrast between "Sons of the Darkness" and "Sons of the Day" in *Hymn to the Third Messenger as Sun God* and the mention of "Sons of Truth" in *Hymn to the Living Soul*. See the translation of these texts in Hans-Joachim Klimkeit, *Gnosis on the Silk Road* (San Francisco: HarperSanFrancisco, 1993). I still contend that Qumran dualism was influenced by the Zurvanites, but the *termini technici* in some of these "gnostic" texts suggest we might well consider some influence from Qumran on post-68 Eastern compositions.

150. *Qumran Studies* (London: Oxford University Press, 1957), 118. Rabin (120-21) suggested that Arabic *mahdî*, "the rightly guided one," may be an attempt to translate מורה הצדק, and *dajjāl*, "the liar," may represent Qumran's "the Man of the Lie." Fascinating is Rabin's report (118) that *bSanh.* 97b refers to the finding of an old messianic scroll which in light of the use of the word מלחמה may suggest some connection with the *War Scroll*.

151. As Hermann Lichtenberger reports, "According to a far-reaching consensus *[weitgehenden Konsens],* the Qumran Community is to be viewed as part of the Essene group"; "Essene/Therapeuten," *RGG,* 4th ed. (Tübingen: Mohr [Siebeck], 1999), 2:1590-91. Also, see the balanced judgments of Jonathan Campbell, "The Qumran Sectarian Writings," in *The Cambridge History of Judaism,* ed. William Horbury, W. D. Davies, and John Sturdy (Cambridge: Cambridge University Press, 1999), esp. 3:813-21, "The Qumran-Essene Hypothesis." As Collins states, "The assumption that Qumran was an Essene settlement remains the most economical way to account for the evidence"; *ABD* 2:619-26; quotation, 623.

152. Long ago, as is well known, Naphtali Wieder indicated that the Karaites wrote commentaries that in many ways are similar to the pesharim. Now, in light of work on the

Were Qumranites Conservative Essenes?

This comment regarding the Qumranites as Essenes needs some discussion. It is clear that by 1980 a consensus regarding this identification had developed in scholarly circles.[153] The consensus was that the Qumran Community was an Essene group. This conclusion now needs more nuance and development. Philip Davies reports that among scholars distinguished in Qumran research "many, perhaps a majority . . . now doubt the Essene identification."[154]

I cannot agree with this assessment. I have often discussed the Essene hypothesis with specialists working in the Israel Museum and in the École Biblique,[155] with some subeditors who are producing an *editio princeps* for the DJD volumes, and with the subeditors who are preparing polished critical editions for the PTSDSSP.[156] Many have confided in me, and I am in full agreement, that the more we learn about the Qumran fragments the more likely it becomes that the best hypothesis is that the Qumran Community belonged to the Essene sect or group.[157] It is evident that the Qumran phenomenon derives from larger and earlier sectarian apocalyptic movements.

Firkowicz collection of manuscripts in St. Petersburg, Russia, Simon Szyszman argues that Wieder has shown that the Karaites inherited the pesher method of interpreting scripture from Qumran; "Une source auxiliaire importante pour les études qumrâniennes: Les collections Firkowicz," in *Qumrân: Sa piété, sa théologie et son milieu*, ed. Mathias Delcor. BETL 46 (Paris: Duculot, 1978), 61-73; see esp. 68.

153. See the summary of this consensus by Campbell in *The Cambridge History of Judaism*, 3:813.

154. Philip R. Davies, "Khirbet Qumran Revisited," in *Scripture and Other Artifacts: Essays on the Bible and Archaeology in Honor of Philip J. King*, ed. Michael D. Coogan, J. Cheryl Exum, and Lawrence E. Stager (Louisville: Westminster John Knox, 1994), 126-42; quotation, 127.

155. Émile Puech is convinced that the cemeteries at Qumran and el-Ghuweir are clearly Essene; "The Necropolises of *Khirbet* Qumrân and 'Ain el-Ghuweir and the Essene Belief in Afterlife," *BASOR* 312 (1998): 21-36. See also Puech, "The Convictions of a Scholar," *NEA* 63 (2000): 160: "They were Essenes." Jean-Baptiste Humbert correctly can refer to "an Essene ritual center on the shores of the Dead Sea"; "Interpreting the Qumran Site," *NEA* 63 (2000): 140. The "Plan of the Aerial View" (143) is one of the clearest and informed layouts of the installations at Qumran.

156. See esp. A. Lange's comment (45) and Hermann Lichtenberger's claim (65) in "Qumran," *Theologische Realenzyklopädie* 27:45-79. See also George J. Brooke, "Essenes," in *A New Dictionary of Religions*, ed. John R. Hinnells (Oxford: Blackwell, 1995), 157.

157. Stegemann, however, is convinced that "the Essenes were indeed the main Jewish Union of late Second Temple times"; "The Qumran Essenes — Local Members of the Main Jewish Union in Late Second Temple Times," in *The Madrid Qumran Congress*, ed. Julio Trebolle Barrera and Luis Vegas Montane. STDJ 11/1 (Leiden: Brill, 1992): 83-166; quotation, 165.

It is likely that the origins of the Qumran Community are to be found "within the Essene movement" which antedates Qumran, but that the settlement at Qumran dates towards the latter half of the 2nd century B.C.E.[158]

Cross has argued that the Greek word "Essene" derives from the Aramaic *hasên* or *ḥasayyâ*, which means "holy ones." He made this point in the first edition of his *The Ancient Library of Qumran.* Now, in the third edition of this work he draws attention to a passage in 4QTLev arb: "And the name of his holy one (is) not blotted out from all names. . . ."[159] The word for "holy one" is חסיה. Cross confides in me that he thinks this passage "proves the etymology of the name" and that the Qumran Essenes "did call themselves 'holy ones' according to both external sources and internal."[160] The connection of the Qumran Essenes with the Hasidim mentioned in 1 and 2 Maccabees is another matter.[161]

Chaos or Consensus?

We are not far from an internationally recognized consensus regarding the *broad contours of the origins* of the Qumran Community. Samuel Iwry and Jerome Murphy-O'Connor's insightful explanation of a Babylonian origin of Qumran needs to be absorbed into a synthesis.[162] Murphy-O'Connor does make a major contribution regarding a schism in early Essenism and the origin of Essenism in other locations. Also, it is clear from primary and secondary sources that the Essenes were a widespread movement in Palestine; and suggestive is Philip R. Davies's contention that the Righteous Teacher left the larger Essene group and resided at Qumran. Many experts rightly suggest that the *Temple Scroll, Jubilees,* and the *Books of Enoch* may represent the earlier parent group of the Essenes.[163]

158. Florentino García Martínez, "The Great Battles Over Qumran," *NEA* 63 (2000): 128.

159. See Cross, *The Ancient Library of Qumran,* 3rd ed., 183.

160. A private letter to me dated 17 June 2001.

161. See the discussion by Joseph Sievers in *The Hasmoneans and Their Supporters: From Mattathias to the Death of John Hyrcanus I.* SFSHJ 6 (Atlanta: Scholars, 1990), 38-40.

162. Esp. the following studies by Murphy-O'Connor: *RB* 76 (1969): 528-49; "An Essene Missionary Document? CD II,14–VI,1," *RB* 77 (1970): 201-29; *RB* 81 (1974): 215-44; *ABD* 5:590-94.

163. See the following works by Davies: *The Damascus Covenant: An Interpretation of the "Damascus Document."* JSOTSup 25 (Sheffield: JSOT, 1982); *Qumran* (Grand Rapids: Wm. B. Eerdmans, 1983); *Behind the Essenes: History and Ideology in the Dead Sea Scrolls.* BJS 94 (Atlanta: Scholars, 1987). Gabriele Boccaccini argues that the Qumranites originated with the Enoch group; *Beyond the Essene Hypothesis: The Parting of the Ways Between Qumran and Enochic Judaism* (Grand Rapids: Wm. B. Eerdmans, 1998).

Even if a Babylonian origin of the Essenes is accepted (and we are seeing more evidence of Babylonian influence in the Qumran horoscopes and calendar), the Essene sect needs to be understood within the world of Jewish apocalypticism. This suggestion was advanced by Cross,[164] and is now advocated by many, including Florentino García Martínez and A. S. van der Woude.[165]

While some scholars hold that there is no consensus regarding the origins of the Qumran Community and the Essenes,[166] there is a solid consensus regarding the Qumran origin of the pesharim and the need to find ways to ascertain the reliability of the historical traditions preserved in these commentaries. It also seems clear that a revision of the old Qumran-Essene hypothesis is being affirmed and developed by many experts.[167] We should not expect Philo and Josephus to present a descrip-

164. Regarding the pesharim, Cross rightly claims that the "technique of exposition in all these sources grows out of the presuppositions of apocalypticism, and can be rightly understood only within the categories of this special type of eschatological thought"; *The Ancient Library of Qumran*, 90.

165. García Martínez and van der Woude, "A 'Groningen' Hypothesis of Qumran Origins and Early History," *RevQ* 14 (1990): 521-41. I would disagree with the "Groningen Hypothesis," which places the origin of Essenism in the late 3rd or early 2nd century B.C.E., by pointing out that the Qumran scrolls seem to place the origin of the Essenes in some connection with the Maccabean Revolt about the middle of the 2d century B.C.E. It seems to result from priestly struggles that can be traced back to the postexilic period; but in its definitive form, it postdates the beginnings of the Maccabean rebellion. For other critics of the Groningen Hypothesis, see Timothy H. Lim, "The Wicked Priests of the Groningen Hypothesis," *JBL* 112 (1993): 415-25. See the response by A. S. van der Woude, "Once Again: The Wicked Priests in the *Habakkuk Pesher* from Cave 1 of Qumran," *RevQ* 17 (1996): 375-84. Van der Woude's insights are a significant defense of some aspects of the Groningen Hypothesis. For me, it is clear that the first Wicked Priest cannot be Judas Maccabeus, but after Jonathan (the first to be called "the Wicked Priest") other Hasmonean high priests could also be seen as "the Wicked Priest" by the Qumranites.

166. Although Schiffman is an expert in Qumran studies, his argument for a Sadducean origin of the Qumranites is ultimately unconvincing; *Reclaiming the Dead Sea Scrolls*, esp. 73-76. Also, see Schiffman's article ("The Sadducean Origin of the Dead Sea Scrolls Sect," 35-49) and VanderKam's rebuttal ("The People of the Dead Sea Scrolls: Essenes or Sadducees?" 50-62) of the Sadducean hypothesis in *Understanding the Dead Sea Scrolls*, ed. Hershel Shanks (New York: Random House, 1992). Far more informed and nuanced is the position of Ya'akov Sussmann, a Talmudist. He perceives remarkable similarities between Qumran legal rules and rabbinics, calls for a more careful study of "Pharisees" and "Sadducees" in rabbinics (and the lack of the term "Essene"), and leans toward the identification of the Qumran sect with the "Essenes." He cannot yet explain how the Qumran sect can be Essene and yet its legal rule "accords with the halakha explicitly described by the rabbinic sources as Sadducean" (192, 200). See his brilliant contribution to Qimron and Strugnell, *Qumran Cave 4.V*: "The History of the Halakha and the Dead Sea Scrolls," 179-200.

167. See the same judgment by Campbell in *The Cambridge History of Judaism*, 3:817:

tion of Essenes that is in full harmony with what we learn from the Qumran scrolls. Their agreement that 4000 Essenes lived in Palestine should not be taken as "gospel truth"; it is rather an example of a Hellenistic topos.[168] Josephus was an outsider, living long after the composition of the pesharim; and he wrote for Greeks and Romans. The Qumran scrolls represent the view of insiders, members of the Community; and they had no desire to communicate with those outside the closed Community.[169]

Phase V (Archaeological Period III)

For some time, perhaps less than a decade, Roman soldiers lived at Qumran. Roman arrowheads were found above the black layer of destruction. The sequence of coins continues up to 73 C.E. The Romans probably added the latrine which used to be quite visible before the mid-1970s; it was just north of the cistern or mikva (loc. 48-49) and in locus 51.[170] Thus, after 68 C.E. Qumran was a Roman garrison, but the Romans lived in only the tower and buildings to the south and east of it. They also curtailed the extent of the aqueducts and cisterns to the use of water for living purposes only. Even later, some Jews may have stayed briefly in the ruins during the Second Jewish Revolt of 132-36,[171] since a pot with 10 coins has been re-

---

"some kind of revised Essene hypothesis seems the most likely candidate to take DSS research into the twenty-first century."

168. See Berndt Schaller, "4000 Essener — 6000 Pharisäer: Zum Hintergrund und Wert antiker Zahlenangaben," in Kollmann, Reinbold, and Steudel, *Antikes Judentum und frühes Christentum,* 172-82.

169. See the similar thoughts of Per Bilde, who affirms that the "accounts in Philo and Josephus should be regarded as revelant sources to the Essenes/the Qumran community, also in cases where they do not *verbatim* correspond with the Dead Sea Scrolls"; "The Essenes in Philo and Josephus," in Cryer and Thompson, *Qumran between the Old and New Testaments,* 32-68; quotation, 68.

170. Magness agrees with de Vaux that this is a latrine. See her comments and references in "Qumran Archaeology," 65.

171. An inscription found near Beit Shean suggests that Bar Kokhba was still alive in 136; see Werner Eck and Gideon Foerster, "Ein Triumphbogen für Hadrian im Tal von Beth Shean bei Tel Shalem," *Journal of Roman Archaeology* 12 (1999): 294-313. For discussion of an occupation at Qumran during the Second Jewish Revolt, see esp. Ernest-Marie Laperrousaz, "L'establissement de Qoumrân près de la Mer Morte: Forteresse ou Couvent?" *ErIsr* 20 [Yigael Yadin Memorial Volume] (1989): 118*-23*. For a superb study of Jewish life in Palestine after Bar Kokhba, see Michael Avi-Yonah, *The Jews under Roman and Byzantine Rule: A Political History of Palestine from the Bar Kokhba War to the Arab Conquest* (New York: Schocken, 1984).

covered. These coins included one denarius of the Second Revolt and three denarii of Trajan.[172]

Results for Reflections

If the above reconstruction of Qumran history is generally correct, then some published suggestions are, if not impossible, at least quite unlikely.[173] Here are the most important hypotheses that seem misinformed.

First, the claim that Qumran was not a community of priests but a villa of a patrician or a *villa rustica* appears ill founded.[174] Even a cursory examination of the ruins at Qumran discloses that the ones who built Qumran had no skill in construction.[175] The contrast between the poor constructions at Qumran and the elegant buildings at Herodian Jericho is highly instructive. Caves IVA, IVB, V, VII, VIII, IX, and X are close to and encircle the lower part of the marl terrace on which Qumran was built. These caves are linked with Qumran by pottery, writing, and time of occupation.[176] Neutron activation analysis (NAA) proves that the pottery

172. Robert A. Kugler rightly states that a letter from Wadi Muraba'at may refer to the site as a "Fortress of the Pious," but it is uncertain that this means people were still living there. See Kugler's excellent "Qumran: Place and History," in *Dictionary of New Testament Background,* ed. Evans and Porter, 883-88. For the Muraba'at papyrus letter, see J. T. Milik in *Les Grottes de Murabba'at,* ed. Pierre Benoit, Milik, and Roland de Vaux. DJD 2 (Oxford: Clarendon, 1961), 163-64: [למצד חסדין]. Milik (163) offered the opinion that "la 'Forteresse des Ḥasidim' (l.6)" should be identified "avec grande probabilité au Ḥirbet Qumrân."

173. I have no problem with Stegemann's claim that Qumran was a publishing house in which manuscripts were produced; but we should think in 1st-century terms, and include Ein Feshka and the manuscript needs of other Essene "camps."

174. The hypothesis of Robert Donceel and Pauline Donceel-Voûte is sometimes marred because they have not participated in excavations of ancient Palestinian sites. See Donceel and Donceel-Voûte, "The Archaeology of Khirbet Qumran," in *Methods of Investigation of the Dead Sea Scrolls and the Khirbet Qumran Site,* ed. Michael O. Wise, John J. Collins, and Dennis G. Pardee (New York: New York Academy of Sciences, 1994), 1-38; Donceel-Voûte, "'Coenaculum' — La salle à l'étage du *Locus* 30 à Khirbet Qumrân sur la Mer Morte," in *Banquets d' Orient.* Res Orientales 4 (Leuven: Bures, 1992), 61-84; for my response, see *Methods of Investigation,* 36-37. If room 30 was a banquet hall, then what was room 77? And the latter, usually seen as the dining room, is contiguous to room 86-89 in which eating dishes were found.

175. See also Magness's reasons why Qumran cannot have been a *villa rustica; "*A Villa at Khirbet Qumran?" *RevQ* 63 (1994): 397-419; "Qumran: Not a Country Villa," *BAR* 22 (1996): 38-47, 72-73; "Qumran Archaeology," 53-57.

176. Thus the numerous *realia* that link the Qumran caves and their contents to the Khirbet disprove Norman Golb's claim that the scrolls in the Qumran caves come only from libraries in Jerusalem; *Who Wrote the Dead Sea Scrolls?* (New York: Scribner, 1995); "The

found in the caves and at Qumran shared the same chemistry; presumably they were almost all made in the Qumran pottery kiln.[177] The scrolls found in the 11 caves are related to the sect described in the *Rule of the Community.*[178]

Second, it is not likely that Qumran was a caravanserai or a place in which balsam was manufactured or that Qumran was a port on the Dead Sea, as Alan D. Crown and Lena Cansdale contend.[179] Qumran was isolated. Despite the misinformation in some publications,[180] there was no ancient road leading past Qumran from Jericho to Ein Gedi.[181]

Third, although some of the Qumran scrolls are on papyrus, Qumran cannot be a center in which papyrus was manufactured, as S. Shapiro claims.[182] Papyrus could grow only far away, more than two days' journey away in the Huleh Valley. Most, if not all, of the papyrus would be ruined before it reached Qumran.[183] Papyrus is manufactured near where it is grown — clearly nowhere near the Dead Sea.

Fourth, the claim that Qumran is a fort and that all the scrolls were brought from Jerusalem to Qumran, as Norman Golb claims, is misleading.[184] Obviously, some of the earliest scrolls were brought to the Community by the first group who followed the Righteous Teacher. More scrolls would have been brought to Qumran by those who joined the Community and gave it their possessions — including what they had acquired to become more acceptable to the authorities in the Community. Additional

---

Dead Sea Scrolls and Pre-Tannaitic Judaism," in *The Cambridge History of Judaism,* 3:822-51.

177. Gunneweg and Balla, "Neutron Activation Analysis."

178. This conclusion is demonstrated by Carol Newsom, "'Sectually Explicit' Literature from Qumran."

179. "Qumran — Was it an Essene Settlement?" *BAR* 20/5 (1994): 24-36, 73-78. See the succinct summary by Magen Broshi, "Was Qumran Indeed a Monastery? The Consensus and Its Challengers: An Archaeologist's View," in Charlesworth, *Caves of Enlightenment,* 19-37.

180. In his informed book, Thiede can claim that Qumran "is situated on a plateau, clearly visible even from a distance on the road which links Jericho with Masada, En Gedi, Sodom and Eilat"; *Scrolls and Jewish Origins;* quotation, 14. The road is modern and not above an ancient road. One could trek over the desert, as the Roman soldiers did as they marched from Jericho to Masada, but the way is often blocked by wadis.

181. Magen Broshi, "Was Qumran a Crossroads?" *RevQ* 74 (1999): 273-76.

182. I am indebted to Broshi for years of discussing such hypotheses. See his "Qumran — Die archäologische Erforschung," in *Die Schriftrollen von Qumran,* ed. Shemaryahu Talmon (Regensburg: Pustet, 1998), 27-50.

183. I am grateful to Broshi for decades of conversations on these issues.

184. See my comments in "Sense or Sensationalism? The Dead Sea Controversy," *Christian Century* 109 (29 January 1992): 92-98.

scrolls could have been brought to Qumran by those who returned to Qumran after 4 B.C.E. Qumran was a center of religious activity that included making leather for scrolls and copying scrolls, but it should not be defined primarily as a center for the manufacture of scrolls.

Fifth, it seems clear that those who deny that the Qumranites were Essenes have failed to explain how two groups could be identical within Early Judaism, yet not the same group.[185] They also have failed to explain how such a group as that known at Qumran could have gone unmentioned anywhere in our sources, especially by Josephus, Dio Chrysostom (Dio Cocceianus), and Pliny the Elder. Josephus was intimate with ancient Palestine before 70; he was inextricably involved in the Revolt of 66-70.[186] Dio Chrysostom could have learned about the Essenes from other written sources or later, perhaps after he was banned from Rome in the early years of Domitian's reign when he wandered in Asia Minor as a Stoic-Cynic philosopher.[187] Pliny the Elder knew Palestine after 70 C.E., since he referred to the ashes that then defined Jerusalem and Ein Gedi;[188] but his record is not to be treated cavalierly.

A further point needs to be clarified, and it is often overlooked in the discussions of Qumran history. Two ancient authors seem to place the Essenes where Qumran is located. First, Pliny the Elder (23/24-79 C.E.) seems to place the Essenes at Qumran: the solitary tribe of the Essenes live on the western shore of the Dead Sea *(Ab occidente litora Esseni)*, and "below it" *(infra hos fuit)* is Ein Gedi, and then Masada.[189] Second, another

185. See, e.g. Laperrousaz, *ErIsr* 20 (1989): 118*-23*.

186. Pliny *Nat.* 2.555-74; Josephus, *War* 2.8.2-13; *Ant.* 18.1.5. Cf. Philo *Prob.* 75-91; *Hypoth.* 11.1-18; and *Contempl.* 1-39, 64-90.

187. See Robert Browning, "Dio Cocceianus," in *The Oxford Classical Dictionary*, 2nd ed., ed. N. G. L. Hammond and H. H. Scullard (Oxford: Clarendon, 1991), 345 (and the works cited in the bibliography there); see also the 3rd ed.

188. "Engada . . . ab Hierosolymis . . . nunc alterum bustum." A *bustum* is literally a place in which corpses are burned. For the text and translation of Pliny's *Natural History* 5.17.4 (73), see Geza Vermes and Martin D. Goodman, eds., *The Essenes According to the Classical Sources* (Sheffield: JSOT, 1989), 32-33.

189. For the Latin text, English translation, and insightful notes, see Menahem Stern, ed., *Greek and Latin Authors on Jews and Judaism* (Jerusalem: Israel Academy of Sciences and Humanities, 1974), 1:465-81. Since Pliny refers to places from the Essene site southward to Ein Gedi and then Masada, it does not seem that Hirschfeld has wisely rejected Qumran as Essene in favor of the 30 huts "above" Ein Gedi as Essene. The Latin *infra* (*Nat.* 5.17.4 [73]) clearly means "below," but it is conceivable some Essenes or desert-dwelling mystics once dwelt in the small "huts" to the west of and above Ein Gedi. I am grateful to Hirschfeld for allowing me to study the "huts" with him. See Yizhar Hirschfeld, "A Settlement of Hermits Above 'En Gedi," *Journal of the Institute of Archaeology of Tel Aviv University* 27 (2000): 103-55. See the rejection of Hirschfeld's position by David Amit and Jodi Magness in "Not a Set-

non-Jew refers to Essenes (τοὺς Ἐσσηνούς) living "near the Dead Water [i.e., the Dead Sea] in the interior of Palestine" (τὴν παρὰ τὸ νεκρὸν ὕδωρ ἐν τῇ μεσογείᾳ τῆς Παλαιστίνης).[190] The author is the "golden-mouthed" orator of Prusa in Bithynia, Dio Chrysostom (ca. 40- after 112 c.e.). While the comments by Dio and Pliny do not prove that Essenes lived at Qumran, they — especially those of Pliny — certainly add plausibility to such a conclusion.

Sixth, only those insufficiently informed think that the Qumranites were Christians, or that all the Essenes lived at Qumran. The *Rule of the Community* contains not only the rules for admission, promotion, and expulsion from Qumran, but also the lore that had to be mastered and memorized by those who sought to join the Community (in my judgment, esp. 1QS 3-4).[191] Most Qumran experts conclude that these rules define the life and high boundaries especially of the celibate Qumran Essenes.[192]

This conclusion is so crucial for a perception of the history of Qumran that we should pause and focus upon it. Thus, we now need to turn to a question high on the agenda of Qumran experts.

Was Qumran a Celibate Monastery?

Important new information has brought considerable new light to bear on this question. The work is focused on the cemetery. If the *Yaḥad* was for mature men only, how do we explain the presence of women and children in the cemetery? The facts need to be clarified. About 1200 graves are in the cemetery. Of these only 53 have been excavated: one by Charles Clermont-Ganneau, 43 by Roland de Vaux, and perhaps 9 by Solomon

---

tlement of Hermits or Essenes," *Tel Aviv* 27 (2000): 273-85. Finally, see Hirschfeld's response to them in "The Archaeology of Hermits," *Tel Aviv* 27 (2000): 286-91. See also de Vaux, *Archaeology and the Dead Sea Scrolls*, 132-38; Jean-Paul Audet, "Qumrân et la notice de Pline sur les Esséniens," *RB* 68 (1961): 346-87; Ernest-Marie Laperroussaz, "'Infra hos Engadda,'" *RB* 69 (1962): 369-80; Christoph Burchard, "Pline et les Esséniens," *RB* 69 (1962): 533-69. Most of the Essenes lived somewhere outside of Qumran, as Philo and Josephus report and as is suggested in or implied by the *Damascus Document* and the *Temple Scroll*.

190. For the text, English translation, and valuable notes, see Menahem Stern, *Greek and Latin Authors on Jews and Judaism*, 1:538-39.

191. Vermes also concluded that the "desert novices . . . were instructed in the doctrine of the 'two spirits'"; *The Dead Sea Scrolls: Qumran in Perspective* (Cleveland: Collins & World, 1978), 105.

192. Stegemann thinks that the Qumranites abstained from marriage for long periods of time perhaps while on priestly duty at Qumran, but not permanently; Stegemann, "Qumran Essenes."

Steckoll.[193] No woman was found in the main cemetery on the central marl terrace.

It seems certain that only a physical anthropologist can professionally analyze the bones from the Qumran cemetery.[194] After more than 50 years, this has finally been accomplished. Joseph Zias has examined the bones of women in the Qumran cemetery and concludes that they are not early Jews but fairly recent bedouin.[195] His method and data are stunning, but — of course — others weigh the evidence differently.[196]

Before subscribing wholesale and uncritically to Zias's conclusion, we need to be certain about some issues. (1) Are Zias's facts, methods, and conclusions balanced and accurate?[197] Is the dating of the bones precise? Are we certain that the bones Zias has examined were the ones de Vaux unearthed in the location specified? (2) Is the "brown dust" found in the anomalous tombs T32-36 the remains of coffins, funeral clothing, and decayed palm branches from a funeral, or something else? These tombs are in the southern extension of the Qumran cemetery — and are uncharacteristically oriented east to west. Such questions are seminal, since only in these five tombs and in the four in the southern cemetery were recovered the remains of children and adult females. (3) Are the two modern bedouin sets of beads, one with a button to hold the beads together, related to the skeletons?[198] Can we be certain when we have neither photographs nor draw-

---

193. I am indebted here to discussion with Émile Puech; see *BASOR* 312 (1998): 21-36; esp. 26.

194. The threats from fundamentalist Jews in Israel make it now impossible to increase the samples derived from the Qumran cemetery.

195. Joseph Zias, "The Cemeteries of Qumran and Celibacy: Confusion Laid to Rest?" *DSD* 7 (2000): 220-53.

196. See esp. the publications by Jürgen Zangenberg: "The 'Final Farewell': A Necessary Paradigm Shift in the Interpretation of the Qumran Cemetery," *Qumran Chronicle* 8 (1999): 213-18; "Bones of Contention," *Qumran Chronicle* 91 (2000): 51-76; "Grave Doubts," *BAR* 26 (2000): 66.

197. I have doubts regarding Zias's claim that no artifacts should be found in Jewish burials from the Second Temple period. The rabbinic source he cites is too late to be trustworthy for the earlier period, and the varieties of Jewish interpretations of Torah preclude such an assumption regarding consistency in Jewish burial practice; see Zias, *DSD* 7 (2000): 226. Moreover, I have acquired for the University of North Carolina, Charlotte, artifacts found in a tomb discovered south of Jerusalem that dates from approximately the 7th century B.C.E. or earlier. In it are zoomorphic statuettes of animals, attesting to the difference between Old Testament theologies and the religion of Israel whose "licentious" practices were the object of derision by the prophets — and thus are proved to have existed among some Israelites. One cannot conclude that all, or even most, Jews living in ancient Palestine observed the halakoth found in later rabbinic works.

198. See the photographs in Zias, *DSD* 7 (2000): 227.

ings of the objects *in situ?* Unfortunately, de Vaux — like Yigael Yadin — in view of new methods and techniques, often moved too much dirt too quickly (that is not to disparage these two geniuses). That is not to claim they should have been so laboriously meticulous as sometimes was Joseph Callaway, yet we cannot be certain about "scientific" results when the provenience and setting of *realia* seem to be too much a matter of faith in revered colleagues. (4) Can we accept as conclusive Zias's conclusions, when some of the human skeletal remains found by de Vaux in 1955 and 1956 in tombs T32-37 are still somewhere in Europe — unpublished and not yet scientifically examined? Can we be certain that these bones are only of adult males? (5) Do other physical anthropologists concur or disagree with Zias's alleged facts and methodology? (6) Has a representative sample of the Qumran cemetery been excavated, and do we have a reliable frame of reference to obtain a general sociological and anthropological conclusion? Hence, until we hear from other physical anthropologists about Zias's analysis we cannot be certain; and obviously there is no way to dig these tombs again, using more modern recording devices and skills.

Yet Zias's conclusion is clear and, for the present at least, compelling. Thus, for the present, Zias's conclusion appears definitive: "There is nothing in the cemeteries that should lead anyone 'along the road to Damascus' to believe that Qumran, lying between Jericho and Ein Gedi, was anything but a monastic community of adult males, preferring the company of palm trees to women."[199] This conclusion is supported by the Qumran scrolls,[200] Pliny, and Philo. Moreover, Qumran celibacy makes sense when one reviews the Torah's rules for abstinence during war and the observation that Qumranites thought they were in a cosmic war (1QS 3, *War Scroll*).[201] Also, a priest on duty was to refrain from sex. Surely, this regulation helps us understand why Qumran priests could have been celibate. Perhaps celibacy could also include those who had sex only for procreation and then lived an ascetic existence, as Josephus reported about the Essenes (*War* 2.161; cf. *History of the Rechabites*).[202]

199. Zias, *DSD* 7 (2000): 253.

200. Thiede claims, e.g., that 4Q249e "confirms the principle of celibacy at Qumran"; *Scrolls and Jewish Origins*, 31.

201. Maybe some of the earliest Qumranites left wives in Jerusalem and most initiates joined the Community before the time of marriage.

202. The motive of the Essenes "in marrying is not (sexual) gratification but the procreation of children" (*War* 2.161). Cf. *Hist. Rech.* 11.4-8: "And we pray also night and day, and this is our entire pursuit. . . . Nor are there any of us taking wives for themselves, (except) until they produce two children. And after they produced two children, they separate from each other and are in chastity, not knowing that they were once in the intimacy of mar-

It seems clear that a group of priests, and other religious Jews, lived at Qumran during three centuries and that they owned (but did not compose all) the manuscripts found near Qumran, especially in Caves IVA and IVB. Whether one wishes to call the Community a "monastery" or the collection a "library" depends on definitions; but it is misinformed to claim that Roman Catholics, especially de Vaux, are responsible for this concept. Today many Israelis, including Magen Broshi, conclude that Qumran was a monastery.[203]

I am convinced that one can talk about the manuscript contents of the 11 caves as constituting a Qumran library. If Qumran is a library, one needs to stress two perspectives. On the one hand, it surprisingly contains works somewhat anathema to Qumran theology. The document most antithetical to Qumran theology and found in the Caves would be the *Prayer of Jonathan*. On the other hand, the Qumran library understandably excludes works that are pro-Hasmonean. Most notably absent from Qumran are the extremely pro-Hasmonean 1 Maccabees and the slightly pro-Hasmonean (or pro-establishment) *Psalms of Solomon*.

If this historical scenario fits the *Rule of the Community*, what should be said about the *Damascus Document?* Most experts conclude, and rightly so, that this document seems to describe the life of non-Qumran Essenes and explains the customs and rules of Essenes who married, as Josephus stated.[204] It seems likely not only that the Essenes originated in the Holy City but that some of them in the 1st century C.E. lived in Jerusalem.[205] It is conceivable that "the Man of Lies" is the epithet for a man who stayed behind in Jerusalem with some "Essenes" when the Righteous Teacher led others into the wilderness (as indicated earlier in this monograph). Perhaps some Essenes left Qumran and joined others living in Jerusalem, when Qumran was burned ca. 40 B.C.E. or later. While these scenarios are conceivable, we are confronted with many unknowns. For example, we do not know what percentage of those who fled Qumran ca. 40, or later, returned to Qumran and lived there until the destruction of 68 C.E.

---

riage; but as if from the beginning being in virginity. One of the children remains for marriage, and the other for virginity." For the Greek text and English translation, see Charlesworth, *The History of the Rechabites*. SBLTT 17; Pseudepigrapha Series 10 (Chico: Scholars, 1982), 64-67. In its present form the *History of the Rechabites* is a Christian redaction and expansion of a Jewish work that probably antedates 136 C.E.

203. Broshi, "Was Qumran, Indeed, a Monastery?" 27.

204. See the authoritative comments by Baumgarten and Schwartz in Charlesworth, *Damascus Document*, 6-7.

205. Along with many experts now affirming that Essenes were living in Jerusalem in the 1st century C.E. is Thiede; *Scrolls and Jewish Origins*, 33.

At times, Essenes may have lived in and near Jericho. That seems possible in light of the ostracon found by James F. Strange which mentions the region of Jericho.[206] It is also conceivable that some Essenes may have lived in the 30 stone "huts" discovered recently above Ein Gedi. There should be no doubt that most Essenes lived in Palestine far from Qumran, the community center. Josephus and Philo report that 4000 Essenes lived in ancient Palestine. No more than 150, and probably less than 100, ever worked and lived near Qumran at any one time.[207]

Seventh, it is misleading to claim that all Essenes died in 68 C.E. One cannot even claim that all Qumranites died in that year.

Eighth, it is almost certain that the origins of Qumran should be dated after 165 and before 102 B.C.E. It is most unlikely that John Hyrcanus I (135/4-104) or a later Hasmonean was the first one called "the Wicked Priest." It is likely, however, that *4QTestimonia* indicates that Jews were already living at Qumran by the time of John Hyrcanus I. This Qumran composition seems to preserve the Qumranites' interpretation of Joshua's curse that the one who rebuilds Jericho will have to pay by the loss of "his firstborn." Hyrcanus's sons, Aristobulus I and Antigonus, both died ca. 104/103 B.C.E. The excavations directed by Ehud Netzer in Jericho seem to prove that south of "Old Testament Jericho" the complex of Hasmonean buildings were built by John Hyrcanus I. Thus, Joshua's curse seems now best to fit John Hyrcanus I and the unexpected demise of his two sons.[208]

Summary

This reconstruction of Qumran history is basically that advocated, *mutatis mutandis,* by most of the experts working in and contributing to the Princeton Theological Seminary Dead Sea Scrolls Project. Yet, we also wish to stress that work continues, and that origins are almost always shrouded

206. Published in Philip S. Alexander and Geza Vermes, eds., *Qumran Cave 4.XIX.* DJD 26 (Oxford: Clarendon, 1998), 497-507.

207. See esp. de Vaux, *Archaeology and the Dead Sea Scrolls,* 86.

208. See Hanan Eshel, "The Historical Background of the Pesher Interpreting Joshua's Curse on the Rebuilder of Jericho," *RevQ* 15 (1992): 409-20. Eshel, contrary to our norm, calls 4QTest a pesher. See also Ehud Netzer, "The Hasmonean and Herodian Winter Palaces at Jericho," *IEJ* 25 (1975): 89-100; "The Winter Palaces of the Judean Kings at Jericho at the End of the Second Temple Period," *BASOR* 228 (1977): 1-14; "Recent Discoveries in the Winter Palaces of Second Temple Times at Jericho," *Qadmoniot* 15 (1982): 22-28 [Hebrew]; and the contributions on Jericho by Netzer and Gideon Foerster in *NEAEHL* 2:681-91.

in the mists of history. We often must flounder, in attempting to reconstuct the past, with frustrating uncertainty amidst what little data have survived from the time. Now that virtually all of the Qumran fragments have been assessed and published, we can no longer imagine that someday we might know the names of the Righteous Teacher, the Wicked Priest, and the Man of Lies. What is known looms much more important: the Qumran scrolls have revealed a side of Judaism that is surprising in light of what was once placarded as certain about Second Temple Judaism. That is to say, the Qumran scrolls have helped us grasp how unreliable sometimes are the historical asides found in Josephus, the New Testament, and the rabbinic corpus.

The Pesharim and Qumran History

It should now be clear that no Qumran scroll is identified as a book dedicated to history or a text defined by an interest in history. The concern to leave a reliable record of monumental events, or to explain the moral lessons to be obtained from history, was an enterprise and occupation more typical of the Greeks and Romans. In Second Temple Judaism (or Early Judaism) the only historical compositions are 1 Maccabees (and to a lesser degree 2 Maccabees) and Josephus's *War* and *Antiquities*.[209] Before turning directly to the ways the pesharim may reflect historical people or events,[210] it is prudent to recognize that we will be *seeing history from within Qumran*. As Shemaryahu Talmon has urged us to see Qumran from within,[211] so we shall be striving to see the history of the world outside of Qumran from the perspective of those living inside the Qumran Community.[212]

---

209. We cannot judge the contents of lost histories mentioned in the Hebrew Scriptures or of the work of Justus of Tiberias. Chronicles is a religious book, and the Gospels theologically proclaim good news about Jesus' life. On Justus of Tiberias, see Yaron Dan, "Josephus Flavius and Justus of Tiberias," in *Josephus Flavius: Historian of Eretz-Israel in the Hellenistic-Roman Period*, ed. Uriel Rappaport (Jerusalem: Yad Izhak Ben Zvi, 1983), 57-78 [Hebrew], VII [Eng. summary].

210. See the survey by Phillip R. Callaway, "The Pesharim and the History of the Qumran Community," in *The History of the Qumran Community*, 135-71.

211. Talmon, *The World of Qumran from Within*.

212. This review of Qumran history is similar to that found in most standard introductions; see, e.g., Vermes, "History of the Sect," in *The Dead Sea Scrolls: Qumran in Perspective*, 137-62. In light of recent research, there also are some dissimilarities between my review and that of others.

What Is a Pesher?

Pesher "interpretation" of Scripture is pneumatic, eschatological,[213] and "fulfillment interpretation"; it is also self-serving and idiosyncratic.[214] *Pēsher,* an Aramaic loanword (פשרא) in Qumran Hebrew, is a noun attested not only at Qumran but also in late biblical books (a *hapax legomenon* in Hebrew in Eccl. 8:1, but in Aramaic numerous times in Daniel).[215] As a noun derived from a verb, it denotes primarily and originally "dissolving" (or "loosening"). In later Mishnaic Hebrew it (פשרה) can denote "agreeing" (or "coming together")."[216] At Qumran — as in Syriac (ܦܫܪ‍ܐ),[217] *Pēsher* primarily denotes "interpretation" and "explanation."[218]

Do the pesharim at Qumran primarily denote the "loosening" of meaning, due to divine revelation? Or do they denote the "coming together" of scriptural meaning, because of the grounding of Qumran theology in the lemmata of Scripture? Any attempt to choose between the two is flawed because they are false alternatives.[219] As S. L. Berrin clarifies,

213. Long ago Karl Elliger clarified the principles of Qumran hermeneutics; *Studien zum Habakkuk-Kommentar vom Toten Meer.* BHT 15 (Tübingen: Mohr [Siebeck], 1953), 150-64.

214. See the helpful outline of issues involved in understanding biblical exegesis at Qumran by Geza Vermes: "Bible Interpretation at Qumran," *ErIsr* 20 (1989): 184-91. See also Devorah Dimant, "Qumran Sectarian Literature," in *Jewish Writings of the Second Temple Period,* ed. Michael E. Stone. CRINT 2/2 (Philadelphia: Fortress, 1984), 483-550; Maurya P. Horgan, *Pesharim.* CBQMS 8 (Washington: Catholic Biblical Association, 1979); George J. Brooke, *Exegesis at Qumran* (Sheffield: JSOT, 1985); and H. Gabrion, "L'interprétation de l'ecriture dans la littérature de Qumrân," *ANRW* 19/1 (Berlin: de Gruyter, 1979): 779-848.

215. See Elisha Qimron, *The Hebrew of the Dead Sea Scrolls.* HSS 29 (Atlanta, Scholars, 1986), 94.

216. See esp. Herbert W. Basser, "Pesher Hadavar: The Truth of the Matter," *RevQ* 13 (1988): 389-405.

217. R. Payne Smith, *Thesaurus Syriacus* 2 (Oxford: Clarendon, 1901), col. 330: *interpretatio somniorum.*

218. See the data amassed in *HAL* 3:982-83. In rabbinics the verb *pshar* can denote "to solve a riddle or dream" (*Tg. Onq.* Gen. 41:15-16), the noun *pashar* means an "interpreter," and the noun *pshar* is an "interpretation." These examples show that Qumran Hebrew is moving away from Biblical Hebrew and towards Mishnaic Hebrew (as Qimron claims; e.g., *The Hebrew of the Dead Sea Scrolls,* 87). Arabic *fassara* denotes "he explained." As Ernest Klein suggests, the Arabic is probably influenced by Syriac; *A Comprehensive Etymological Dictionary of the Hebrew Language for Readers of English* (New York: Macmillan, 1987), 535.

219. See esp. George Brooke, "Qumran Pesher: Towards the Redefinition of a Genre," *RevQ* 10 (1979-1981): 483-503; *Exegesis at Qumran,* 149-56.

The room most scholars judge to be the scriptorium,
in which many of the Dead Sea Scrolls were copied

Photo by James H. Charlesworth

The binding, exegetical methodology provides the language in which the loosening, revelatory content is expressed. The synthesis of these two aspects is seen in the formal structure of pesher which consists of (1) the biblical citation, (2) an introductory formula, and (3) the pesher interpretation.[220]

Two perspectives are paramount in the pesharim. First, according to the Qumranites the ancient men of wisdom, especially the prophets, focused their thoughts on the latter days. Second, the Qumranites believed they were living in the latter days of time and history.[221] According to the pesharim (esp. 1QpHab 7), only the Qumranites or the Righteous Teacher knew the meaning of the prophetic books. Even the authors of Scripture did not know what had been revealed through them. God disclosed the full meaning, in the latter days, only to the Righteous Teacher and thence to his group.

We may now explore the ways the pesharim and other Qumran commentaries may preserve a Qumranic view of history and earlier traditions regarding the history of the Qumran group. If we do not struggle to ascertain the degree of reliability of history in the pesharim, we have virtually nowhere else to turn to learn about Qumran history. We do have access to the asides preserved in the *Rule of the Community*, the *Damascus Document*, and some innuendoes in the *Temple Scroll*. However, these references are oblique, in the judgment of most Qumran experts. History, especially of the origins of the Qumran group, is primarily preserved in the pesharim.

Methodology

Long ago Frank M. Cross gave voice to the consensus[222] that has dominated Qumranology from the mid-1950s until the present. Cross contended that "the allusions in biblical commentaries can be utilized in reconstructing the history of the sect."[223] He offered only a generic methodology for discerning history in the pesharim. He did, however,

220. S. L. Berrin, "Lemma/Pesher Correspondence in Pesher Nahum," in Schiffman, Tov, and VanderKam, *The Dead Sea Scrolls Fifty Years after Their Discovery*, 1:341.

221. This consensus was stated long ago by Cross in *The Ancient Library*, 90.

222. As is well known, it has been challenged by some, especially by Philip R. Davies and George J. Brooke. See esp. Davies, *The Damascus Covenant*, 204; and Brooke, "The Pesharim and the Origins of the Qumran Community," in Wise, Collins, and Pardee, *Methods of Investigation*, 339-53.

223. Cross, *The Ancient Library of Qumran*, 93.

The plastered "benches" found in the scriptorium

Photo by James H. Charlesworth; courtesy of the
Department of Antiquities of the Hashemite Kingdom of Jordan

point out the need to utilize "outside controls to limit the framework within which our sources operate" and to determine "the time period set by archaeological data, by paleographical evidence, and by other more objective methods before applying the more subjective techniques of internal criticism."[224] Without forcing or distorting the intent and character of our primary sources, let us seek ways to curb subjective speculations and approximate reliable results in reconstructing history from Qumran's point of view.

The Qumranites did not create *ex nihilo* a view of their origins without any controls. Among the most important internal controls for preserving somewhat reliable traditions of the history of their movement, the following seem most important. (1) Qumranites were required to memorize Qumran lore, and that surely included an inward perception of the origins of the Community. (2) The rigid sociological barriers of the Community would have protected, to a certain degree, the flow of traditions from ca. 150 to at least 40 B.C.E. (3) The conservative nature of such priestly communities indicates a desire to preserve accurately prior traditions. (4) The

224. Cross, *The Ancient Library of Qumran*, 93.

hierarchical nature of the Community would have helped to control the dissemination of lore. (5) The power of the Righteous Teacher would have galvanized and shaped memories of origins and of common enemies; and he was not a distant figure of the murky past but a contemporary of many who composed and edited Qumran scrolls. (6) The Qumranites' passionate claim that their history was special, that their movement was divinely ordained, and that they alone had received, through the Righteous Teacher, the proper means to understand Scripture (esp. 1QpHab 7) would cumulatively have focused reflections on the meaning of contemporaneous events. Thus, the Jews at Qumran, while scarcely rational historiographers like Polybius, most likely preserved somewhat reliable traditions of their special sacred history. They claimed that they were chosen to live in the wilderness to fulfil God's word and to prepare for "the latter days."[225] They also were a closed community devoted to learning that protected the secret knowledge of God's "renewed covenant" for Israel.

One might postulate that what the Qumranites report about their own closed group's history is more reliable than what they reported about others. On the one hand, they were passionate about their unique place in the economy of salvation. On the other, they hated "the Sons of Darkness." Those outside the renewed covenant were viewed with less reliable objectivity; in fact, they were cursed in the covenant renewal ceremony. Such emotions clearly distort history, and perhaps in ways we cannot now discern.

It is imperative to comprehend the sociological dimensions of knowledge and language developed within the Community. One might miss some dimensions of Qumran history and sociology by seeking to discern the identities of those named only by sobriquets.[226] One dimension of Qumran theology is anonymity. New members of the Community were taught to think and express themselves using sobriquets and epithets.

I think it unwise to devise a *set methodology* for discerning the reliability of history in the pesharim. A systematic method might force data into a created coherent system, miss the context of allusions, and ignore the fact that we are not working with something like Polybius's histories but with pneumatic interpretations of Scripture.[227] This axiom, however,

225. See Rietz, *Collapsing of the Heavens and the Earth.*

226. See Bengtsson, *What's in a Name?*

227. Michael Fishbane insightfully discerns various literary forms among the pesharim (viz. lemmatic, anthological, pseudepigraphical) and points to different techniques for interpreting (scribal, legal, homiletical, and prophetic); "Interpretation of Mikra at Qumran," in *Mikra*, ed. Martin Jan Muilder. CRINT 2/1 (Philadelphia: Fortress, 1988), 339-77.

should not preclude the development of some clear, yet fluid, means of proceeding to discern and evaluate historical innuendoes and allusions in the pesharim. Thus, it does seem wise to introduce a methodology that will serve exegetically to help us obtain reliable historical nuggets from the pesharim. Thus, I shall proceed with six methods for discerning history in the pesharim. It is imperative, at the outset, to stress that we must proceed with caution in weighing the validity of historical information in the pesharim.[228]

(1) *Multiple attestation within Qumran literature.* This method pertains especially to the well-known sobriquets such as "the Righteous Teacher," "the Wicked Priest," "the Man of the Lie," and "the Spouter of the Lie." It also applies to pervasive Qumran *termini technici.*

Among the most important technical terms are the ways the Qumranites refer to themselves. They called themselves "the Poor Ones," "the Good Ones," "the Sons of Aaron," "the Sons of Light," "the Sons of Truth," "the Sons of the Dawn," "the Sons of Zadok," "the Sons of Righteousness," "the Righteous Ones," "the Perfect Ones," "the Perfect in the Way," "the Holy Ones," and "the Most Holy Ones." The "Many" and "the Holy Ones" live in the "House of Holiness," because "the Holy Spirit" has left Jerusalem and dwells on earth with them.

They consider their Community not only "the House of Holiness," but also "the Community" — the abode of those who are united and one. Other terms for their ruling body are "the Council of the Community" and perhaps "the Congregation of the Community." Some of the rules of the Community were conceived by "the Righteous Teacher." The daily life at Qumran is run by "the Examiner," "the Master," "the Overseer," and "the Men of the Council."

The Qumranites (a term not found in the Qumran scrolls) celebrate "the Day of Atonement," live in "the Endtime," and look forward to "the Day of Judgment," and "the Day of Vengeance." Their enemies, historically speaking, are "the Kittim," who are almost always the Romans.[229] The evil angels are under the power of "the Spirit of Deceit" and "the Angel of Darkness." Both are probably names for Satan or "Belial." The ruling good angel is called "the Angel of Truth" and "the Spirit of Truth."

---

228. Wise, but also too pessimistic regarding the presence of reliable historical information in the pesharim, is the caution suggested by Davies; *Behind the Essenes*, 90; *The Damascus Covenant; Qumran*, esp. 80-81 (a more positive assessment of the consensus and "the major working hypothesis").

229. The identification of the Kittim with the Romans is so obvious to most Qumran experts today that a mere footnote signals this fact. See Johann Maier, *Die Texte vom Toten Meer* (Munich: Reinhardt, 1995), 2:89.

We know these are *termini technici* at Qumran because of their unifying perspective and the multiple attestations of such terms in the Qumran scrolls. These terms give a basis for understanding the Qumran perspective and the historical allusions preserved within it. The pervasiveness of such terms reveals that the Qumranites hated the Romans, "the Kittim," and spewed forth even more passionate invectives against the priests, under the rule of "the Wicked Priest," who had corrupted the sacrifices in the Temple (see 5Q10).

(2) *Multiple attestation from non-Qumran literature in Early Judaism.* The Qumran sectarian scrolls mention figures that can be identified or linked with individuals known from non-Qumran literary sources. The scholar can then compare and contrast what is learned from each source. We should not assume that non-Qumran references to historical events are more objective; for example, the authors of the *Psalms of Solomon* refer to Pompey as a snake or dragon and a man of "insolence" (Ps. Sol. 2:25-26).[230]

(3) *Coherence within Qumran sectarian literature.* By comparing what can be known in all the Qumran sectarian sources about a figure, we do not obtain factual and reliable historical data; but we do begin to grasp the mindset of the Qumranites. This information then needs to be assessed in terms of the likely date of each composition. Sometimes a lack of coherence may be due to different periods in the life of the Qumran Community.

By collecting first all the references to such figures in the pesharim and related commentaries we can obtain some initial information. Then, we can ascertain what is known from other Qumran compositions. In much previous investigation, some confusion has been caused by mixing together conceptions and references in documents whose composition is spread over more than one century of work in the Qumran scriptorium and elsewhere. Here, as in most publications on Qumran history, pride of place for historical information goes to the pesharim.

Almost all the hymns in the *Thanksgiving Hymns* are earlier than the pesharim. Numerous hymns preserve "historical and biographical" information about the Righteous Teacher. The hymns were well known and recited habitually in the Community. References to the Righteous Teacher in the pesharim may be shaped, in some places, by liturgy and not by valid

---

230. On Pompey and revolts, see E. Mary Smallwood, *The Jews Under Roman Rule: From Pompey to Diocletian.* SJLA 20 (Leiden: Brill, 1976), which is a little dated; and Amy-Jill Levine, "Visions of Kingdoms: From Pompey to the First Jewish Revolt," in *The Oxford History of the Biblical World,* ed. Michael D. Coogan (Oxford: Oxford University Press, 1998), 467-514.

historical reminiscences.[231] The *Thanksgiving Hymns* do intermittently contain passages in which we can discern the Righteous Teacher's autobiographical comments, but that does not mean the pesharim have only these as avenues to early history. Such would demand the impossible. It would presuppose, incorrectly, that the Righteous Teacher was the only learned man in the origins of Qumran history, that all who participated in the origins of Qumran died with him, and that all historical knowledge evaporated with them. Thus, coherence at Qumran indicates that the Righteous Teacher may have had an exalted view of his place in history, and passed on to those in his community the claim that he alone had been given special revelations by God (see 1QpHab 7 and 1QH 16).

(4) *Coherence with non-Qumran literature.* One goal in searching for historical information in the pesharim and related commentaries is to learn something about historical persons or events. That entails sifting through all known non-Qumran early Jewish literature and all relevant ancient literature. Pride of place, outside Qumran, in terms of historical data, goes to 1 Maccabees and Josephus's *War* and *Antiquities.* It would be impossible to proceed further if we did not already have a universally accepted grid of persons and dates to understand events and persons in antiquity. This grid has been constructed over centuries by looking at sources that are not found at Qumran. It is the coherence such works present, and which may be supplemented from Jewish sources, that is usually ignored by classicists as they work on ancient history.

(5) *Coherence with archaeological insights obtained from excavations at and near Qumran.* The events that shaped Qumran history from ca. 150 B.C.E. to 68 C.E. were not completely isolated from what was happening elsewhere. Thus, what is learned from archaeological research elsewhere is essential. We need to synthesize what has been learned archaeologically from Qumran, the Qumran caves, Ein Feshka, Ein Ghuweir,[232] Jericho, Ein Gedi,

---

231. I am indebted to, but have modified, an insight introduced by Davies; *Behind the Essenes,* 90.

232. See the three publications by Pessaḥ Bar-Adon: "Chronique archéologique: Rivage de la Mer Morte," *RB* 77 (1970): 398-400; "Another Settlement of the Judaean Desert Sect at 'Ein Ghuweir on the Dead Sea," *ErIsr* 10 (1971): 72-89 [Hebrew]; "Another Settlement of the Judean Desert Sect at 'En el-Ghuweir on the Shores of the Dead Sea," *BASOR* 227 (1977): 1-25. Many scholars have voiced the desire to have heard what de Vaux thought about Bar-Adon's claim that el-Ghuweir was an Essene settlement; in fact he did express his opinion. He considered it "rash to apply the designation 'Essene' to the building excavated near 'Ain el-Ghuweir or to the cemetery which may have been attached to it"; *Archaeology and the Dead Sea Scrolls,* 89. Instrumental neutron activation analysis (INAA) of pottery found at Qumran and at El Ghuweir does not reveal that the latter was manufactured at Qumran; in fact, a surprising amount of the pottery derives from Jerusalem. This finding

Masada, Muraba'at, Naḥal Ḥever,[233] and Jerusalem (esp. in what was before 70 C.E. the southwestern portion of the city and the graves at Talpiyot).[234] Then, we need to add to our perception and synthesis what has been learned by archaeologists from excavations of the Roman strata at Sepphoris, Nazareth, Capernaum, Bethsaida, Gamla, the Herodium, and elsewhere. It is imperative to enrich research focused on literary remains with *realia* and insights obtained from archaeological excavations and study.

(6) *Historical allusions not generated by Qumran theological tendencies.* We may be closer to reliable historical information if we do not discern the concerns of Qumran theology shaping the presentation. With the pesharim we are faced with theological exaggerations caused by Qumran theology; hence, we are dealing in these compositions with degrees of historical distortion.

Summary

Militating against discerning reliable history in the pesharim is the observation that practically the only reason the Qumranites use the prophets to explain their own history is the conviction that the prophets were speaking about or alluding to the time of the Qumranites, the latter days. Following the *lemma* (a scriptural citation) is a *pesher* (an interpretation) that explains Scripture. The interpretation often refers to events contemporary with, or slightly prior to, the commentator. We are not confronted with an either-or as if we have history or we do not have history. As Cross said long ago, in the "commentaries the inner history of the sect is bewilderingly mixed with external political events."[235] As he warned, we must not force

---

will lead some scholars to conclude that there is now further evidence of Essenes living in Jerusalem and others to deny the Essene hypothesis. See Magen Broshi, "The Archaeology of Qumran — A Reconsideration?" in *The Dead Sea Scrolls: Forty Years of Research*, ed. Devorah Dimant and Uriel Rappaport (Leiden: Brill, 1992), 103-15; and Joseph Yellin, Magen Broshi, and Hanan Eshel, "Pottery of Qumran and Ein Ghuweir: The First Chemical Exploration of Provenience," *BASOR* 321 (2001): 65-78.

233. Not only 2nd-century but also 1st-century *realia* have been discerned in the "Cave of Letters." See Richard C. Freund and Rami Arav, "Return to the Cave of Letters: What Still Lies Buried?" *BAR* 27/1 (2001): 24-39.

234. See the discussion in this essay on "the Essene Gate." In Talpyot, near Teddy (Kollek) Stadium, there are graves dissimilar to those outside the walls of Jerusalem and from the early Roman period but similar to those in the cemeteries at Qumran. I am grateful to Magen Broshi for helping me examine these graves. See Amos Kloner and Y. Gat, "Burial Caves in the Region of East Talpiyot," *'Atiqot* 8 (1982): 74-76 [Hebrew].

235. Cross, *The Ancient Library of Qumran*, 3rd ed., 92.

into the apocalyptic mind of the Qumranites categories familiar to us but foreign to them.

Coherence both within Qumran sectarian compositions and with historical events known from reliable Hellenistic sources seems to be the best guide for finding historical information in the pesharim.[236] We are not presented with *bruta facta;* only to a certain extent do historical data found in more than one scroll, and in coherence with related allusions found in other Qumran sectarian writings, have a better chance of being historically reliable than one mere aside that seems ambiguous. Nevertheless, a mere allusion to an event that is coherent with a recorded trustworthy historical account is not to be dismissed lightly. Thus, it is simply the nature of the reference that will help us discern how historically reliable a comment may be.

The Date of the Pesharim

The issue of the date of the pesharim has been variously assessed. Some scholars point out that the pesharim seem to be late compositions in the life of Qumran, and that this fact militates against their historical veracity. That is, some Qumran experts claim the record in the pesharim is unreliable, since they are 100 years removed from the events they describe.

Other Qumran experts rightly point out that 100 years is not that long a time when we observe the continuity of Qumran lore and life and the conservative nature of priestly communities. Indeed, we need to realize that we are evaluating the traditions of a group that has been cohesive, continuous, and in one place. The pesharim were composed at Qumran and antedate the exodus from the site in the late 1st century B.C.E.

Since the 1950s many scholars have concluded that all the pesharim are autographs. In a gracious, informative, and supportive letter of 17 June 2001, Frank M. Cross brought me up to date regarding his own position: "As I argued in the introduction to *Scrolls from Qumrân Cave I* (the AIAR edition), all of the pesharim appear to be autographs. We had when I wrote no instance of multiple copies, and corrections appeared to be contemporary or later." Thus, he supports his earlier published conclusion that the pesharim are autographs:

236. Still to be mined for valuable information and its importance for understanding the pesharim are the insights published by Shimon Applebaum in *Judaea in Hellenistic and Roman Times: Historical and Archaeological Essays.* SJLA 40 (Leiden: Brill, 1989).

The exegetical lore, bearing elements coming from many periods of the sect's life, evidently was transmitted orally until finally precipitated into writing, under *lemmata* from a biblical scroll. Such a setting can be reconstructed thanks to . . . the existence of single copies only of the commentaries, as over against multiple copies of works belonging to other categories of literature, suggesting that many if not all of the *pĕšarîm* are autographs.[237]

To be taken with utmost seriousness is Cross's insight that the pesharim preserve exegetical lore that had been transmitted orally within the Qumran Community for some time. It is also evident that he did not claim all the pesharim were autographs, leaving open the door for the suggestion that one or more might be a copy of an earlier work. That conclusion might add some credence to historical asides found in a pesher, since the original work would move closer to the date of an event mentioned in it. In any case, moving the date of a pesher closer to the date of an event described in it certainly removes the claim that the pesharim preserve unreliable historical data because they are far removed from the events they mirror.

The main reasoning for all the pesharim being autographs is the fact that for each of them we have only one copy. The logic is very strong, especially when we have so many copies of some documents, notably many of the biblical books, *More Precepts of the Torah,* the *Rule of the Community,* the *Damascus Document, Enoch,* and *Jubilees.* Obviously however, this analysis is not conclusive in itself. The contention that we have only one copy of each pesher and therefore each is an autograph is itself a blatant *non sequitur.* When we add that all of the pesharim were composed at Qumran, the argument increases in force; but we cannot conclude either that all material written at Qumran was placed in the caves or that we have most of what was hidden in 68 C.E.

We must then closely examine the pesharim themselves for clues. Eschewing the supposition that "all" pesharim are autographs, can we find evidence that one or more may be a copy and that, therefore, there is evidence that some of them originated within or near the time of the Righteous Teacher?

First, in *4QPesher Isaiah^c* (4Q163) we may find evidence of copying. In frg. 23, col. 2, line 14 a scribe has added above the line "As the raider[s] lie in wait for a man." This, however, may be an error of copying from a

---

237. Frank M. Cross, David Noel Freedman, James A. Sanders, eds., with John C. Trever, *Scrolls from Qumrân Cave I* (Jerusalem: Albright Institute of Archaeological Research and The Shrine of the Book, 1972), 5.

manuscript of Hosea 6:9a. A much better example is found in *4QPesher Isaiah^e* (note the interlinear correction in 4QpIsa^e frg. 5.5). Here a scribe clearly erred in copying Isaiah 21. He (or another scribe) omitted the words מפני חרבות נדד and inserted them above the line. The error can easily be explained as haplography due to copying. It seems to be a case of a copying error caused by *parablepsis;* the eye of the copying scribe went from the first to the second מפני, inadvertently omitting the words later added in the supralinear line. Another copying error is also evident at this point, and it is also due to the appearance of another מפני. This composite prepositional form, in fact, appears four times in Isaiah 21:15. Thus, we find evidence of errors due to copying in the pesharim; but to ground the hypothesis that a pesher is a copy of an earlier work we must not focus on the lemmata, which are obviously copied, but only on the interpretation.

Second, a scribal correction in 4QpIsa^b (4Q162) is arresting. In col. 1, line 4 we find evidence that a scribe wrote ואשר אשר, which makes no sense. He (or another scribe) then added a ו above and before the second אשר, but this also gives us only the nonsense "when, and when." Then the scribe (or another one) put dots above and below each consonant in the second ואשר . . . (including the supralinear ו). We are obviously confronted with some type of correction of a scribal error.

This scribal correction could be an example of dittography. While it is not impossible that dittography can occur in an autograph, it often is a classic means of detecting an error caused by copying from another manuscript. Perhaps this form indicates that a scribe had been copying from an earlier copy of this Isaiah Pesher.

The error could have arisen as a scribe wrote a well-known formula for introducing the commentary. That is, ואשר אשר looks suspiciously like the formula ואשר אמר. Three observations strengthen this speculation: this formula is found in the preceding line, a lemma seems to be introduced, and in Hasmonean scripts a medial *mem* with a partially eroded right foot might look like a *shin* (both often have serifs and the slanting left foot of the *mem* often looks like the slanting strokes of the *shin*). We do have an example of a scribal error. Is it due to copying or simply an error in writing? It is conceivable, and perhaps probable, that a scribe saw ואשר אמר in an earlier copy of this pesher and absentmindedly wrote ואשר אשר.

We might conclude that while dittography is possible in an autograph, the example isolated here suggests that 4QpIsa^b may be a copy of an earlier work. Thus, we should no longer assume that all the pesharim are autographs. Perhaps we should contemplate that some of them may be copies of works that go back to the time of the Righteous Teacher.

Other pesharim, especially *4QPesher Psalms^a* (observe the interlinear correction in frgs. 1-10, col. 3.5), give reason to surmise that the scribal corrections may be due to errors in copying an earlier, presumably Hasmonean, manuscript. They are not caused by an error in composing but perhaps by an error in copying. The pesher formula and the beginning of the interpretation in *4QPesher Psalms^a* are germane to the work and would easily have been assumed to have been written already or over-looked in copying (and then later corrected upon proofing). Thus, the older view of some experts that the pesharim were all autographs pro-duced late in the life of the Community seems in need of revision.[238]

We also learn from a study of the critical texts of the pesharim that some of these works seem to antedate the end of the 1st century B.C.E. We now have textual evidence that some pesharim may have been copied from earlier sources (even if not strictly a pesher). Some pesharim are indeed in the late Hasmonean script. In need of correction is the prevalent claim that all the pesharim are extant in Herodian scripts.

Some passages with the "pesher-method" of interpreting Scripture, and the formulae that introduce the commentary, can be found in early works of the sect, notably 1QS (esp. 1QS 8.15; cf. also CD 4.14), as is clear from the list by C. D. Elledge published in PTSDSSP 6B.[239] Perhaps these new insights prove, or at least strengthen, Cross's insightful suggestion, of-fered in the late 1950s,[240] that the Righteous Teacher directly initiated the tradition of Essene exegesis, and that he "was heavily indebted to earlier apocalyptic materials, especially to Daniel."[241]

Historical Allusions in the Pesharim

As was reported in the first section of this monograph, *The Pesharim, Other Commentaries, and Related Documents* has been prepared to help the scholar avoid fanciful suggestions about historical episodes mirrored in

238. Milik, *Ten Years of Discovery,* 41; Cross, *The Ancient Library of Qumran,* 3rd ed., 91-92. Cross judges that "*most* of the commentaries are autographs" (92; italics mine). The "most" is also in the first edition (1958) of his work. Thus, he leaves open the possibility that some may have been copied. It also seems evident to me that most of the pesharim are auto-graphs.

239. Also, see Moshe J. Bernstein, "Introductory Formulas for Citation and Re-citation of Biblical Verses in the Qumran Pesharim," *DSD* 1 (1994): 30-70.

240. Dimant follows Cross: "some of these pesharim, or their sources, may be attrib-uted to an early stage in the community's history, or even to the founder of the community himself"; *ABD* 5:245. If such writings may not derive from the Righteous Teacher, the exegetical traditions most likely do.

241. Cross, *The Ancient Library of Qumran,* 90-91.

the commentary. Four features of the new edition, and reflections upon them, now seem to be in order. First, the restorations in the new critical edition of the pesharim are *pro forma*. They are attempted only when we have a base text (the document is preserved at this point elsewhere [*lemmata*, intertext, etc.]), formulae,[242] known *termini technici*, or when a word is anchored by the remains of ink (before, after, above, or below) the lacuna. Second, the new method highlights the preserved portions of each pesher or commentary graphically on the printed page. Third, the extant interpretations are often characterized by a pastiche of scriptural allusions that remain frustratingly elusive.[243] Fourth, after studying the 17 pesharim, one learns that only a few of them seem to preserve historical allusions (viz. the pesharim on Habakkuk and Nahum).

As scholars assess the degree that the traditions preserved in the pesharim preserve reliable history, we ought to keep in mind five perspectives. (1) Jewish historiography in the 2nd and 1st centuries B.C.E., with the exception of 1 Maccabees and to a lesser extent 2 Maccabees, tends to be creative historiography.[244] Past events were presented with a creative imagination that was fired by apocalypticism and an increasing belief that God would soon fulfill all his promises to Israel, his chosen people.

(2) The rhetoric that shaped our sources was fired by polemics among various factions within Early Judaism. Factional forces and extreme variety of thought characterize the early Jewish compositions, especially those composed from the Maccabean Revolt (167-165 B.C.E.), which is portrayed by Elias Bickerman, Victor Tcherikover, and Martin Hengel as primarily a Jewish civil war,[245] to the death of Bar Kokhba in 135 or 136 C.E., which was a Jewish revolt against Rome that was localized south of Jerusalem. The fiery invectives against fellow "Christians" or Jews deposited

242. See Elledge, "Graphic Index."

243. For "the house of Judah," see 4QFlor frg. 4.4. For "Ephraim and Judah," see 4QTest 27. For "the offspring of Judah," see 4QCata 12.

244. I am indebted to Doron Mendels for decades of discussing this perspective; see "'Creative History' in the Hellenistic Near East in the Third and Second Centuries BCE: The Jewish Case," *JSP* 2 (1988): 13-20; also see his comments in *The Rise and Fall of Jewish Nationalism*, 45.

245. Elias Bickerman, *The God of the Maccabees*. SJLA 32 (Leiden: Brill, 1979); Victor Tcherikover, *Hellenistic Civilization and the Jews* (Philadelphia: Jewish Publication Society, 1959); Martin Hengel, *Judaism and Hellenism* (Philadelphia: Fortress, 1974). Luc Dequeker is convinced that the Maccabean Revolt was caused by "Antiochus IV's attack on the holy city in 169 and 168 B.C.E."; "Jason's *Gymnasium* in Jerusalem (2 Mac. 4:7-17)," *Bijdragen, Tijdschrift voor Filosofie en Theologie* 54 (1993): 371-92. See also the judicious review of secondary discussions and insightful comments about the Maccabean Revolt by Sievers in *The Hasmoneans and Their Supporters*, esp. 15-38.

in the Gospels of Matthew and John pale in comparison to the polemics against other Jews found in the Qumran scrolls, especially in the pesharim.

(3) With the exception of 1 Maccabees, the extant Jewish sources should not be judged in terms of Polybius's historiography. The Jewish authors in Second Temple Judaism were often deliberately recasting historical events in a way that was self-serving for their own group.

(4) As we examine the pesharim for deposits of reliable history, we should recall what is clear in the Old Testament Pseudepigrapha that we have labeled "Expansions of the 'Old Testament' and Legends," especially *1 Enoch, Jubilees,* and the *Martyrdom of Isaiah.*[246] From these pseudepigrapha we learn that present historical events, including relationships among Jews and Idumeans, various tribes, and priestly cultic groups, were retrojected into the antediluvian, patriarchal, or monarchical past.

(5) The converse is also true. In many early Jewish compositions, the past was mined to serve the present. Particularly in the pesharim the biblical records, stories, and especially prophecies were given new life. They were reinterpreted to serve a variety of needs, including nationalistic activities. For the Qumranites, such re-interpretation was necessary to obtain rationale for meaningful existence and survival in the wilderness.[247]

On the one hand, we should not expect the pesharim to preserve inviolate objective history. The Jewish authors portrayed the events surrounding the career of the Righteous Teacher *sub specie aeternitatis.*[248] On the other hand, it is unwise to take a posture of dehistoricizing the pesharim, even if we are confronted with patterns from the Hebrew Scriptures. At least the Qumranites were convinced that there was solid history embedded within their interpretations of Scripture. As there is a mirror of reliable history in the story that shaped the *Letter of Aristeas,*[249] so there are real events embedded in the interpretation of Scripture found in the pesharim. Thus,

---

246. One should also add the Semitic sources behind the Greek *Testaments of the Twelve Patriarchs.*

247. Here I am indebted to Mendels, *The Rise and Fall of Jewish Nationalism,* 45.

248. Ida Fröhlich claims that the "general consensus is that the Qumran *pesharim* are the work of a single author"; *"Time and Times and Half a Time": Historical Consciousness in the Jewish Literature of the Persian and Hellenistic Eras.* JSPSup 19 (Sheffield: Sheffield Academic, 1996), 155, n. 5. This claim is incorrect.

249. Scholars (notably, Sidney Jellicoe, Harry M. Orlinsky, and R. J. H. Shutt) have clarified that the *Letter of Aristeas* is neither history nor fiction, but a defense of Judaism by a Jew who lived in Alexandria ca. 170 B.C.E. See Shutt in *OTP* 2:7-34; esp. 9-11. Dov Gera is convinced that the Tobiad history in *Ant.* 12.156-222 is simply "a piece of propaganda written by a Jew of Ptolemaic Egypt"; "On the Credibility of the History of the Tobiads (Josephus, *Antiquities* 12, 156-222)," in *Greece and Rome in Eretz Israel,* ed. Aryeh Kasher, Uriel Rappaport, and Gideon Fuks (Jerusalem: Yad Izhak Ben-Zvi, 1990), 21-38; quotation, 38.

the two extremes to avoid are the posture of denying any historical data in these works and the desire to prove them to be faithful historical narratives. Perhaps the best posture is not skepticism, but caution. To what extent can we learn about past events by studying Qumran's pesharim? With this methodology and question we can now review *some* of the most important passages in the pesharim that allude to historical events.[250]

Historical Allusions within Palestinian Judaism

The Unparalleled Authority of the Righteous Teacher

so that he can run who reads it, Its interpretation concerns the Righteous Teacher, to whom God made known all the mysteries of the words of his servants the prophets.[251] (1QpHab 7.3-5)

This is the most important passage in the pesharim concerning the Righteous Teacher. According to this text, he is the only one to whom God has revealed "all the mysteries of the words of his servants the prophets." That is, the Righteous Teacher alone has the ability to teach to his elect few the meaning of God's actions in time and history and the right interpretation of God's will. All other contemporary teachers, and even the prophets themselves, did not know what God revealed only to the מורה הצדק. In the whole history of salvation God revealed only to the Righteous Teacher כול רזי דברי עבדיו הנבאים.

It is conceivable that "the Interpreter of Knowledge" (4QPs[a] frgs. 1-10, col. 1.27) is the Righteous Teacher. It is equally possible, and to me more probable, that this person and the דורש התורה of CD 6.7 and 7.18 are not the Righteous Teacher. They seem to refer to the real founder of the movement that eventually went to Qumran and became the Community.[252] The "Interpreter of Torah" seems different from the Righteous Teacher. Note CD 7.18: "And the 'star' is the interpreter of Torah who came to Damascus, as it is written: 'A star stepped forth out of Jacob and a staff arose out of Israel.'" As in the pesharim, so in CD an historical event is explained by an interpretation of Scripture (the *lemma* is Num. 24:17).[253]

---

250. It is not helpful to divide the next section into "internal historical allusions" and "external historical allusions," since the two are intertwined in the pesharim.

251. The lemmata are printed in bold script.

252. See Davies, "Teacher of Righteousness."

253. For the text and translation, see Baumgarten and Schwartz in Charlesworth, *Damascus Document*.

Pesher Habakkuk (1QpHab 7)

Photo courtesy of John C. Trever/Claremont School of Theology
with the Ancient Biblical Manuscript Center

The person known as "the Interpreter of Knowledge" may be identified with "the Interpreter of Torah," who is the founder of the movement that much later was led to Qumran by the Righteous Teacher.

The Righteous Teacher was endowed by God with special knowledge that is divinely inspired truth. He was opposed by "the Man of the Lie" (CD 1.26). Karl Elliger and Bilha Nizan rightly clarify that, according to the Qumran sect, the Righteous Teacher possessed prophetic visionary powers and was directly inspired and guided by God.[254]

254. Elliger, *Studien zum Habakkuk-Kommentar*, 154-55; Bilha Nizan, *Pesher*

84

Throughout the Qumran scrolls, especially those composed at Qumran, there are references to "mysteries" (Heb *rzym;* e.g., 1QpHab 7.8; 1QS 3.23; 1QH 2.13; 1QM 3.9; cf. CD 3.18 and Dan. 2:29, et al.). Dimant rightly contends that "these enigmatic mysteries. . . could. . .only be unraveled by an inspired person living close to the time of the actual events."[255] It should be obvious that the Righteous Teacher lived during the events described in the pesharim — even if all these commentaries were composed after his death. Furthermore, we have already seen that some of the pesharim seem to have been copied from other earlier compositions, and it seems *prima facie* obvious that the Righteous Teacher had taught his followers "the pesher method." To a certain extent, historical references found not only in these alleged copies but also in all the pesharim are thus more reliable than if all the pesharim were written by later members of the Community who had not lived through the crises mirrored in the texts. This assumption or observation seems warranted because of the continuity and coherency of thought and community represented by the pesharim — all were written during the uninterrupted occupancy of Qumran during Phases I and II and before the abandonment of Qumran.

In studying the meaning of historical references too many scholars look only at the section that is the interpretation of a scriptural citation. It is imperative to stress that sometimes the "interpretation" does not begin only after the *lemma.* Some of the meaning of the pesher is embedded in the biblical citation. Any phenomenological indwelling of Qumran and the full text of one of the pesharim discloses that its author is only pointing out what is to be seen in the scriptural citation; thus, the meaning of a historical event is implicit in the text and more explicit in the pesher. This fact that historical meaning is found in *lemma* and subsequent interpretation will be true of most of the following excerpted passages.

The excerpted text *(lemma)* was not treated cavalierly, and the interpretation (pesher) is not arbitrary. As George J. Brooke states, the

> scriptural text takes priority. It can be played with, adjusted, punned, reordered, but it is the control. Secondly, the commentary is just such a skilled literary enterprise as the notice of some exegetical techniques points out. It is not arbitrary and should not encourage modern interpreters to treat it arbitrarily. It is carefully constructed with all manner

Habakkuk: A Scroll from the Wilderness of Judaea (1QpHab) (Jerusalem: Bialik Institute, 1986), 24-27 [Hebrew].

255. Dimant, *ABD* 5:248.

of allusions primarily to other scriptural texts which have not only suitable vocabulary but also suitable literary contexts of their own.[256]

The interpretation of Qumran's interpretation demands learning the rules of exegesis and hermeneutics in the pesharim. That is, one must strive to think as if one were a member of the Community.

The pesharim are only to a certain degree *sui generis;* they share much with other Jewish texts that are commentaries on Torah.[257] Similar to other early Jewish compositions that interpret *sacra scriptura,* the pesharim are shaped by incorporating the biblical text (intertextuality, *lemmata*) and echo or allude to memorized Scripture. The pesharim are also defined by a limited set of literary genres (only selected biblical books and only sections of them).[258]

The historical reflections in the pesharim are within a hermeneutical continuum that includes the reviews of history in the apocalypses. Metaphorical images are found not only in the pesharim; for example, history in *1 Enoch* is recited in metaphors and epithets. Moses is "a man who built a house for the Lord of the sheep." David is "another sheep" who was "promoted" to a ram, a judge, and a leader. Judas Maccabeus, the last leader reflected metaphorically, is "that ram" who battles nations represented by vultures, kites, eagles, and ravens. The Enoch author seems to identify "the Lord of the sheep" as God. He is the one who "revealed" to "that man, who writes down the names of the shepherds" not only some secrets but "everything." This thought in *1 Enoch* is strikingly reminiscent of the later concept in the pesharim that God revealed all the mysteries to the Righteous Teacher (compare 1QpHab 7 with "the Dream Visions" of *1 En.* 83–90).[259]

There is much that is unique about the pesharim also. These features reside not only in hermeneutical techniques but also in historical reminiscences — as we shall see.

The unique and unparalleled knowledge of the Righteous Teacher, found in 1QpHab 7.3-5, is supported by a coherence with other Qumran compositions. He alone can understand the meaning of Torah (1QpHab 8.1-3; 1QpMic frg. 8-10, 6-7).

The Community seems to conceive of two aspects of Torah. First, the

256. "Pesharim and the Origins," 350.

257. Two main books should be consulted: Daniel Patte, *Early Jewish Hermeneutic in Palestine* (Missoula, Mont.: Scholars, 1975); and David Instone Brewer, *Techniques and Assumptions in Jewish Exegesis before 70 C.E.* (Tübingen: J. C. B. Mohr [Siebeck], 1992).

258. See the similar reflections by Dimant in "Literary Typologies and Biblical Interpretation," in Talmon, *Jewish Civilization in the Hellenistic-Roman Period,* 77-78.

259. The excerpts are from Isaac in *OTP* 1:66-70.

Community possesses the well-known Scriptures (virtually all the *Biblia Hebraica*), but only the Righteous Teacher can interpret accurately Torah. Second, the Community is guided not only by Torah but also by further revelations made known only to the Righteous Teacher and through him to the Men of the Community and even the Many. Some Qumranites may have thought about the Righteous Teacher as a messenger from God (1QpHab 2.1-3). His followers must adhere to his teachings (1QpHab and CD 20.32).

There are inconsistencies between some statements in the pesharim and other texts, and some of these are related to the Essene group. According to 4QpPs[a] 3.15-16, the Righteous Teacher was the "founder" of the Community.

> for Ya[hweh supports his hand.] Its interpretation concerns the Priest, the [Righteous] Teacher, [whom] God [ch]ose as the pillar. F[or] he established him to build for him a congregation of [. . .]. (4QPs[a] frgs. 1-10, col. 3.15-16)

The idea that the Righteous Teacher founded the Community seems to be a concept later developed at Qumran,[260] which is assumed to be fact by too many scholars.[261] It clashes with the more reliable ideas found in the *Damascus Document* that the Righteous Teacher inherited an already existing group (CD 1.9-11).[262] While this aspect of the *Damascus Document* should be taken seriously, since it is corroborated by other historical work on Qumran history, the document should not always be taken literally.[263] For example, the 390 years, mentioned in CD 1.5-6, is not a mathematical computation but an adaptation from Ezekiel 4:5 which may be, nevertheless, not far off the mark.[264]

260. Scholars continue to perpetuate the misconception that the Righteous Teacher was the founder of the Qumran movement; he inherited a previously existing group. Contrast Fishbane: "The group is founded by one called the Unique Teacher"; he then cites CD 20.1 (361). See his otherwise excellent work in "Interpretation of Mikra at Qumran."

261. For example, Wacholder can open one of his erudite articles with the comment that the Righteous Teacher "founded the Dead Sea Scroll sect"; *BRev* 15/2 (1999): 26-29; quotation, 26.

262. Philip R. Davies, long ago, rightly warned about "treating" the pesharim as "documents of primary historical value." I have tried to avoid a positivistic historicism and to portray these works as commentaries that do mirror (but also distort) historical events. See Davies, *The Damascus Covenant*, 204.

263. See Phillip R. Callaway, "CD and the History of the Qumran Community," in *The History of the Qumran Community*, 89-133.

264. See Charlesworth, *Damascus Document*, 13, n. 4. Regarding the editing of CD here, see Michael A. Knibb, *The Qumran Community* (Cambridge: Cambridge University Press, 1987), 20.

The Righteous Teacher Was a Priest

for Ya[hweh supports his hand.] Its interpretation concerns the Priest, the [Righteous] Teacher, [whom] God [ch]ose as the pillar. F[or] he established him to build for him a congregation of [. . .]. (4QPs^a frgs. 1-10, col. 3.15-16)

Pesher Psalm^a is the only text that calls the Righteous Teacher "the Priest (הכוהן)." The Righteous Teacher probably had officiated in the Temple cult, and may have served there as high priest.[265] Now he was one of "the Poor Ones" living in exile in the wilderness near the unattractive vapors of the Dead Sea and without the luxuries of the Temple cult. The sumptuous nature of the Temple, and especially the elegance of the high priest, was described in a rather idealized,[266] yet somewhat reliable, way, *mutatis mutandis,* perhaps in about 170 B.C.E., when the Righteous Teacher may have been active in the cult, by an Alexandrian who visited Jerusalem:

It was an occasion of great amazement to us when we saw Eleazar engaged on his ministry, and all the glorious vestments, including the wearing of the "garment" with precious stones upon it in which he is vested; golden bells surround the hem (at his feet) and make a very special sound. Alongside each of them are "tassels" adorned with "flowers," and of marvelous colors. He was clad in an outstandingly magnificent "girdle," woven in the most beautiful colors. On his breast he wears what is called the "oracle," to which are attached "twelve stones" of different kinds, set in gold, giving the names of the patriarchs in what was the original order, each stone flashing its own natural distinctive color — quite indescribable. Upon his head he has what is called the "tiara," and upon this the inimitable "mitre," the hallowed diadem having in relief on the front in the middle in holy letters on a golden leaf the name of God, ineffable in glory. The wearer is considered worthy of such vestments at the services. Their appearance makes one awe-stuck and dumbfounded: a man would think he had come out of this world into another one. I emphatically assert that every man who comes near the spectacle of what I have described will experience astonishment and

265. The argument that the Righteous Teacher was the reigning high priest during the *intersacerdotium* was advanced by Stegemann and adopted by Murphy-O'Connor. Along with many, I am a little skeptical about this conclusion. The Righteous Teacher was clearly "the priest" for the Qumranites, but nowhere at Qumran is he called the high priest.

266. See J. M. G. Barclay, "The Letter of Aristeas," in *Jews in the Mediterranean Diaspora: From Alexander to Trajan (323 BCE–117 CE)* (Edinburgh: T. & T. Clark, 1996), 138-50.

amazement beyond words, his very being transformed by the hallowed arrangement on every single detail. (*Let. Aris.* 96-99; Shutt, *OTP* 2:19; cf. also Sir. 50:1-21)

Faith in the Righteous Teacher

[. . . **And the righteous man will live by his faithfulness.**] Its interpretation concerns all those who observe the Torah in the House of Judah, whom God will save from the house of judgment on account of their tribulation and their fidelity to the Righteous Teacher. (1QpHab 7.17–8.3)

The "House of Judah" seems to be a metaphor for the Qumran Community; this term appears again elsewhere in the biblical commentaries.[267] What is stated here is faithfulness to the Righteous Teacher. We should resist the temptation to equate this passage with the later "Christian" concept of faith in Jesus of Nazareth. At Qumran faith is not grounded in a person, as in the New Testament.[268] The contexts are the tribulations caused by the Wicked Priest and the unfaithfulness of the Man of the Lie. It is not possible to explain all of the numerous cryptograms; they were intentionally hidden from all except the one who had joined "the Many" at Qumran.[269]

The Persecution of the Righteous Teacher and the Calendar of His Group

making (them) drunk in order that he might look upon their feasts. (VACAT) Its interpretation concerns the Wicked Priest, who pursued the Righteous Teacher — to swallow him up with his poisonous vexation — to his house of exile. And at the end of the feast, (during) the repose of the Day of Atonement, he appeared to them to swallow them up and to make them stumble on the fast day, their restful sabbath. (1QpHab 11.3-8)

---

267. See esp. 4QFlor frg. 4.4.

268. Much has been written on this subject and is either well known or easily accessible in numerous publications. See now esp. Heinz Feltes, *Die Gattung des Habakukkommentars von Qumran (1QpHab)*. FB 58 (Würzburg: Echter, 1986), 47.

269. E.g., "Lebanon" may refer to the temple, but more likely to the Community as the temple. It also may have been given more than one meaning at Qumran.

The wicked one lies in ambush for the righteous one and seeks [to mur-der him. Yah]weh [will not abandon him into his hand,] n[or will he] let him be condemned as guilty when he comes to trial. Its interpreta-tion concerns [the] Wicked [Pri]est, who l[ay in ambush for the Righte[ous Teach]er [and sought to] murder him [. . .]. (4QPs* frgs. 1-10, col. 4.7-8)

The Righteous Teacher was persecuted by הכוהן הרשע. The pesher known as the *Pesher Habakkuk* (1QpHab) helps solve the problem whether the Righteous Teacher ever went to Qumran. This pesher clarifies that he did indeed go to Qumran and was in exile there. The Wicked Priest seems to have gone to Qumran to disturb and undermine the worship of the Righ-teous Teacher and his group. The two priests clearly observed different li-turgical calendars, since the Wicked Priest as the ruling high priest could not leave the Temple cult during his own Yom Hakippurim.[270]

It is possible that the Righteous Teacher was significantly injured when the Wicked Priest allegedly sought to murder him (compare 1QpHab 11 with 4QPs[a]). There is no evidence in the Qumran scrolls that the Wicked Priest killed the Righteous Teacher, even though there is abun-dance evidence in the *Thanksgiving Hymns,* in the sections identified as likely autobiographical compositions by the Righteous Teacher, that he was severely wounded by his adversary, the Wicked Priest. André Dupont-Sommer incorrectly claimed that the Righteous Teacher had been killed.[271] Jean Carmignac astutely showed that this hypothesis was without merit.[272]

Coherence with much that is learned about the Righteous Teacher in the *Pesher Habakkuk* can be obtained from the *Damascus Document.* Four significant points of coherence seem most important. First, the Righteous Teacher was "the unique Teacher" (מורה היחיד; CD 20.1).[273] Second, he

270. This fact was first pointed out by Talmon; see his "Yom Hakippurim in the Habakkuk Scroll," repr. in *The World of Qumran from Within,* 186-99. Since Yom Hakippurim in Early Judaism was either a day of mourning (*Jub.* 34:19) or the day of rejoic-ing (*m. Yoma* 7.4, *m. Ta'an.* 4.8), the clash between the Righteous Teacher and the Wicked Priest might include not only calendrical differences but also the nature of the day. See this argument by Joseph M. Baumgarten, "Yom Kippur in the Qumran Scrolls and Second Tem-ple Sources," *DSD* 6 (1999): 184-91. One cannot be certain that the Mishnaic tradition can be taken back into the 2nd century B.C.E.

271. André Dupont-Sommer, *Aperçus preliminaires sur les Manuscrits de la Mer Morte* (Paris: Maisonneuve, 1950), 121-22.

272. Jean Carmignac, *Christ and the Teacher of Righteousness* (Baltimore: Helicon, 1962).

273. The Hebrew מורה היחיד is a construct chain that means literally "the teacher of the only one (or solitary one)." It can, of course, mean "the unique Teacher" because of syn-

died before the coming of "the Messiah from Aaron and from Israel" (CD 20.1) in the end of days. Thus, at least this part of the *Damascus Document* postdates the death of the Righteous Teacher. Third, the Righteous Teacher probably taught his followers to confess their sins before God (CD 20.28). This passage also makes it clear that he was the quintessential legislator for the Community.[274] Fourth, faithfulness to his teachings, and to them alone, is the means of salvation (CD 20:32).

The Wicked Priest

On account of human bloodshed and violence (done to) the land, the town and all who inhabit it. The interpretation of the passage concerns the Wicked Priest — to pay him his due inasmuch as he dealt wickedly with the Poor Ones. . . . (1QpHab 12.1-3)

It is apparent that mentioning the Righteous Teacher demands a reference also to the Wicked Priest. Who was this person? Within the first decade of Qumran research, options regarding the identity of הכוהן הרשע had polarized between two main candidates, both of whom were Hasmonean priests. Milik thinks the Wicked Priest is Jonathan;[275] Cross contends that he is Simon. The latter scholar pointed to *Psalms of Joshua*, which mentions the demise of two sons. Cross interpreted the text to denote Simon's two sons, Judas and Mattathias, who died in Jericho. He also interpreted 1QpHab 11.12-15 to refer to "Simon's drunken demise."[276]

Geza Vermes was actually the first to suggest that the Wicked Priest was Jonathan, but added that the sobriquet applied also to Simon.[277] Vermes later changed his mind and opted for Jonathan rather than Simon, "because he alone suffered the vengeance of the 'Chief of the Kings of Greece' and died at the hands of the 'violent of the nations,' whereas Simon was murdered by his son-in-law (1 Macc. 16:14-16)."[278]

---

tax and context. Perhaps the construct chain was chosen to draw attention to the grammatical form of "the Righteous Teacher," which is also a construct form; i.e., the Righteous Teacher, the unique Teacher, has died (CD 20.1). Also, היחיד may have been chosen because it is an echo of יחד. Perhaps these insights help us understand why the scribe wrote the construct chain and not the expected המורה היחיד.

274. This point has been made previously by Schiffman, *Reclaiming the Dead Sea Scrolls*, 117.

275. Milik, *Ten Years of Discovery*, 84-87.

276. Cross, *The Ancient Library of Qumran*, 115.

277. Vermes, *Cahiers Sioniens* 7 (1953): 71-74.

278. Vermes, *The Dead Sea Scrolls: Qumran in Perspective*, 11. This position is reiter-

It is clear that the Wicked Priest was some Hasmonean high priest ruling in the Temple. Most likely the first one denoted as the Wicked Priest was Jonathan. The Wicked Priest only subsequently at Qumran could be imagined as Alexander Jannaeus (Delcor and Nizan)[279] or Hyrcanus II (Dupont-Sommer).[280] I. R. Tantlevskij contends that two different high priests are labeled "the Wicked Priest." He claims that 1QpHab 8.3–10.5 and 11.2-8 refer to Jonathan, but that 1QpHab 11.8–12.10 denotes Alexander Jannaeus.[281] It is conceivable, perhaps highly probable, that Jonathan was the first to be branded as the "Wicked Priest" and that later the term was applied to the presently ruling Hasmonean high priest.

The Rise and Fall of the Wicked Priest

Woe to the one who multiplies what is not his own! How long will he weigh himself down with debt? (VACAT) Its interpretation concerns the Wicked Priest, who was called by the true name at the beginning of his standing, but when he ruled in Israel, his heart became large, and he abandoned God, and betrayed the statutes for the sake of wealth. (1QpHab 8.7-11)

One main reason Jonathan is most likely the Wicked Priest, in the judgment of most scholars now, is that he was *once honored* (even if he was not a Zadokite).[282] It is apparent from 1QpHab 8 that the Wicked Priest "was called by the true name at the beginning of his standing," but that this praise pertains only to the beginning of his tenure as high priest. Later he "abandoned God, and betrayed the statutes." The earliest possible candidate for the Wicked Priest is Jonathan; all those who followed him would not have been considered to have "the true name at the beginning of his standing." From the perspective of the Qumranites, Jonathan became corrupt and defiled the Temple.

On account of human bloodshed and violence (done to) the land, the town and all who inhabit it. The interpretation of the passage concerns

---

ated in a book that bears a new title but is essentially the same book: *An Introduction to the Complete Dead Sea Scrolls* (Minneapolis: Fortress, 1999); quotation, 140.

279. Mathias Delcor, "Le Midrash d'Habacuc," *RB* 58 (1951): 521-48; Nizan, *Pesher Habakkuk,* 132-36.

280. André Dupont-Sommer, *Les Écrits Esséniens découverts près de la mer Morte,* 4th ed. (Paris: Payot, 1980), 274 n. 1.

281. I. R. Tantlevskij, "The Two Wicked Priests in the Qumran Commentary on Habakkuk," *Qumran Chronicle* 5 (1995): 1-39; see esp. 2.

282. The last Zadokite high priest was Onias III.

the Wicked Priest — to pay him his due inasmuch as he dealt wickedly with the Poor Ones; for "Lebanon" is the Council of the Community, and the "beasts" are the simple ones of Judah, those who observe the Torah — (he it is) whom God will condemn to complete destruction because he plotted to destroy completely the Poor Ones. And when it says, **On account of the bloodshed of the town and violence (done to) the land,** its interpretation: the "town" is Jerusalem, where the Wicked Priest committed abominable deeds and defiled God's sanctuary. **And violence (done to) the land** (refers to) the cities of Judah, where he stole the wealth of the Poor Ones. (1QpHab 12.1-10)

The Poor Ones refer to the Qumranites. This passage generally is in coherence with 1QpHab 11.3-8 and 4QPs³ frgs. 1-10, col. 4.7-8. The Wicked Priest acted violently against them, and "plotted to destroy completely the Poor Ones." He resides in Jerusalem, here called "the town." He "committed abominable deeds" in Jerusalem and "defiled God's sanctuary" (see 5Q10). Such passages help one better to understand the hatred of the Qumranites for the Wicked Priest and all the Sons of Darkness associated with him in the corrupted cult.

The End of the Wicked Priest

On account of human bloodshed and violence (done to) the land, the town, and all its inhabitants. Its interpretation concerns the [Wi]cked Priest, whom — because of wrong done to the Righteous Teacher and the men of his counsel — God gave into the hand of his enemies to humble him with disease for annihilation in bitterness of soul, beca[u]se he had acted wickedly against his chosen ones. (1QpHab 9.8-12)

This passage fits the demise of the two Hasmonean high priests, Jonathan and Simon — either of them or conceivably both of them consecutively. Many other names could also be mentioned after them, including King Herod who died of a horrible sickness; but, of course, the palaeography of the Qumran scrolls and the archaeology of Qumran make names after Simon unlikely and at times impossible. The Wicked Priest had "acted wickedly against" God's "chosen ones," obviously the Qumranites (and perhaps other Essenes). The coherence here among the Qumran documents is impressive.

The Man of the Lie (= Scoffer, the Spouter of the Lie)

"The Man of the Lie" is most likely identical with "the Spouter of the Lie." This sobriquet probably derives from Micah 2:11:

> If a man were to go about uttering
> Windy, baseless falsehoods (רוח ושקר כזב):
> "I'll preach to you in favor of wine and liquor" —
> He would be a preacher [acceptable] to that people. (NJPS)

Vermes has been convinced that "the Wicked Priest," "the Man of the Lie," and "the Spouter of the Lie" refer to "the same individual."[283] As he states, this conclusion is "not unreasonable"; but is it the best solution? Vermes focuses on 1QpHab 8.8-9, which states that the Wicked Priest began his career with "the name of truth." That is correct, but to contend "the inference being that later he changed into a 'Liar'" is perhaps a *non sequitur*. Moreover, one should ask about the functions of the Wicked Priest, who is clearly outside the Righteous Teacher's group, and the Man of the Lie, who appears to be within it. It is more likely, therefore, as Murphy-O'Connor has shown, that "the Man of the Lie" resisted the Righteous Teacher within the early Essene Movement.[284] Among the most important passages are the following:

> [. . . Look, O traitors, and] s[ee;] [and wonder (and) be amazed, for I am doing a deed in your days that you would not believe if] it were told. (VACAT) [. . .] the traitors together with the Man of the Lie. For (they did) not [. . .] the Righteous Teacher from the mouth of God. And it concerns the trait[ors to] the new [covenant,] f[o]r they were not faithful to the covenant of God [. . .] his holy name. (1QpHab 1.16–2.4)

This passage suggests that the Man of the Lie (איש הכזב) belonged to a group called "the traitors" (הבוגדים). What is the identity of the group designated as "the traitors" and who is the Man of the Lie?

The word "the traitors" was supplied to the Qumran interpreter by the *lemma* from Habakkuk. Who are "the traitors" (הבוגדים)? Hartmut Stegemann focused his early research on this question, clarifying that the group singled out as "the traitors" can denote as many as three different groups, or it can denote one group with three distinct characteristics.[285]

---

283. Vermes, *Introduction,* 139.
284. See Murphy-O'Connor's comments, and publications cited, in *ABD* 6:340-41.
285. Stegemann, *Die Entstehung der Qumrangemeinde,* 57.

The central issue is faithfulness to the Righteous Teacher and the revelation of divine truths given only to him by God. It is possible that the author of the *Pesher Habakkuk* is referring to two groups of traitors. First, it clearly refers to those who earlier opposed the Righteous Teacher and supported "the Man of the Lie."[286] Second, it is possible that it denotes, sometimes, those who continue to resist his group and are contemporaneous with the author of the *Pesher Habakkuk*. The multivalency of some Qumran epithets needs to be appreciated.

The history behind "the traitors" is obscure. Phillip Callaway rightly points out that probably there are not three, but "two temporally distinct groups of traitors," and "disobedience to the Teacher" is in "the past."[287] He may be correct to understand that all verbs in the perfect in this passage refer to past actions. But Biblical and Qumran Hebrew intermittently preserve perfect tenses that are *perfectum propheticum*[288] (*perfectum futurum* or *perfectum confidentiae*). The verb is in the "past" tense but it refers to a present or future time; that is, the verb denotes a not completed action that is for humans in the future. It is also possible that different things are the object of the traitors; thus, Elliger rightly draws attention to the difference between resistance to the Righteous Teacher in early times in the *Pesher Habakkuk*, and rejection of God's "renewed covenant" in subsequent times.[289]

It appears that the Man of the Lie had once been a member of the group that is now controlled by the Righteous Teacher, those who claim to constitute "the renewed covenant." The concept of "traitor" applies better to one that had been inside a group than to one who was always an enemy outside it. Even here we are devoid of certainty, since the Righteous Teacher's group may have thought that Jonathan, the Wicked Priest, had once been good but betrayed his calling.

Why do you heed traitors, but are silent when a wicked one swallows up one more righteous than he? (VACAT) Its interpretation concerns the

---

286. Davies rightly contends that "the traitors" denotes "those who refused to acknowledge the 'Teacher'"; *Sects and Scrolls*, 93. That valid insight does not preclude the possibility that later another meaning was given to this term.

287. Callaway, *The History of the Qumran Community*, 145; Callaway's review of this issue is clear and informative.

288. See *WO* 20.2j and 21.2c. See the examples in GKC, 312-13, and in P. Joüon-T. Muraoka, *A Grammar of Biblical Hebrew* (Rome: Pontifical Biblical Institute, 1991), 363 (§112f-h). Some of the best examples of the prophetic perfect, really a rhetorical technique, are in Isaiah (cf. 9:1; 9:5).

289. Elliger, *Studien zum Habakuk-Kommentar vom Totem Meer*, 171.

> House of Absalom and the men of their counsel, who were quiet at the
> rebuke of the Righteous Teacher and did not support him against the
> Man of the Lie (VACAT) who rejected the Torah in the midst of all their
> counsel. (1QpHab 5.8-12)

It is clear that the Righteous Teacher was rebuked, presumably by the Man of
the Lie. This passage in the *Pesher Habakkuk* adds support for the supposition that the Man of the Lie seemed to belong formerly to the same group as
the Righteous Teacher. The rebuke occurred "in the midst of all their counsel" (assuming that concept does not refer to a general council in Jerusalem).
The reference to the rejection of the Torah should not be left without interpretation. The author of 1QpHab 5 seems to be referring to the Righteous
Teacher's *interpretation* of Torah and that — not Torah — is what was rejected. This passage in 1QpHab 5 is in stunning coherence with 4QMMT,
which is dedicated to explaining Qumran's interpretation of Torah and how
it differs from, and is superior to, that practiced within the Temple cult.

The Man of the Lie seems to perform the same functions as the
Spouter of the Lie. The similar opposition to the Righteous Teacher and
the similarity of the sobriquets suggest that these virtually identical terms
refer to the same distinct person. Note the following passage (italics high-
light the echoes in the pesher that are derived from the intertext of
Habakkuk):

> **Woe to the one who builds a city with blood and founds a town on iniq-
> uity. Are not these from Yahweh of Hosts? Peoples toil for fire and na-
> tions grow weary for nothing.** (VACAT) The interpretation of the pas-
> sage concerns the Spouter of the Lie, who caused many to err, *build*ing *a
> city* of emptiness with *blood*shed and establishing a congregation with
> falsehood, for the sake of its glory making many *toil* in the service of
> emptiness and saturating them with w[o]rks of falsehood, with the re-
> sult that their labor is *for nothing;* so that they will come to the judg-
> ments of *fire,* because they reviled and reproached the elect of God.
> (1QpHab 10.5-13; cf. 10.17–11.2)

These comments are clearly reminiscent of the charge that the Man of the
Lie was a traitor. The Spouter of the Lie mainly is charged with causing
many to err, building a city of emptiness, establishing a congregation with
falsehood, and reviling and reproaching the elect of God. Most likely "the
city" is Jerusalem, in which this Man of the Lie resides, probably refusing
to go into the wilderness with the Righteous Teacher and his remnant. The
latter are certainly "the elect of God." It is important to observe that "Lie"

and "falsehood" *(bis)* are not echo words. That is, they are not in the intertext. The latter evoked in the mind of the author of the pesher what had transpired when the Spouter of the Lie reviled and reproached the Righteous Teacher (who is not explicitly mentioned in the commentary, but he is mentioned in the preceding column).

> [Moa]n before [Yahweh and] writhe before him. And do not be angry with the one who makes his way prosperous, with the man [who doe]s evil plans. Its [interpretation] concerns the Man of the Lie, who led many astray with words of deceit, for they chose empty words and did not lis[ten] to the Interpreter of Knowledge, so that they will perish by the sword, by famine, and by plague. (4QPs³ frgs. 1-10, col. 1.25–col. 2.1; cf. 4QPs³ frgs. 1-10, col. 4.13-15)

The Man of the Lie is the one "who led many astray" and who is now suffering from sword, famine, and plague. He does not seem to oppose the Interpreter of Knowledge. He is the leader of those Jews who later "did not lis[ten] to" him. We have already seen that the Interpreter of Knowledge seems to be the "interpreter of Torah" in the Qumran scrolls. This individual is not the Righteous Teacher who led a group later to Qumran and alone had special knowledge (cf. esp. 1QpHab 7). Thus, the Interpreter of Knowledge seems to be the founder of the movement that became Essene and from which a group left Jerusalem to live in the wilderness.

The Crucifixion of Some Seekers-After-Smooth-Things

The Man of the Lie (the Spouter of the Lie) may once have been associated with what is now the Righteous Teacher's group. But Stegemann has amassed evidence, focusing on the *Damascus Document* (esp. CD 1.18-20) and the *Pesher Nahum*, to indicate that the Man of the Lie also belongs to the Seekers-After-Smooth-Things.[290] It seems likely that this group, דורשי החלקות, which probably derives from Isa. 30:10 (cf. Ps. 12:3; Dan. 11:32), are now to be identified as Pharisees,[291] as many scholars have concluded.[292] The Pharisees are mentioned clearly first in history during the

---

290. Stegemann, *Die Entstehung der Qumrangemeinde*, 72.

291. I can agree with this possible identification, but that does not mean we should assume the *Psalms of Solomon* is a Pharisaic composition. For decades I have endeavored to urge caution in claiming that any pre-70 Jewish composition is Pharisaic.

292. See esp. Callaway, *The History of the Qumran Community*, 170-71; Dimant correctly states that the Seekers-After-Smooth-Things are the Pharisees (Dimant, *ABD* 5:246); Anthony J. Saldarini, *Pharisees, Scribes and Sadducees in Palestinian Society* (1988, repr.

time of John Hyrcanus; if they originated near that time that would be decades after the Righteous Teacher had most likely left Jerusalem and was already at Qumran.[293]

What does the metaphorical expression "Seekers-After-Smooth-Things" symbolize? It seems to embody the Qumranites' disdain, even hatred, of a powerful group of Jews, most likely Pharisees (or at least mostly Pharisees).[294] According to the Qumranites, these Jews are too liberal; with too much smoothness they accommodate themselves to Hellenistic influences and compromise the demands of Torah.[295] As Hengel demonstrates in numerous publications, the Qumran Essenes were "the most fervent enemies of the Greek way of life and thought in Eretz Israel."[296] In this context, it is imperative to observe that there are almost no Greek loanwords in the documents composed at Qumran, but the Mishnah is replete with Greek loanwords — and obviously much of the Mishnah derives from the Pharisaic schools of Shammai and especially Hillel.[297] Thus, the conservative Qumranites, strict constructionists, shunned the Pharisees and those like them who were the liberals in Early Judaism.

Grand Rapids: Wm. B. Eerdmans, 2001), 278-79 (but also note his caution); and Schiffman, "Pharisees and Sadducees in *Pesher Nahum*," in *Minhah le-Nahum: Biblical and Other Studies Presented to Nahum M. Sarna in Honour of His 70th Birthday*, ed. Marc Brettler and Michael Fishbane. JSOTSup 154 (Sheffield: JSOT, 1993), 272-90.

293. De Vaux reported that archaeological evidence, found *in situ*, indicates that the buildings of Period Ib at Qumran "may have been constructed under John Hyrcanus, 135-104 B.C."; *Archaeology and the Dead Sea Scrolls*, 5. Period Ia antedates these dates; it is the first Hellenistic buildings that should be identified as the first work at Qumran by the Righteous Teacher and his followers.

294. The task of discerning the Pharisees within Second Temple Judaism is complex. See John P. Meier, "The Quest for the Historical Pharisee: A Review Essay on Roland Deines, *Die Pharisäer*," *CBQ* 61 (1999): 713-22.

295. See the similar comments by Saldarini in *Pharisees, Scribes and Sadducees in Palestinian Society*, 279. Consult the works of Hengel, who demonstrated the influence of Hellenism within ancient Palestine; see esp. *Judaism and Hellenism: Jews, Greeks and Barbarians*, trans. John Bowden (Philadelphia: Fortress, 1980); "Die Begegnung von Judentum und Hellenismus im Palästina der vorchristlichen Zeit" (151-70) and "Qumran und der Hellenismus" (258-94) in *Judaica et Hellenistica: Kleine Schriften I*. WUNT 90 (Tübingen: Mohr [Siebeck], 1996). I fully concur with Hengel's insight that "Zwar ist die essenische Bewegung eine besonders radikale Frucht der Gegenreaktion auf den hellenistischen Reformversuch, der die Makkabäerkämpfe auslöste" (294).

296. Martin Hengel, "Qumran and Hellenism," in Collins and Kugler, *Religion in the Dead Sea Scrolls*, 46-56; quotation, 55.

297. See the discussions in James H. Charlesworth and Loren L. Johns, eds., *Hillel and Jesus* (Minneapolis: Fortress, 1997).

Alexander Jannaeus

Most scholars rightly conclude that the *Pesher Nahum* refers to King Alexander Jannaeus (103-76) because he, according to Josephus, crucified about 800 Jews at one time. No other Maccabean or Hasmonean ruler has gone down in record as having crucified fellow Jews.

Some of these Jews must have been Pharisees (cf. *War* 1.113),[298] whom Qumran most likely calls "Seekers-After-Smooth-Things" (as we have just seen). According to Josephus, the Hasmonean Jannaeus crucified Jews inside (a shocking error for "near") Jerusalem: τῶν γὰρ ληφθέντων ὀκτακοσίους ἀνασταυρώσας ἐν μέσῃ τῇ πόλει (*War* 1.97; cf. *Ant.* 13.380).[299] This hideous act that occurred in 88 B.C.E. immediately shocked the nation and later disturbed Josephus, who was a Hasmonean. It was so horrible, especially near the time of its occurrence, that the following account, most likely, was written soon after the event:

> [. . . And it fills up] its cave [with prey,] and its den with torn flesh. Its interpretation concerns the Lion of Wrath, [. . .]*mwt* in the Seekers-After-Smooth-Things; he would hang men up alive [. . .] in Israel before, for regarding one hanged alive upon the tree [it] reads: **Behold I am against [you]** say[s **Yahweh of Hosts. And I shall burn up yo]ur [abundance in smoke,] and the sword will devour your lions. And [I] shall cut off its [p]rey [from the land,] and [the voice of your messengers] will no [longer be heard.]** Its [inter]pretation: **your abundance** — they are the detachments of his army th[at (are) in Jerusale]m; and **his lions** — they are his great ones [. . .] and **his prey** — that is the wealth that the [prie]sts of Jerusalem have amas[sed,]. . . . (4QpNah frgs. 3-4, col. 1.6-11)

Clearly, the man who hung "men up alive" and hung men "alive upon the tree" is the Lion of Wrath who crucified men. This occurred in or near "Jerusalem." He is connected with the priests of Jerusalem. There should be no doubt that the Lion of Wrath is a sobriquet for Alexander Jannaeus.

There is considerable coherence to the supposition that this pesher refers to Alexander Jannaeus and the events of 88 B.C.E. He was the second Hasmonean who claimed the title "king." Coherence with the *Pesher*

---

298. See the similar judgment by Lester L. Grabbe in *Judaism from Cyrus to Hadrian* (Minneapolis: Fortress, 1992), 2:471; and see the insights by Saldarini in *Pharisees, Scribes and Sadducees in Palestinian Society,* 89-95, 278 (n. 2).

299. I doubt this report, and prefer to follow *Antiquities;* the crucifixions most likely occurred outside the walls of Jerusalem, not "in the midst of the city." As Strugnell points out to me *viva voce,* 4QMMT is concerned about what may be allowed inside Jerusalem.

Nahum is found in the *Temple Scroll.* This scroll contains a section focused on limiting the functions of a king, including his deployment of an army[300] (חוקת המלך in 11QT 56.12ff.). Sometimes the high priest is elevated over the king and controls his actions. Real, rather than ideal or imagined, offenses by a king seem to be in the mind of the redactor of this scroll. The final redaction of this work refers to a real king who seems to be none other than King Jannaeus (see Josephus *Ant.* 13.398: ὁ Βασιλεὺς Ἀλέξανδρος).[301] The only viable candidate seems to be Jannaeus; and this also makes eminent sense since the Hasmoneans were the despised enemies of the Qumranites.[302] Both the *Pesher Nahum* and the *Temple Scroll* mention one Jew crucifying (hanging on a tree) another Jew (יתלו אותו

---

300. On the Hasmonean army, see Israel Shatzman, *The Armies of the Hasmonaeans and Herod: From Hellenistic to Roman Frameworks.* TSAJ 25 (Tübingen: Mohr [Siebeck], 1991).

301. Some of Jannaeus's coins are overstruck with the Hebrew "Jonathan the High Priest" or "veḥever hayehudim" almost obliterating the previous Hebrew or Greek inscriptions that hail him as "king." An explanation for this overstriking, as Schwartz contends, is to assume that under Jewish pressure, probably from Pharisees, Jannaeus relinquished the title "king"; *Studies in the Jewish Background of Christianity,* 46, esp. n. 14. Uriel Rappaport points out that a coin dating to 78 B.C.E. (i.e., near to the end of the reign of Jannaeus) and bearing in Aramaic *Alexandros Malka,* suggests that the overstriking occurred posthumously. That makes sense, since his wife Alexandra favored Jannaeus's enemies, namely the Pharisees who opposed his kingship. See Rappaport, "Numismatics," in Davies and Finkelstein, *The Cambridge History of Judaism* 1:25-59, esp. 1:38-39.

302. See Martin Hengel, James H. Charlesworth, and Doron Mendels, "The Polemical Character of 'On Kingship' in the Temple Scroll: An Attempt at Dating 11QTemple," *JJS* 37 (1986): 28-38. Strugnell disagrees with our dating of the redaction of the *Temple Scroll.* He informs me *viva voce* that the author of the *Temple Scroll* probably had a text of Deuteronomy before him that had many of the characteristics now seen in the *Temple Scroll,* including the use of the first person pronoun for God. Strugnell is convinced that this lost text of Deuteronomy may date from the 3rd century B.C.E. He is also convinced that the section "On Kingship" is related to the 3rd-century Greek writings. He is persuaded that the earliest copy of the *Temple Scroll* dates from ca. 150 to 125 B.C.E. I certainly agree with Strugnell that the *Temple Scroll* is a composite document, preserving many divergent traditions. See his students' publication on the composite nature of the *Temple Scroll:* A. M. Wilson and L. Wills, "Literary Sources of the Temple Scroll," *HTR* 75 (1982): 275-88. It is not easy to differ with Strugnell; however, perhaps the palaeographical dating is too close to be definitive in settling this debate between us. We may also be focusing on a section of the *Temple Scroll* that is not from the final redaction (see the various versions of the *Rule of the Community*). Furthermore, the section "On Kingship" is probably not shaped by earlier τύποι but seems to represent restrictions placed on the actions of a real king (i.e., a Hasmonean "king"). In the *Temple Scroll* we are confronted with priests dictating the actions of a king; this makes sense in terms of the crises Jews were facing after ca. 103 B.C.E. With Strugnell, however, I am convinced that the final redaction of the *Temple Scroll* may have taken place somewhere besides Qumran.

העץ; 11QT 64.9). Both texts cohere; they point to none other than Jannaeus. The Qumran condemnation of Jannaeus makes sense in light of the restrictions placed on the ruling high priest who is a king in the *Temple Scroll* — and Alexander Jannaeus claimed to be both high priest and king,[303] as we know from his coins.[304]

The references to "the Lion of Wrath (כפיר החרון)" and "his lion-esses" in *Pesher Nahum* also point to Jannaeus. We learn that "the Lion of Wrath" and "the Lion" are nicknames of Alexander Jannaeus in the pesharim.[305] Thus, conceivably referring to him also is the following passage from the *Pesher Hosea*[b]:

> For I am like a young l[ion to Eph[rai]m [and like a lion] [to the house of Judah. Its interpretation con]cerns the last priest, who will stretch out his hand to smite Ephraim. . . . (4QpHos[b] frg. 2.2-3)

It is possible that Ephraim refers to the Pharisees (as we shall see) and the "lion," in the text of Isaiah, denotes Jannaeus. While the document is too fragmentary and the allusions too oblique and metaphorical for us to be certain about any clear scenario,[306] the link between "the last priest" who will "smite Ephraim" in the interpretation and the "lion" in the *lemma* seems cumulatively to point to the actions by Jannaeus in 88 B.C.E.

Another reference to Alexander Jannaeus is possibly found in *Pesher Isaiah*[a]:

> He has passed [through Migron.] At Michma[sh] [stores his baggage. They have crossed] over the pass. Geba is a lodging place for them.

303. See Hengel, Charlesworth, and Mendels, *JJS* 37 (1986): 28-38.

304. See Ya'akov Meshorer, *Ancient Jewish Coinage* (Dix Hills, N.Y.: Amphora, 1982), 1:57 and 118-34 for the inscriptions; for Jannaeus's coins, see pl. 4-24. See also Meshorer's corrections and new perceptions published in "Ancient Jewish Coinage: Addendum I," *Israel Numismatic Journal* 11 (1990-91): 104-32, pl. 17-32.

305. This is the view of many; see the excellent article, "Alexander Jannaeus," by Hanan Eshel in Schiffman and VanderKam, *Encyclopedia of the Dead Sea Scrolls*, 1:16-18. Gregory L. Doudna rejects Jannaeus as the "Lion of Wrath." He opts for a Nebuchadnezzar-like foreign invader who will deliver God's wrath on Israel; *4Q Pesher Nahum: A Critical Edition*. JSPSup 35 (Sheffield: Sheffield Academic, 2001). I had access only to unpaginated proofs.

306. Eshel presents a quotation of this text that is restored, without indication, and concludes that its author is "speaking of the execution of the rebels by the 'Lion of Wrath,' designating Alexander Jannaeus"; "Alexander Jannaeus," 1:17. See also Eshel, "The History of the Qumran Community and Historical Details in the Dead Sea Scrolls," *Qadmoniot* 30 (1997): 86-93 [Hebrew].

[Ramah becomes] ill. [Gibeah of] [Saul has fled. Cry] aloud, O daughter Gallim! Hearke[n, O Laishah! Answer her, O Anathoth!] Madmenah
[is in flight.] The [in]habitants of Gebim seek refuge. This very [day he
will halt at Nob. He will shake] his fist (at the) mount of daughter Zion,
the hill of Jerusalem. [The interpretation of the] matter with regard to
the latter days concerns the coming of o[. . .] [. . .]*rh* when he goes up
from the Valley of Acco to fight against Phil[istia . . .] [. . .]*dh*, and there
is none like it, and among all the cities of *h*°[. . .] and even up to the
boundary of Jerusalem [. . .] (4QpIsa° frgs. 2-6, col. 2.21-29)

Basing his interpretation on Isaiah 10:28-32, the author of the *Pesher Isaiah°*
seems to refer to an enemy army who will come like the Assyrian or Syro-
Ephraimite army (Isa. 10:24),[307] during his lifetime, "the latter days," from
the north and east, to the walls of Jerusalem. Like the Assyrian army (Isa.
10:24), the author apparently celebrates, *post eventum*, that the enemy will
not succeed in taking the city, because of God's intervention (Isa. 10:33-34).
This passage in *Pesher Isaiah°* shows some coherence with *4QFlorilegium*,
which interprets Ps° 1:1 in light of what "is written in the book of Isaiah the
prophet concerning the latter days . . ." (4QFlor frgs. 1-2, col. 1.15).

As most Qumran scholars have concluded, this passage is more than
a simple figure of speech; it embodies more than an amorphous apocalyptic image. It seems to allude to a real historical event. There is obviously
more than one option to suggest for this ostensibly historical event.[308]
Palaeographical dating of the fragments and coherence with the other
pesharim indicate that this event most likely refers to the invasion of Palestine in 103 B.C.E. by Ptolemy IX (Soter II) Lathyrus of Cyprus.[309] He was
invited, then rebuffed by the citizens of Ptolemais. "The Valley of Acco" in
the interpretation most likely refers to Ptolemais.[310] Acco is a synonym for

307. The route from the north to Jerusalem is logical, but there is no proof an Assyrian army took such a route. That point would, of course, be irrelevant for evaluating the
later work of the author of the *Pesher Isaiah*. For an informative and succinct study of the
Assyrian army, see Ephraim Stern, "The Assyrian Army," in *Archaeology of the Land of the Bible 2: The Assyrian, Babylonian, and Persian Periods, 732-332 B.C.E.* ABRL (New York:
Doubleday, 2001), 2:4-10.

308. A. S. van der Woude thought the event referred to the coming of the Romans
(but they do not come from the northeast); *Bijbelcommentaren en Bijbelse Verhalen* (Am-
sterdam: Proost en Brandt, 1958), 75-76 (I am indebted to Horgan for this reference).

309. See Joseph D. Amoussine, "A propos de l'interprétation de 4Q161 (fragments 5-
6 et 8)," *RevQ* 8 (1974): 381-92. See also his book on Qumran, in Russian, that was published
in Moscow in 1983, esp. 77 and 121.

310. See the recent surveys of Acco, and the discovery of a 4th-century B.C.E. red-
figured kylix, by A. Muqari, "'Akko," *Excavations and Surveys in Israel* 15 (1996): 27-28.

Ptolemais, which was just north of Jannaeus's kingdom.[311] Our text thus most likely refers to Ptolemy Lathyrus's invasion of 103.[312]

Ptolemy Lathyrus and his army approached Palestine from the northwest and eventually Judea and Jerusalem from the northeast, moving from "Asochis" in Galilee, having battles with Jannaeus at Sepphoris, "Asophon" near the Jordan, and some villages of Judea (*War* 1.86; *Ant.* 13.324-55). Thus, in line with Isaiah's prophecy, Ptolemy approached Jerusalem from the northeast; but he was driven back by something quite extraordinary. His opponent turns out to be his mother. Cleopatra III sent her troops northward from Egypt to stop him.[313] This event seems to have been interpreted as the fulfillment of Isaiah's prophecy[314] and clear evidence of divine intervention by the author of the *Pesher Isaiah*ᵃ.[315] If this document does refer to Ptolemy Lathyrus, then the Kittim, mentioned in the interpretation in frgs. 8-10, col. 3.7-12, must refer to those from Kittim, properly the city on the southern shores of Cyprus. The authors of later pesharim transferred this term to the Romans, since it almost always denotes them (see the following section).

The Jews, especially those living in Jerusalem, and probably some Qumranites would have been pleased with Jannaeus — at this early period in his kingship. God had heard his pleas and those of other Jews and saved Jerusalem from the invading army of Ptolemy Lathyrus. The coherence among the Qumran sectarian writings and also with those outside of the Qumran corpus helps us evaluate the historical crises of 103 B.C.E.

The *Prayer for King Jonathan* (4Q448), which quotes from Psalm 154 and contains words and concepts familiar from 1QS 10 and 11, is frustratingly mutilated and ambiguous; but it is of potential historical importance. A man, "King Jonathan," is celebrated. He seems to be in Zion or Jerusalem (col. A). He receives the following stunning blessing: יהו שלום כלם ועל ממלכתך "May there be peace (on) all of them, (indeed peace)[316] on your kingdom" (col. B). Who is "King Jonathan" (col. B and col. C)?

---

311. This is the judgment of Horgan in *Pesharim*, 81.

312. Hanan Eshel and Esther Eshel now conclude that 4QpIsa refers to the events of 103-102 B.C.E.; "4Q448, Psalm 154 (Syriac), Sirach 48:20, and 4QpIsa," *JBL* 119 (2000): 645-59; see esp. 652-53.

313. She had driven her son out of Egypt and desired to banish him from Cyprus also; see Josephus *Ant.* 13.328-32.

314. See Isa. 10:5, in which it is clear that Assyria functions as God's fury, but the Lord of Hosts will also send sickness to destroy the Assyrian army (Isa. 10:16-19).

315. Hanan Eshel judges that this *Pesher* appears to refer to the invasion of Palestine by Ptolemy Lathyrus in the time of Alexander Jannaeus; "Alexander Jannaeus," 1:17.

316. The *waw* is not clear.

Vermes thinks he is Jonathan Maccabeus.[317] This Hasmonean, however, was never a "king" and the reading יונתן המלך in col. B line 2 is, as Émile Puech states, clear and not in question.[318] Puech also thinks the text refers to Jonathan; but neither expert sufficiently explains why Jonathan Maccabeus can be identified as a "king."[319]

The words יונתן המלך could refer to the king known as Alexander Jannaeus (Yannai) (*War* 1.85; *Ant.* 13.320), whose first name was also Jonathan or Yehonathan (or Yehonatan). Jannaeus (Yannai) is the hypocoristicon of Yonathan. His Hebrew name was יהנתן, as is clear from a study of the coins (esp. the small bronze coin called פרוטה) that Jonathan Jannaeus minted.[320] Some of his coins have on the obverse in Greek "King Alexander" (ΑΛΕΞΑΝΔΡΟΥ ΒΑΣΙΛΕΩΣ) and on the reverse in Paleo-Hebrew "the King Jonathan" (המלך יהונתן).[321] This document refers favor-

<hr />

317. Vermes, "The So-called King Jonathan Fragment (4Q448)," *JJS* 44 (1993): 294-300.

318. "A la l.2, la lecteur *'l ywntn hmlk* est indiscutable"; Émile Puech, "Jonathan le Prêtre Impie et les débuts de la Communauté de Qumrân: *4QJonathan (4Q523)* et *4QPsAp (4Q448)*," *RevQ* 17 (1996): 241-70; quotation, 253. See also Puech, "Le grand prêtre Simon (III)."

319. Vermes does not provide an explanation. Puech offers the opinion that, "Si Jonathan n'a pas officiellement porté le titre le roi, ce fut probablement dû à la situation de son temps et à la domination séleucide, voir *1 Macc* 12,53"; *RevQ* 17 (1996): 261-62. While this possibility cannot be denied, I would prefer to work with what is presented in our historical records. Josephus reported that Jonathan was a "high priest," not a "king." Jonathan Alexander Jannaeus certainly claimed both titles, as his coins clarify. Finally, I do not think that the *Prayer of King Jonathan* refers to "the Wicked Priest," and I am convinced that Jonathan may well have been the first Hasmonean who was labeled as "the Wicked Priest" (on that point I concur with Puech and many).

320. See esp. J. Chaim Kaufman, *Unrecorded Hasmonean Coins from the J. Chaim Kaufman Collection* (Jerusalem: Israel Numismatic Society, 1995), 27-42, 61-80, pl. 26-67.

321. For obvious reasons I represent the Paleo-Hebrew Script by square characters. Some coins have, in Paleo-Hebrew, only יהונתן הכהן הגדל, "Jonathan, the High Priest." As Ya'akov Meshorer points out, the use of "obverse" and "reverse" is defined inconsistently by numismatists, and is arbitrary for early Jewish coins; *Ancient Jewish Coinage* 1:118-34 for the inscriptions; for Jannaeus's coins, see pl. 4-24. Meshorer informed me that excavations in Samaria have changed his opinion that no coins were minted by John Hyrcanus; but that point does not change what I have reported here. One must be cautious in using Meshorer's earlier books; some coins attributed to Jannaeus probably belong to Hyrcanus I. Meshorer published some of his new insights and corrected some of his earlier conclusions in *Israel Numismatic Journal* 11 (1990-91), esp. 106 ("I am now convinced that all the coins of יהונתן [YHWHNN] were struck by John Hyrcanus I") and 131-32 (corrections). For a discussion of the Yehonatan coins in this publication, see 117-18 and pl. 21 and 23. Sometimes Jannaeus's name is the expected יהונתן, sometimes יונתן, sometimes ינתן, and sometimes יהונת; there are unexplainable anomalies also (some are caused by the ignorance of the en-

ably to Jannaeus; hence it — like so many documents found in Cave 4 — is not a Qumran composition and probably was not even copied there.[322]

The work entitled the *Prayer for King Jonathan* was most likely composed in Jerusalem, during the first of the three phases of Jannaeus's reign (according to Josephus).[323] In this first phase he fought against Ptolemy Lathyrus, the king of Cyprus, in 103 and before the second phase, when he turned his rage against his fellow Jews, notably Jews who included the Pharisees in 88, 15 years later.

What is the text doing in the Qumran caves? We have no way of being certain. Perhaps the author or one fond of the work — probably the psalmic passages within it (viz. Ps. 154) — brought it with him to Qumran sometime ca. 88 B.C.E. This would most likely have occurred during, or better just after, the time when Jonathan Alexander Jannaeus brutally killed and even crucified fellow Jews not far away outside the walls of Jerusalem. Josephus reports that during this time 8000 Jews fled Jerusalem (*War* 1.98). There should be no doubt that some Jews could have gone towards Qumran and remained in that area. There are ample reasons to conclude that some of these Jews most likely joined the Community, brought new compositions and older works with them, and contributed to the expansion of the compound.[324]

It has become clear that we have three possible references to Jonathan Alexander Jannaeus in the pesharim. First is the relatively clear reference to him as "the Lion of Wrath" who "will hang men up alive . . . in Israel"; these words are found in the *Nahum Pesher* (4QpNah frgs. 3-4, col. 1.6-11). This link is strengthened by coherence with the events of 88 B.C.E. that are recorded in other documents. The passage probably alludes to

---

gravers). In McCarter's brief discussion, the obverse and reverse of the Jannaeus coin are reversed; *Ancient Inscriptions*, 150-51.

322. This is the argument of Esther Eshel, Hanan Eshel, and Adam Yardeni, "A Scroll from Qumran Which Includes Part of Psalm 154 and a Prayer for King Jonathan and His Kingdom," *Tarbiz* 60 (1991): 295-324 [Hebrew], I [Eng. summary]; *IEJ* 42 (1992): 199-229. See also their work in DJD 11.403-25, pl. XXXII. See the following discussion which draws attention to Esther and Hanan Eshel's change of position.

323. Hanan and Esther Eshel now lean toward the hypothesis that 4Q448 may have been composed in Jerusalem and "among the followers of Alexander Jannaeus. . . . the scroll was written by a non-Qumranite scribe and imported to Qumran"; *JBL* 119 (2000): 656. They also endorse the probability that this prayer was composed shortly after Ptolemy Lathyrus's campaign and before the Pharisaic revolt in 88.

324. See Charlesworth, *RevQ* 10 (1980): 224. Most likely some of those who expanded Qumran were Pharisees. See J. T. Milik, *Tefillin*, in Roland de Vaux and Milik, *Qumrân grotte 4.II*. DJD 6 (Oxford: Clarendon, 1977), 17; and Lawrence H. Schiffman, *The Halakah at Qumran*. SJLA 16 (Leiden: Brill, 1975), esp. 134-36.

Jannaeus because of the coherence with the *Temple Scroll,* which antedates Qumran but was redacted near the beginning of the 2nd century B.C.E.

Second, the reference to the "lion" in *Pesher Hosea*[b] may possibly refer to Alexander Jannaeus (4QpHos[b] frg. 2.2-3) and the events of 88 B.C.E. The possibility for this identification is raised by the coherence with the *Nahum Pesher.*

Third, *Pesher Isaiah*[a] seems to refer to the invasion of Ptolemy Lathyrus from Cyprus in 103 B.C.E. According to this author, the prophecy of Isaiah was once again fulfilled as God protected his people and his Holy City. The *Prayer of Jonathan* also seems to reflect this wonderful beginning to Jannaeus's reign, but it represents non-Qumran perspectives (even concepts anathema to Qumran [perhaps it was admired at Qumran because of the concepts shared with 1QS and Ps. 154]).

Judah, Ephraim, and Manasseh

One pesher refers to three groups in Second Temple Judaism:

> Its interpretation concerns the Seekers-After-Smooth-Things, whose wicked deeds will be revealed to all Israel at the end of time, and many will discern their sin, will hate them, and consider them repulsive on account of their guilty insolence. But when the glory of Judah is [re]vealed, the simple ones of Ephraim will flee from the midst of their assembly. And they will abandon those who led them astray and will join [I]srael. (4QpNah frgs. 3-4, col. 3.3-5)

What is *prima facie* evident? "The Seekers-After-Smooth-Things" are wicked, sinful, and guilty. They seem identical with "Ephraim" who "led" some astray. Thus, in light of previous reflections, the Seekers-After-Smooth-Things and Ephraim seem to be sobriquets for the Pharisees.[325] "Israel" does not denote all the Jews, but most likely the Qumranites, because "the simple ones of Ephraim," that is some Pharisees, will "flee" the assembly and "join" Israel. "Judah" also seems to refer to Qumran, since the *Pesher Nahum* was composed at Qumran. It would be surprisingly unprecedented for a Qumranite to talk about "the glory of Judah" being any other group than the Qumranites; they alone are those whose glory will be revealed at the end of time.

---

325. This is the conclusion of many experts; see the clear and authoritative statements by Dimant, *ABD* 5:247; and Hanan Eshel, "Demetrius III Eukerus," in Schiffman and VanderKam, *Encyclopedia of the Dead Sea Scrolls,* 1:189.

The third group is "Manasseh." Who is this group? Here is a crucial text for seeking answers to this perplexing question:

> **Will you do better than Am[on, situated by] the rivers?** Its interpretation: "Amon" — they are Manasseh, and "the rivers" — they are the gr[ea]t ones of Manasseh, the honored ones of the. . . . [. . . P]ut and the **[Libyans are your help.]** Its interpretation: they are the wicked one[s of Manass]eh, the House of Peleg, who are joined to Manasseh. . . . [her] g[rea]t **[ones were bound]** in fetters. Its interpretation concerns Manasseh at the last time, whose reign over Is[rael] will be brought down. . . . **[You too will be drunk]** and you will be hidden. (VACAT) Its interpretation concerns the wicked ones of E[phraim . . .] whose cup will come after Manasseh. . . . (4QpNah frgs. 3-4, col. 3.8-9, 12-col. 4.6)

Despite the numerous references to Manasseh, the truncated nature of the fragments and the ambiguity of the remaining words bring more obfuscation than clarification. What is certainly clear is that the meaning of Manasseh is not clear to the interpreter today.[326]

Pondering on the *Pesher Nahum*, it seems obvious that "Manasseh" denotes those despised by the Qumranites. But who is meant by this sobriquet? They are the great ones and those who have already received "honor." They are wicked ones and associated with "the House of Peleg (בית פלג)." They now "reign over" Israel, but they "will be brought down." All of these references are best suited to denote the precursors of the group known later as the Sadducees.[327]

"The House of Peleg" appears only twice in the Qumran scrolls, in CD 20.22 and in the text just cited, the *Pesher Nahum*. It denotes, literally, "the house of separation." What does it connote figuratively? Does it represent the same thing in both texts? The key seems to be the major concept of "separation." Scholars are sharply divided as they attempt to identify "the House of Peleg." Six different suggestions are found in the secondary literature. (1) Richard T. White thinks the House of Peleg denotes Onias IV and his supporters who separated from the Jerusalem cult and built a temple at Leontopolis in Egypt.[328] (2) Carmignac thought that

---

326. See the similar judgment of Dimant, *ABD* 5:247.

327. Schiffman has been famous for the claim that in 4QMMT can be found a type of "halakhic" exegesis that is associated in the Mishnah with Sadducees. See now his more nuanced claim that this text, *More Works of the Torah,* arises "from the hermeneutical assumptions of the Sadducees or as a result of their priestly and Temple-centered piety"; "The Dead Sea Scrolls and the History of Judaism," *NEA* 63 (2000): 154-59; quotation, 156.

328. Richard T. White, "The House of Peleg in the Dead Sea Scrolls," in Davies and

it denoted a group within the Qumran Community who defected to the opponents.[329] (3) Dupont-Sommer identified the House of Peleg with division between Hyrcanus II and Aristobulus II.[330] (4) Richard Ratzlaff speculates that the House of Peleg denoted a "group who left Jerusalem at a time when Israel sinned by defiling the Temple, but who later returned to the ways of the people (Judaism at large)."[331] (5) Stegemann and Murphy-O'Connor contend the House of Peleg should be identified with Ephraim.[332] (6) Maurya Horgan thinks it refers to an unknown group somehow "joined to Manasseh, presumably then a group of Sadducee-sympathizers."[333] While some of these solutions are distinctly different, a few are not mutually exclusive.

Obviously, some of these scholars have CD in focus; in this text "the House of Peleg" denotes those "who went out of the holy city. And they depended upon God during the time of Israel's trespass. But (although) they considered the sanctuary impure, they returned to the way of the people in some few ways" (CD 20.22).[334] Horgan's understanding seems to make the best sense of the allusive reference in *Pesher Nahum*, especially when one thinks about coherence with other Qumran references in the pesharim. It is also clear that the author may have denoted one adversarial group but later Qumran readers would have thought about others.

It is tempting to conclude that the three groups mentioned in *Pesher Nahum* are to be identified with the Essenes, the Pharisees, and the Sadducees. This conclusion, however, is far from certain. The references are confusingly ambiguous. We know too little about the various groups within

---

White, *A Tribute to Geza Vermes,* 67-98. Paul A. Rainbow speculates that the Onias who established Leontopolis may not be Onias III and that the latter is linked to the Righteous Teacher; "The Last Oniad and the Teacher of Righteousness," *JJS* 48 (1997): 30-52. I think that Rainbow rightly points to the parallels between the establishment of Leontopolis and Qumran, but while both originate from struggles within the temple cult there is little else that connects them.

329. Jean Carmignac, "Notes sur les Peshârîm," *RevQ* 3 (1961-62): 505-38; *Les Textes de Qumrân traduits et annotés* (Paris: Letouzey et Ané, 1963), 2:85-92.

330. André Dupont-Sommer, "Le Commentaire de Nahum découvert près de la Mer Morte (4Q p Nah): Traduction et notes," *Sem* 13 (1963): 55-88.

331. Richard Ratzlaff, "Peleg, House of," in Schiffman and VanderKam, *Encyclopedia of the Dead Sea Scrolls,* 2:641-42.

332. Hartmut Stegemann, "Weitere Stücke von 4 Q p Psalm 37, von 4Q Patriarchal Blessings und Hinweis auf eine unedierte Handschrift aus Höhle 4Q mit Exzerpten aus dem Deuteronomium," *RevQ* 6 (1967-69): 193-227, esp. 195-96; Murphy-O'Connor, *RB* 81 (1974): 239-44.

333. Horgan, *Pesharim,* 190.

334. Baumgarten and Schwartz in Charlesworth, *Damascus Document.*

Judaism in the 2nd century B.C.E., and Josephus's accounts and those in the Mishnah should not be read as anything more than later syntheses of vast differences that existed within Judaism before 70 C.E. It is unwise to make sweeping generalizations upon poorly founded speculations.

We should not be misled by Josephus's summary of history. He wrote in the second half of the 1st century C.E. He sought to make Judaism a logical system, and one that would be understandable to and appreciated by his Roman audience. Josephus by no means represented the vast variety of Jews in Second Temple Judaism. He reported that the Jews have "three sects of philosophy" (*Ant.* 18.11). This is far from representative of what we now know from studying the Old Testament Pseudepigrapha and the scrolls found to the west of the Dead Sea. Josephus simply ignored so many significant Jewish groups, even though we learn from him, and elsewhere, of baptist groups, hermits and ascetics, and the Samaritans.[335] What can be gleaned from Josephus must be supplemented by what can be learned from other literary and nonliterary sources. These clarify the existence of groups: especially the Enoch groups and remnants of earlier groups (namely the Nazirites[336] and the Rechabites[337]).

Historical Allusions Outside Palestinian Judaism: The Greeks and Romans

It is now clear that many sobriquets and ambiguous groups mirrored in the pesharim can be linked, with some probability, to persons and groups known from non-Qumran sources. Sometimes these groups represent previously unknown Jewish groups; sometimes they seem to mirror reflections from other previously known groups of Jews, especially the Pharisees. Can the same be said about non-Jewish groups or people?

The Kittim

There once was a major rift among scholars as attempts were published to identify "the Kittim, w[ho ar]e swift and strong in battle" (1QpHab 2.12). Now, most scholars concur that הכתיאים almost always refers to the

---

335. Gösta W. Ahlström thinks that the Samaritan temple was built "after Alexander's conquest of Palestine," and that it "should not be labeled a sectarian temple"; *The History of Ancient Palestine* (Minneapolis: Fortress, 1994), 902-3.

336. See Judg. 13:4-7; 4Q51 *(Samuel)*, which salutes Samuel as a permanent Nazirite; and Acts 21:18-26, which seems to report that Paul and others took a Nazirite vow.

337. See James H. Charlesworth, "History of the Rechabites," *OTP* 2:443-61.

The caves dug in the marl terrace north of Khirbet Qumran.
Some of the Qumranites lived here where the evaporation
of water in the soil would "air condition" the room.

Photo by James H. Charlesworth; courtesy of Magen Broshi and Hanan Eshel

Romans.[338] It is clear that the Kittim in the pesharim are enemies of the
Qumranites and that they are usually Romans, who are distinct from
Greeks.[339]

We should be aware of the prevalent and misleading tendency to
speak about the Romans as if they appeared for the first time in history in
63 B.C.E. That is the date when Pompey entered Jerusalem, exasperated the
establishment, and curtailed the power and territory controlled by
Hyrcanus II[340] (*Pss. Sol.* 1; cf. also 1QpHab 6.10-11).[341] Long before that

338. See the judicious report by Moshe J. Bernstein, "Pesher Habakkuk," in Schiffman
and VanderKam, *Encyclopedia of the Dead Sea Scrolls,* 2:649.

339. 1QpHab may antedate the invasion of Palestine by the Parthians in 40 B.C.E.;
otherwise one might expect the author to mention that God did not allow them to take Jerusalem [see *1 En.* 56].

340. Pompey reinstated Hyrcanus II as high priest, but he was most likely only an
ethnarch (certainly not a king). What powers this title bore is unclear, but the territory once
controlled by Jannaeus was drastically reduced. Surely, much of this diminution of power
and province was not only due to Roman incursion; it was a result of the civil war between
Hyrcanus II and Aristobulus II. See Shatzman, *The Armies of the Hasmonaeans and Herod,*
129-38.

341. 1QpHab was most likely composed sometime after the Roman plundering of

date, and prior to the Maccabean period, Polybius wrote about the rise of the incomprehensible might of Rome and the dawning of its awesome dominance. A few decades later, during the Maccabean period (167-152), the Romans were "the friends and allies of the Jews" (τοὺς φίλους ἡμῶν τοὺς συμμάχους Ἰουδαίους; 1 Macc. 8:31). Their might protected the otherwise exposed Maccabees in Palestine. Scholars now tend to agree that Judah Maccabeus sent ambassadors to Rome ca. 161 B.C.E.,[342] and that, *mutatis mutandis*, 1 Maccabees 8:23-30 does preserve somewhat reliably a Roman document.[343] The following words were sadly short-lived:

> May all go well with the Romans and with the nation of the Jews at sea and on land forever; and may sword and enemy be far from them. (1 Macc. 8:23)

Some of the friendly relations with Rome continued during the Hasmonean period, since Simon and John Hyrcanus (*Ant.* 13.259) sought and received Roman support.

If the Romans were the friends of the Maccabees and early Hasmoneans, then it is easy to comprehend how they became Qumran's enemies. While it is likely that some early references to the Kittim refer to Greek enemies, especially Ptolemy Lathyrus, coming from Cyprus — also known as Kition — most references to the Kittim are to the Romans.

For me there are further keys to unlocking the identity of the Kittim; they are found in the *Pesher Habakkuk*. One is found that points to further 1st-century B.C.E. crises, most significantly a reference to the plundering of the Temple by the Kittim:

> **For you have plundered many nations, but all the rest of the peoples will plunder you.** (VACAT) Its interpretation concerns the latter priests of Jerusalem, who amass wealth and profit from the plunder of the peoples; but at the latter days their wealth together with their plunder will be given into the hand of the army of the Kittim. (1QpHab 9.3-7)

This is more than an oblique and obscure notation. It has specifics: plundering of the Jerusalem Temple, which is rich because priests have plundered the Jewish people, and a foreign army has plundered the Temple.[344]

---

the temple in 54 B.C.E. (compare 1QpHab 9.2-7 with *Ant.* 14.105-109). So also Stegemann, *Die Essener*, 184.

342. See esp. Sievers, *The Hasmoneans and Their Supporters*, 68-70.

343. This was first argued by Eugen Täubler, *Imperium Romanum: Studien zur Entwicklungsgeschichte des römischen Reichs* (Leipzig: Teubner, 1913), 1:239-54.

344. Sometimes debates among scholars obscure the simple historical meaning of the

All these actions, as we have already discerned, are most likely to be dated sometime after ca. 100 B.C.E. The best option is the actions by Crassus in 55 B.C.E. In *Antiquities* Josephus describes how Crassus enters Judea, plunders the Temple of the money (χρήματα) left there by Pompey, and even breaks an oath he had made to a certain Eleazar, who was custodian of the Temple treasures, and plunders the Temple further (*Ant.* 14.105-9). This historical event seems alluded to in *Pesher Habakkuk.*

A second key is an oblique reference that makes sense only in connection with the Romans, who were identified by the eagle. Note the reference to their symbol in *Pesher Habakkuk:* "Its inter[pretation] concerns the Kittim, who trample the land with [their] horses and with their beasts. And from a distance they come, from the islands of the sea, to devour all the peoples like an eagle, and there is no satiety" (1QpHab 3.9-12). The geographical reference — from a distance and across the sea — denotes the world to the west of Palestine, and that indicates Italy and Rome.

A third key in the pesharim that the Kittim are to be identified as Romans is the reference to their worshipping their standards:

> **Therefore he sacrifices to his net and burns incense to his seine;** (VACAT) Its interpretation is that they sacrifice to their standards, and their weapons of war are the objects of their reverence. (1QpHab 6.2-5)

While this notation is not pellucid, it does seem to mirror what Qumranites probably thought about the Roman army and their devotion to their standards.[345]

Demetrius

The appearance of names, and known names not indicating biblical persons, is unusual in the Qumran scrolls. For names that cannot be identified in other documents, see the *Decrees* (4Q477), which is the only scroll that contains the name of members of the Congregation (or Community), the two ostraca found by James F. Strange in 1996,[346] and the *List of Netinim* (4Q340).

---

text that should be in clear focus. Kevin McCarron, a specialist in English literature, rightly points to the pyromania (my word) in publications on the Qumran scrolls that take over the text, as in Nabokov's *Pale Fire,* so that "there is nothing left of the text"; McCarron, "History and Hermeneutics: The Dead Sea Scrolls," in Porter and Evans, *The Scrolls and the Scriptures,* 107-20; esp. 119.

345. This judgment has been expressed by many other scholars before; see Bernstein, "Pesher Habakkuk," 2:649.

346. See Alexander and Vermes, *Qumran Cave 4.XIX,* 497-507.

Known nonbiblical names are found only in the *Prayer for King Jonathan* (4Q448), in *Apocryphon 3* (or *4QHistorical B;* i.e., 4Q468g), and in *Pesher Nahum*. Only three political figures are mentioned by name in the Qumran scrolls. The first is Jonathan Alexander Jannaeus. The Qumranites singled him out, because he stood out in Jewish history. He was notorious, committing abominable acts that horrified the Jews, including crucifying fellow Jews near the walls of Jerusalem. His notoriety is reflected in the pesharim and reported by Josephus (esp. *Ant.* 13.377-86).

The second name is probably "Peitholaos (Πειθόλαος)," the commander of Jewish troops during the struggle between Hyrcanus II and Aristobulus II (i.e., between 56 and 51 B.C.E.).[347] The name "Peitholaos" may appear, with different spelling, in a fragment of a Qumran work that is perhaps a portion of a pesher.[348] The document is named *Apocryphon 3* (or *4QHistorical;* i.e., 4Q468g). The fragment refers to a *pwtl'ys* or more likely *pytl'ws*. The first suggestion is that this man is to be identified with "Ptollâs," a courtier of Archelaus (ca. 4 B.C.E.). This hypothesis was suggested by Broshi.[349] Ptollas is rather an insignificant person in history, and the Hebrew is more likely "Peitholaos." Thus, the text probably refers to a Peitholaos who was quite prominent in Jewish history, a Jewish general and occasionally *hypostratēgos* of Jerusalem (*War* 1.162, 172, 180; *Ant.* 14.93 [Πειθόλαος γοῦν τις, ὑποστράτηγος ἐν Ἱεροσολύμοις ὤν]). Probably, Peitholaos is the man mentioned in *Apocryphon 3*. This probable identification is suggested by Strugnell.[350]

The third name belongs to a Greek person named "Demetrius." He is mentioned explictly in *Pesher Nahum*.

> **Where the lion went to enter, the lion's cub [. . .]o [and no one to disturb.** Its interpretation concerns Deme]trius, King of Greece, who sought to enter Jerusalem on the advice of the Seekers-After-Smooth-Things, [. . .] into the hand of Greece from Antiochus until the rise of the rulers of the Kittim. . . . (4QpNah frgs. 3-4, col. 1.1-3)

347. See Josephus *War* 1.162, 172, 180; *Ant.* 14.84, 93, 124.

348. See 4Q468g and Strugnell, "The Historical Background to *4Q468g* [= *4Qhistorical B*]," *RevQ* 73 (1999): 137-38. During conversations with Strugnell, I became persuaded that he may be correct to think that 4Q468g could be from a lost pesher. Strugnell's insight was not presented in his note.

349. Magen Broshi, "Ptolas and the Archelaus Massacre (4Q468g = 4Qhistorical text B)," *JJS* 49 (1998): 341-45.

350. Strugnell, *RevQ* 73 (1999): 137-38.

The restoration of "Demetrius" is guided by the remaining letters that anchor the restoration and the context that refers to a "King of Greece." As we have seen, the Seekers-After-Smooth-Things are probably the Pharisees. The man named "Antiochus" is most likely Antiochus IV (Epiphanes).[351] He is mentioned to clarify that Demetrius lived between the times of Antiochus and those of the Kittim, the Romans. The person is clearly one of the Greeks that controlled the Seleucid Empire north of Palestine; and the Seleucid control of Palestine and its social setting ca. 200 B.C.E. is clarified by the Greek inscription found near Hefzibah.[352] According to Strabo, the Seleucids claimed that the Hasmoneans controlled a "robber state."[353]

Among the works that are clearly pesharim, the mention of personal names occurs only in *Pesher Nahum*.[354] While it seems clear that "Kittim" usually denotes the Romans, it is not obvious, *prima facie,* who was meant by "Demetrius." There are three known Greek kings called Demetrius. Most scholars now[355] are convinced that the text refers to Demetrius III (Eukerus) who had been crowned king in Damascus. He reigned from 96 to 88 B.C.E.[356] Demetrius invaded Palestine and defeated Alexander Jannaeus at Shechem in 88 B.C.E. He then lost 6000 of his Jewish supporters to Jannaeus. Why? According to Josephus, they felt "pity" for Jannaeus (*Ant.* 13.379). This explanation is scarcely convincing. Most likely, as Cross long ago suggested, the reason for the desertion of Jews from Demetrius to Jannaeus, is that Demetrius intended to march on

351. See Otto Mørkholm, "Antiochus IV," in Davies and Finkelstein, *The Cambridge History of Judaism,* 2:278-91. See also Daniel R. Schwartz, "Antiochus IV Epiphanes in Jerusalem," in Goodblatt, Pinnick, and Schwartz, *Historical Perspectives,* 45-56.

352. At the beginning of the Fourth Syrian War, Ptolemaios, son of Thraseas στρατηγοῦ [καὶ] ἀρχιερέως, appeals to "King Antiochus" and reveals that travelers are plundering his villages, which consist of those he owns outright, those he leases from the king, and those that the king has assigned to him (see IVa [20] to [25]). For a study with text, translation, transcription, and facsimile, see Y. H. Landau, "A Greek Inscription Found Near Hefzibah," *IEJ* 16 (1966): 54-70.

353. Strabo *Geogr.* 16.2.37 C 761; see T. Fisher, in Kasher, Rappaport, and Fuks, *Greece and Rome in Eretz Israel,* 9.

354. This insight was expressed earlier by others, esp. Stegemann, *Die Essener,* 183.

355. See esp. Cross, *The Ancient Library of Qumran,* 3rd ed., 99; André Paul, *Les manuscrits de la Mer Morte* (Paris: Bayard, 1997), 99; Grabbe, *Judaism from Cyrus to Hadrian,* 1:234; Callaway, *The History of the Qumran Community,* 170; Dimant, *ABD* 5:246; Eshel, "Demetrius III Eukerus," 1:189.

356. Horgan also makes this identification in her introduction to the *Nahum Pesher* in Charlesworth et al., *The Pesharim, Other Commentaries, and Related Documents;* Luigi Moraldi, *I Manuscritti di Qumrân,* 2nd ed. (Turin: Unione tipografia-editrice Torinese, 1986), 546-47, also claims that "Demetrio" is Demetrius III.

"the Holy City" (*Ant.* 13.377-79).[357] There seems every reason, as I have previously clarified, to opt for Jannaeus as "the Lion of Wrath," since the latter "would hang men up alive" (4QpNah frgs. 3-4, col. 1.7).[358] This alludes to Jannaeus's crucifixion of 800 Jews, especially Pharisees, as previously discussed. Thus, the chronological period fits only Demetrius III (Eukerus).

We have seen that historical gems are embedded in the coded language of some of the pesharim.[359] Each book was chosen for select passages or chapters that can be used to prove that prophecy pointed to the historical events that had already occurred or were transpiring.[360] These works are not an attempt at objective history or a rationalistic history as in Thucydides' *Peloponnesian War* (310).[361] They are not like the practical history or "history of events" *(pragmatikē historia)* written by Polybius. They are not an apology for Judaism as in Josephus's histories. They are not "creative" histories like the passages from Hecataeus of Abdera, Artapanus, and Eupolemus. They are not like the universalistic histories found in Ephorus and Diodorus Siculus. They certainly are not similar to the "media history" created by Eusebius, according to Doron Mendels.[362] While they contain intermittently biographical information, especially concerning the Righteous Teacher, they are not biographies like the works of Suetonius and Plutarch.

What are the pesharim, then? They are first and foremost pneumatic commentaries on Scripture,[363] or historicizing allegories of Scripture —

357. Cross, *The Ancient Library of Qumran*, 99.

358. As Luigi Moraldi states: the majority of leading scholars (he lists Milik, Allegro, Cross, Maier, Dupont-Sommer, Lohse, and Carmignac) rightly identify the "leoncello furioso" with Alexander Jannaeus; *I Manuscritti di Qumrān*, 546.

359. In her introduction to *Pesher Psalm I* (see 4Q171, which precedes), Horgan rightly states that in it there are "no clear allusions to identifiable historical events"; Charlesworth et al., *The Pesharim, Other Commentaries, and Related Documents.*.

360. Fröhlich correctly states that the main requirement of the genre of *pesher* is "to draw a parallel between all the events he [the Qumran author] wishes to deal with in the *pesher* and all the events mentioned in the prophetic text"; *"Time and Times and Half a Time,"* 159.

361. In these reflections on historiography, I am indebted to my colleagues at the Hebrew University in Jerusalem and for fruitful discussion during my tenure as Lady Davis Professor, and I am especially grateful to Doron Mendels for decades of engaging reflections on Hellenistic historiography.

362. See the challenging book by Mendels, *The Media Revolution of Early Christianity: An Essay on Eusebius's "Ecclesiastical History"* (Grand Rapids: Wm. B. Eerdmans, 1999).

363. Patte correctly sees that the Qumranites emphasized Scripture as the "locus of the new revelation" and that accordingly "the mysteries of the contemporary history" are to be expressed "in inspired biblical commentaries: the so-called pesharim"; *Early Jewish Hermeneutic in Palestine*, 299. In *Techniques and Assumptions in Jewish Exegesis Before 70 CE*,

that is, *fulfillment exegesis*.[364] They are different from historical works;[365] yet, some of them mirror history by refracting the facts pneumatically and eschatologically for an in-group cut off from the mainstream.

Conclusion

The historical data mirrored in the pesharim can be recovered and understood only within a balance of delicate possibilities and probabilities. As Hanan Eshel states, anyone "who studies the scrolls from Qumran is aware of how difficult it is to understand historical allusions embedded in the text, allusions which must have been perfectly clear to readers in the Second Temple Period."[366] To a certain extent this perspective may be a little misleading. The historical allusions in the pesharim were most likely clear to the informed at Qumran and perhaps a few others, but they were not necessarily obvious to many, even other Jews living in ancient Palestine in the Second Temple period.

We have seen that of all the Qumran commentaries only *Pesher Nahum* contains the names of historical individuals; otherwise anonymity and sobriquets characterize the pesharim. Within this veritable maze of historical allusions, Qumran lore can be detected. Some history is present in the pesharim, as if in a fogged mirror.

While one should only cautiously seek data on which to speculate about historical events, it is clear that most scholars now conclude that events mirrored in the pesharim can sometimes be linked with historical events known from non-Qumran sources, especially 1 Maccabees and Josephus's histories. Thus, for example, with requisite caution, we have seen that the *Pesher Nahum* refers to "Demetrius," who is probably Demetrius III, "the Lion of Wrath," who is clearly Jannaeus, and to "the Seekers-After-

---

Instone Brewer rightly claims that the "one concept which sums up the Qumran approach to Scripture is inspiration. They [the Qumranites] regarded the whole of the Law, Prophets and Psalms as inspired prophecy which was to be interpreted by inspired exegetes and even copied with some inspired creativity" (198). Worth exploring is Brewer's claim that Qumran exegetical techniques are closer to Philonic than scribal traditions.

364. Strugnell tells me he prefers "historicizing allegories" or "fulfillment exegesis."

365. Brooke wisely warns about lumping all the pesharim into a set mold and confusing them with other Qumran commentaries. Among his numerous publications, see esp. "Pesharim," in Evans and Porter, *Dictionary of New Testament Background,* 778-82. The publications of the PTSDSSP warn against using *pesher* loosely and distinguish it from other types of biblical interpretations extant from Qumran and elsewhere.

366. Eshel, *RevQ* 15 (1992): 419.

Smooth-Things."[367] The latter is synonymous with "Ephraim," and along with it most likely denotes the early Pharisees.[368]

The three pesharim that most clearly mirror historical events are the *Pesher Habakkuk, Pesher Psalm^a*, and *Pesher Nahum*. Along with the *Damascus Document* they contain and share *termini technici* that denote historical individuals. Note the distribution of the most significant terms:

	1QpHab	4QpPs 37	4QpNah	CD
Righteous Teacher	x	x		x
Wicked Priest	x	x		
Man of the Lie	x	x		x
Seekers-AST			x	x
Kittim	x		x	
Ephraim		x	x	
Manasseh		x	x	
traitors	x			x
Demetrius			x	
Antiochus			x	

We have observed an attractive coherence among the various areas of research that has been devoted to different aspects of Qumranology. All the datable events in the pesharim can be identified with historical people who were active after the death of the Righteous Teacher and before Herod the Great. The events can be dated between 103 and 55 B.C.E. Note especially the following sequence:

B.C.E. (ca.)	Person	Event
110	Righteous Teacher	dies
103	Ptolemy Lathyrus	invades Palestine
88	Demetrius III	invades Palestine, defeated by Jannaeus
88	Alexander Jannaeus	crucifies fellow Jews
56-51	Peitholaos	Jewish general in Judea
55	Crassus	plunders the Jerusalem Temple

No sure dates before 103 or after 55 are preserved in the pesharim. This discovery of a sequence of historical dates mirrored in the pesharim is re-

367. After completing this work, I noted that Horgan makes these same identifications in her introduction to the *Nahum Pesher* in Charlesworth et al., *The Pesharim, Other Commentaries, and Related Documents.*.

368. This judgment is well received, e.g., by Callaway in *The History of the Qumran Community*, 170; and by Saldarini in *Pharisees, Scribes and Sadducees in Palestinian Society*, 278-79.

inforced by the coherent insights obtained by both palaeographical and archaeological studies. It is undergirded by the date assigned to the manuscripts that preserve the pesharim; all are in late Hasmonean or early Herodian scripts. All the pesharim were composed at Qumran during Phase II (Archaeological Period Ib) or ca. 100 to 40 B.C.E., with the possibility that one or two pesharim were composed near the end of Phase I (Archaeological Period Ia), probably sometime between approximately 110 and 100 B.C.E.

When one reads the pesharim one learns much about how the Qumranites remembered the origins of the Qumran Community. One also learns much about the way the later Qumranites revered the Righteous Teacher, who most likely left his own autobiographical reflections in some of the *Thanksgiving Hymns*. The Qumranites lived out the belief that they were chosen by God. The divine Voice had called them to prepare the Way in the wilderness. They were preparing for the future day in which God's promises found in Scripture would be fulfilled. The Qumranites devoted the day and the night to preparing "the Way of YHWH," studying Torah, seeking to understand God's hand in contemporaneous events — that is, by composing pesharim. The life of the Qumranite was shaped by realizing expectations for the full dawning of the end of the age. The second generation of those who lived at Qumran probably added another concept. They also expected the coming of the Messiah or the Messiahs of Aaron and Israel.[369]

369. For texts and discussions on Qumran messianism, see James H. Charlesworth, Herman Lichtenberger, and Gerbern S. Oegema, eds., *Qumran-Messianism* (Tübingen: Mohr [Siebeck], 1998).

Index of Biblical Quotations in the Pesharim, Other Commentaries, and Related Documents

compiled by

LIDIJA NOVAKOVIC

Below is the list of biblical passages that are either quoted or alluded to in the pesharim, other commentaries, and related documents. The third column contains the information about other Dead Sea scrolls in which these quotations are fully or partially extant. The references are limited to the published material (see the attached bibliography).

Biblical Passage	Pesharim, Other Commentaries, and Related Documents	Other DSS
Gen 6:3a	4Q252 frgs. 1-2 1.1-2	—
Gen 6:3b	4Q252 frgs. 1-2 1.2-3	—
Gen 6:15b	4Q254a frgs. 1-2 lines 2-3	—
Gen 7:10b	4Q252 frgs. 1-2 1.3	—
Gen 7:11a	4Q252 frgs. 1-2 1.3-4	—
Gen 7:11b-12	4Q252 frgs. 1-2 1.5-6	—
Gen 7:24	4Q252 frgs. 1-2 1.7	—
Gen 8:3b	4Q252 frgs. 1-2 1.8-9	—
Gen 8:4	4Q252 frgs. 1-2 1.10	—
Gen 8:5a	4Q252 frgs. 1-2 1.11	—
Gen 8:5b	4Q252 frgs. 1-2 1.12	—
Gen 8:6a	4Q252 frgs. 1-2 1.12	—
Gen 8:6b	4Q252 frgs. 1-2 1.13	—

Biblical Passage	Pesharim, Other Commentaries, and Related Documents	Other DSS
Gen 8:8a	4Q252 frgs. 1-2 1.14	—
Gen 8:9a	4Q252 frgs. 1-2 1.14-15	—
Gen 8:10a	4Q252 frgs. 1-2 1.15-16	—
Gen 8:11a	4Q252 frgs. 1-2 1.16	—
Gen 8:11b	4Q252 frgs. 1-2 1.17-18	—
Gen 8:12	4Q252 frgs. 1-2 1.18-19	—
Gen 8:12b	4Q252 frgs. 1-2 1.20-21	—
Gen 8:13a	4Q252 frgs. 1,3 2.1	—
Gen 8:13b	4Q252 frgs. 1-2 1.22	—
Gen 8:13c	4Q252 frgs. 1-2 1.21-22	—
Gen 8:14	4Q252 frgs. 1,3 2.1-2	—
Gen 8:18a	4Q252 frgs. 1,3 2.2	—
Gen 8:19c	4Q252 frgs. 1,3 2.2	—
Gen 9:1a	4Q252 frgs. 1,3 2.7	—
Gen 9:24-25	4Q252 frgs. 1,3 2.5-6	—
	4Q254 frg. 1 lines 2-4	—
Gen 9:27b	4Q252 frgs. 1,3 2.7	—
Gen 11:31b	4Q252 frgs. 1,3 2.8-9	—
Gen 12:4b	4Q252 frgs. 1,3 2.9	—
Gen 15:13	4Q464 frg. 3 2.3-4	—
Gen 18:32b	4Q252 frgs. 1,3-5 3.5	—
Gen 22:10a	4Q252 frgs. 1,3-5 3.6-7	—
Gen 22:11b	4Q252 frgs. 1,3-5 3.7-8	—
Gen 22:12c	4Q252 frgs. 1,3-5 3.8-9	—
Gen 28:3a	4Q252 frgs. 1,3-5 3.12	—
Gen 28:4a	4Q252 frgs. 1,3-5 3.13	—
Gen 36:12a	4Q252 frg. 5 4.1	4Q1 frg. 5 line 20
Gen 49:3-4	4Q252 frg. 5 4.3-5	4Q1 frgs. 15-16 lines 3-4
Gen 49:10a	4Q252 frg. 6 5.1	—
Gen 49:15b	4Q254 frgs. 5-6 line 1	—
Gen 49:16	4Q254 frgs. 5-6 line 3	—
Gen 49:17	4Q254 frgs. 5-6 lines 4-5	—
Gen 49:20b	4Q252 frg. 6 6.1	—
Gen 49:24a	4Q254 frg. 7 line 2	—
Gen 49:24d	4Q254 frg. 7 line 3	—
Gen 49:25c	4Q254 frg. 7 line 4	—
Gen 49:26b	4Q254 frg. 7 line 5	—
Exod 15:17b-18	4Q174 frgs. 1-2,21 1.3	4Q14 frgs. 32-34 line 41
Exod 20:22a	4Q175 line 1	1Q2 frgs. 2-3 line 3

Index of Biblical Quotations in the Pesharim

Biblical Passage	Pesharim, Other Commentaries, and Related Documents	Other DSS
Exod 20:22a		4Q11 21.4
		4Q22 20.30
Lev 25:9	11Q13 2.25	—
Lev 25:13	11Q13 2.2	—
Num 24:15-17	4Q175 lines 9-13	—
Deut 5:28b-29	4Q175 lines 1-4	4Q37 3.13-4.2
		4Q38 1.1-3
Deut 7:15a	4Q177 frgs. 1-4,14,24,31 line 2	5Q1 frg. 1 1.1
Deut 15:2	11Q13 2.2-4	4Q30 frgs. 26-27 lines 2-3
		Mur 2 frg. 3 lines 1-2
Deut 18:18-19	4Q175 lines 5-8	4Q33 frgs. 10-12 lines 1-2
Deut 25:19b	4Q252 frg. 5 4.2-3	4Q34 frgs. 6-9 line 7
Deut 33:8-11	4Q174 frgs. 6-7 lines 3-6	4Q35 frgs. 11-15 lines 1-4
	4Q175 lines 14-20	4Q45 frgs. 42-43 line 7
Deut 33:12a	4Q174 frg. 8 line 3	4Q35 frgs. 11-15 line 5
		1Q5 frg. 20 line 12
Deut 33:20-21	4Q174 frgs. 9-10 lines 3-4	4Q35 frgs. 11-15 lines 10-12
		1Q5 frg. 22 line 21
2Sam 7:10b-11a	4Q174 frgs. 1-2,21 1.1-2	—
2Sam 7:11b	4Q174 frgs. 1-2,21 1.7	—
2Sam 7:11c	4Q174 frgs. 1-2,21 1.10	—
2Sam 7:12b	4Q174 frgs. 1-2,21 1.10	—
2Sam 7:13b-14a	4Q174 frgs. 1-2,21 1.10-11	—
Ps 1:1a	4Q174 frgs. 1-2,21 1.14	—
Ps 2:1-2	4Q174 frgs. 1-2,21 1.18-19	—
Ps 6:2-3a	4Q177 frgs. 12-13 1.4	—
Ps 6:3b-5a	4Q177 frgs. 12-13 1.5	—
Ps 7:8b-9a	11Q13 2.10-11	—
Ps 11:1-2a	4Q177 frgs. 5-6 lines 7-8	—
Ps 12:1a	4Q177 frgs. 5-6 line 12	—
Ps 12:7	4Q177 frgs. 7,9-11,20,26 line 1	—
Ps 13:2-3	4Q177 frgs. 7,9-11,20,26 lines 8-9	—
Ps 13:5a	4Q177 frgs. 7,9-11,20,26 lines 11-12	—
Ps 16:3a	4Q177 frgs. 1-4,14,24,31 line 2	—
Ps 17:1a	4Q177 frgs. 1-4,14,24,31 line 4	—
Ps 37:7	4Q171 frgs. 1-10 1.25-26	—
Ps 37:8-9a	4Q171 frgs. 1-10 2.1-2	—
Ps 37:9b	4Q171 frgs. 1-10 2.4	—
Ps 37:10a	4Q171 frgs. 1-10 2.5	—

Biblical Passage	Pesharim, Other Commentaries, and Related Documents	Other DSS
Ps 37:10b	4Q171 frgs. 1-10 2.7	—
Ps 37:11	4Q171 frgs. 1-10 2.9	—
Ps 37:12-13	4Q171 frgs. 1-10 2.13-14	—
Ps 37:14-15	4Q171 frgs. 1-10 2.16-17	—
Ps 37:16	4Q171 frgs. 1-10 2.22	—
Ps 37:17	4Q171 frgs. 1-10 2.24-25	—
Ps 37:18-19a	4Q171 frgs. 1-10 2.26-27	—
Ps 37:19b-20a	4Q171 frgs. 1-10 3.2-3	—
Ps 37:20b-c	4Q171 frgs. 1-10 3.5a	—
Ps 37:20d	4Q171 frgs. 1-10 3.7	—
Ps 37:21-22	4Q171 frgs. 1-10 3.8-9	—
Ps 37:22b	4Q171 frgs. 1-10 3.11-12	—
Ps 37:23-24	4Q171 frgs. 1-10 3.14-15	—
Ps 37:25-26	4Q171 frgs. 1-10 3.17-18	—
Ps 37:28	4Q171 frgs. 1-10 3.27-4.1	—
Ps 37:29	4Q171 frgs. 1-10 4.2	—
Ps 37:30-31	4Q171 frgs. 1-10 4.3-4	—
Ps 37:32-33	4Q171 frgs. 1-10 4.7	—
Ps 37:34	4Q171 frgs. 1-10 4.10-11	—
Ps 37:35-36	4Q171 frgs. 1-10 4.13-14	—
Ps 37:37	4Q171 frgs. 1-10 4.16	—
Ps 37:38	4Q171 frgs. 1-10 4.17-18	—
Ps 37:39-40	4Q171 frgs. 1-10 4.19-20	—
Ps 45:1	4Q171 frgs. 1-10 4.23	—
Ps 45:2a	4Q171 frgs. 1-10 4.24-25	—
Ps 45:2b	4Q171 frgs. 1-10 4.26-27	—
Ps 60:8-9	4Q171 frg. 13 lines 3-4	—
Ps 68:13	1Q16 frg. 3 line 3	—
Ps 68:26b-27a	1Q16 frg. 8 line 2	—
Ps 68:30	1Q16 frg. 9 line 1	—
Ps 68:31	1Q16 frg. 9 lines 2-3	—
Ps 82:1	11Q13 2.10	Mas1e 2.4
Ps 82:2	11Q13 2.11	Mas1e 2.5
Ps 118:20	4Q173a (4Q173 frg. 5 *olim*) line 4	—
Ps 129:7-8	4Q173 frg. 4 lines 1-2	11Q5 5.8-9
Isa 1:1	3Q4 lines 1-2	1QIsa^a 1.1-2
		4Q55 frg. 1 line 1
		4Q56 frg. 1 lines 1-2
		4Q63 lines 1-2

Index of Biblical Quotations in the Pesharim

Biblical Passage	Pesharim, Other Commentaries, and Related Documents	Other DSS
Isa 1:2a	3Q4 line 4	1QIsa^a 1.2-3
		4Q55 frg. 1 line 2
		4Q56 frg. 1 line 2
Isa 5:5b-6a	4Q162 1.1-2	1QIsa^a 4.17-18
Isa 5:6aγ	4Q162 1.3-4	1QIsa^a 4.18
Isa 5:11-14	4Q162 2.2-6	1QIsa^a 4.26-5.1
		4Q60 frg. 7 lines 1-2
Isa 5:24c-25	4Q162 2.7-10	1QIsa^a 5.11-14
		4Q56 frg. 3 2.10-12
Isa 5:29b-30	4Q162 3.1-3	1QIsa^a 5.19-20
		4Q69 frgs. 1-2 lines 2-4
Isa 6:9b	4Q162 3.9	1QIsa^a 6.3
Isa 6:9c	4Q162 3.8	1QIsa^a 6.3
Isa 8:7-8	4Q163 frg. 2 lines 2-4	1QIsa^a 7.27-8.1
		4Q60 frgs. 12,14,15 lines 20-23
Isa 8:11b	4Q174 frgs. 1-2,21 1.15-16	1QIsa^a 8.4
Isa 9:11	4Q163 frgs. 4,6-7 1.7-8	1QIsa^a 8.30-9.1
		4Q57 frgs. 1-2,49 line 10
		4Q56 frg. 4 line 11
Isa 9:13-16	4Q163 frgs. 4,6-7 1.9-14	1QIsa^a 9.3-7
Isa 9:17-20	4Q163 frgs. 4,6-7 1.17-22	1QIsa^a 9.8-13
		4Q59 frgs. 7,11-16 lines 1-4
Isa 10:12-13b	4Q163 frgs. 6-7 2.1-2	1QIsa^a 9.25-27
Isa 10:19	4Q163 frgs. 6-7 2.8	1QIsa^a 10.5-6
Isa 10:19b	4Q163 frgs. 6-7 2.4	1QIsa^a 10.6
Isa 10:20-22bα	4Q163 frgs. 6-7 2.11-14	1QIsa^a 10.7-9
Isa 10:22-23	4Q161 frgs. 2-6 2.1-3	1QIsa^a 10.8-10
		4Q57 frgs. 3-5,50 line 1
Isa 10:22	4Q161 frgs. 2-6 2.6-7	1QIsa^a 10.8-9
Isa 10:22a-bα	4Q163 frgs. 6-7 2.17	1QIsa^a 10.8-9
Isa 10:22bβ-23	4Q163 frgs. 6-7 2.19-20	1QIsa^a 10.9-10
		4Q57 frgs. 3-5,50 line 1
Isa 10:24-27	4Q161 frgs. 2-6 2.10-15	1QIsa^a 10.11-14
		4Q57 frgs. 3-5,50 lines 2-5
Isa 10:24a	4Q163 frgs. 6-7 2.22	1QIsa^a 10.11
		4Q57 frgs. 3-5,50 line 2
Isa 10:28-32	4Q161 frgs. 2-6 2.21-25	1QIsa^a 10.15-17
		4Q57 frgs. 3-5,50 lines 6-9
Isa 10:33-34	4Q161 frgs. 8-10 3.1-3	1QIsa^a 10.18-19

Biblical Passage	Pesharim, Other Commentaries, and Related Documents	Other DSS
Isa 10:33-34		4Q57 frgs. 3-5,50 line 10
Isa 10:33b	4Q161 frgs. 8-10 3.9	1QIsa^a 10.18
		4Q57 frgs. 3-5,50 line 10
Isa 10:34	4Q161 frgs. 8-10 3.6-7	1QIsa^a 10.19
Isa 10:34a	4Q161 frgs. 8-10 3.10	1QIsa^a 10.19
Isa 10:34b	4Q161 frgs. 8-10 3.11-12	1QIsa^a 10.19
Isa 11:1-5	4Q161 frgs. 8-10 3.15-20	1QIsa^a 10.20-24
		4Q57 frg. 6 lines 1-2
Isa 11:3b	4Q161 frgs. 8-10 3.26-27	1QIsa^a 10.21-22
Isa 11:11-12a	4Q165 frg. 11 lines 3-5	1QIsa^a 10.29-11.1
Isa 14:8	4Q163 frgs. 8-10 lines 1-3	1QIsa^a 12.9-10
		4Q59 frgs. 20-22 line 6
Isa 14:19b	4Q165 frg. 3 line 1	1QIsa^a 12.20
Isa 14:26-27	4Q163 frgs. 8-10 lines 4-7	1QIsa^a 12.28-30
Isa 14:28-30	4Q163 frgs. 8-10 lines 11-14	1QIsa^a 12.31-13.3
		4Q68 frg. 1 lines 1-3
Isa 15:4b-5	4Q165 frg. 4 lines 1-2	1QIsa^a 13.10-12
		1Q8 frg. 3 lines 3-4
Isa 19:9b-12	4Q163 frg. 11 2.1-5	1QIsa^a 15.13-16
		1Q8 frg. 4 lines 3-5
		4Q56 frgs. 10-13 lines 15-18
Isa 21:10	4Q165 frg. 5 lines 1-2	1QIsa^a 16.25-27
		4Q55 frgs. 10-14 line 30
Isa 21:11-15	4Q165 frg. 5 lines 3-5	1QIsa^a 16.28-17.1
		4Q55 frgs. 10-14 lines 32-35
Isa 22:13b	4Q177 frgs. 5-6 line 15	1QIsa^a 17.18-19
		1Q8 frg. 5 line 3
Isa 29:10-12a	4Q163 frgs. 15-16 lines 1-4	1QIsa^a 23.18-21
Isa 29:15c-16b	4Q163 frg. 17 lines 1-2	1QIsa^a 23.26-27
Isa 29:18b-23a	4Q163 frgs. 18-19 lines 1-6	1QIsa^a 23.29-24.4
Isa 30:1-5	4Q163 frg. 21 lines 9-15	1QIsa^a 24.6-10
Isa 30:15-18	4Q163 frg. 23 2.3-9	1QIsa^a 24.25-30
Isa 30:19-21	4Q163 frg. 23 2.15-19	1QIsa^a 24.30-25.3
Isa 30:23b	4Q163 frg. 22 line 4	1QIsa^a 25.5-6
Isa 31:1	4Q163 frg. 25 lines 5-7	1QIsa^a 25.23-25
Isa 32:5-7	4Q165 frg. 6 lines 2-6	1QIsa^a 26.13-17
Isa 32:7b	4Q177 frgs. 5-6 line 6	1QIsa^a 26.16-17
Isa 35:10a	4Q177 frg. 19 line 6	1QIsa^a 28.27
Isa 37:30a	4Q177 frgs. 5-6 line 2	1QIsa^a 31.8-9

Index of Biblical Quotations in the Pesharim

Biblical Passage	Pesharim, Other Commentaries, and Related Documents	Other DSS
		4Q56 frgs. 22-23 line 2
Isa 40:1-5a	4Q176 frgs. 1-2 1.4-9	1QIsaᵃ 32.29-33.5
		4Q56 frgs. 24-25 lines 14-16
		1QS 8.14
Isa 40:12	4Q165 frgs. 1-2 lines 3-4	1QIsaᵃ 33.12-13
Isa 41:8-9	4Q176 frgs. 1-2 1.9-11	1QIsaᵃ 34.11-13
		4Q56 frg. 27 lines 2-3
Isa 43:1-2	4Q176 frg. 3 lines 1-3	1QIsaᵃ 36.9-10
		4Q61 frgs. 1-8 lines 14-15
Isa 43:4-6	4Q176 frgs. 4-5 lines 1-4	1QIsaᵃ 36.13-15
		4Q61 frgs. 1-8 line 18
Isa 49:7	4Q176 frgs. 1-2 2.1	1QIsaᵃ 41.6
Isa 49:13-17	4Q176 frgs. 1-2 2.2-6	1QIsaᵃ 41.12-16
		4Q58 frgs. 6-10 4.22-24
Isa 51:22-23a	4Q176 frgs. 6-7 lines 1-3	1QIsaᵃ 43.11-13
Isa 52:1-3	4Q176 frgs. 8-11 lines 2-4	1QIsaᵃ 43.14-18
		4Q56 frg. 37 line 1
Isa 52:1a-b	4Q176 frgs. 42,12-13 lines 2-3	1QIsaᵃ 43.14-15
Isa 52:1c-2a	4Q176 frgs. 42,12-13 lines 5-6	1QIsaᵃ 43.15-16
Isa 52:7	11Q13 2.15-16	1QIsaᵃ 43.22-23
		4Q56 frg. 38 lines 1-2
		4Q58 frg. 11 1.23
Isa 52:7c	11Q13 2.23	1QIsaᵃ 43.23
		4Q56 frg. 38 line 2
		4Q58 frg. 11 1.23
Isa 54:4-10a	4Q176 frgs. 8-11 lines 5-12	1QIsaᵃ 44.27-45.8
		4Q57 frg. 40 lines 2-3
		4Q57 frgs. 41-42 lines 1-3
		4Q57 frg. 43 line 1
		4Q57 frgs. 44-47 lines 1-2
		4Q58 frg. 12 lines 3-10
Isa 54:11c	4Q164 frg. 1 line 1	1QIsaᵃ 45.10-11
		4Q57 frgs. 44-47 line 3
Isa 54:12a	4Q164 frg. 1 lines 3-4	1QIsaᵃ 45.11
Isa 54:12b	4Q164 frg. 1 line 6	1QIsaᵃ 45.11
		4Q69a line 3
Isa 65:22b-23b	4Q174 frg. 15 lines 2-3	1QIsaᵃ 53.5-6
Jer 5:7b	4Q182 frg. 1 line 5	—
Jer 18:18b	4Q177 frgs. 12-13 1.3	4Q70 frg. 11 line 5

Biblical Passage	Pesharim, Other Commentaries, and Related Documents	Other DSS
Jer 33:17b	4Q252 frg. 6 5.2	4Q72 25.1-2
Ezek 25:8b	4Q177 frgs. 7,9-11,20,26 line 14	—
Ezek 37:23a	4Q174 frgs. 1-2,21 1.16-17	—
Dan 9:25b	11Q13 2.18	—
Dan 11:32b	4Q174 frgs. 1 and 3 2.4a	—
Hos 2:8a,c	4Q166 1.7-8	—
Hos 2:9bβ,c	4Q166 1.15-16	—
Hos 2:10	4Q166 2.1-2	—
Hos 2:11-12	4Q166 2.8-11	—
Hos 2:13	4Q166 2.14-15	4Q78 1-2.1
Hos 2:14	4Q166 2.17-19	4Q78 1-2.2
Hos 5:8aα	4Q177 frgs. 1-4,14,24,31 line 13	—
Hos 5:13b	4Q167 frg. 2 line 1	—
Hos 5:14a	4Q167 frg. 2 lines 2-3	—
Hos 5:15	4Q167 frg. 2 lines 5-6	—
Hos 6:4a	4Q167 frgs. 5-6 line 3	—
Hos 6:7a	4Q167 frgs. 7-8 line 1	—
Hos 6:9a	4Q163 frg. 23 2.13a	—
Hos 6:9bβ-10	4Q167 frgs. 10 and 26 lines 1-2	—
Hos 6:11a	4Q167 frgs. 4,10a,18 and 24 line 1	—
Hos 8:6	4Q167 frgs. 11-13 lines 3-4	—
Hos 8:6b	4Q167 frgs. 11-13 line 5	—
Hos 8:7-8	4Q167 frgs. 11-13 lines 6-8	—
Hos 8:13bγ-14b	4Q167 frgs. 15,33 and 4Q168 frg. 2 2.1-2	—
Amos 9:11a	4Q174 frgs. 1-2,21 1.12	Mur 88 8.26
Mic 1:2b-5a	1Q14 frgs. 1-5 lines 1-5	Mur 88 11.36-12.1
Mic 1:5b	1Q14 frg. 10 line 2	Mur 88 12.1
Mic 1:5c	1Q14 frg. 10 lines 3-4	Mur 88 12.1-2
Mic 1:6a	1Q14 frg. 10 line 8	Mur 88 12.2
Mic 1:9b	1Q14 frg. 11 line 3	Mur 88 12.6-7
Mic 4:8c-12	4Q168 frgs. 1 and 3 lines 1-6	—
Mic 6:15-16	1Q14 frgs. 17-18 lines 2-5	Mur 88 15.12-14
Nah 1:3b	4Q169 frgs. 1-2 2.1	Mur 88 16.10-11
Nah 1:4aα	4Q169 frgs. 1-2 2.3	Mur 88 16.11
Nah 1:4aβ-b	4Q169 frgs. 1-2 2.4-5	Mur 88 16.11-12
Nah 1:5-6	4Q169 frgs. 1-2 2.9-11	Mur 88 16.12-14
Nah 2:11b	4Q177 frgs. 1-4,14,24,31 line 3	Mur 88 16.37
Nah 2:12b	4Q169 frgs. 3-4 1.1-2	Mur 88 16.39
Nah 2:13a	4Q169 frgs. 3-4 1.4	Mur 88 17.1

Biblical Passage	Pesharim, Other Commentaries, and Related Documents	Other DSS
Nah 2:13b	4Q169 frgs. 3-4 1.6	Mur 88 17.1-2
Nah 2:14	4Q169 frgs. 3-4 1.8-10	Mur 88 17.2-4
Nah 3:1a-bα	4Q169 frgs. 3-4 2.1	Mur 88 17.6
Nah 3:1bβ-3	4Q169 frgs. 3-4 2.3-4	Mur 88 17.6-9
Nah 3:4	4Q169 frgs. 3-4 2.7	Mur 88 17.9-10
Nah 3:5	4Q169 frgs. 3-4 2.10-11	Mur 88 17.11-12
Nah 3:6-7a	4Q169 frgs. 3-4 3.1-2	Mur 88 17.12-13
Nah 3:7b-c	4Q169 frgs. 3-4 3.5-6	Mur 88 17.14-15
Nah 3:8a	4Q169 frgs. 3-4 3.8	Mur 88 17.15
Nah 3:8b	4Q169 frgs. 3-4 3.10	Mur 88 17.16
Nah 3:9a	4Q169 frgs. 3-4 3.11	Mur 88 17.16
Nah 3:9b	4Q169 frgs. 3-4 3.12	Mur 88 17.17
Nah 3:10	4Q169 frgs. 3-4 4.1-3	Mur 88 17.17-19
Nah 3:11a	4Q169 frgs. 3-4 4.4-5	Mur 88 17.19
Nah 3:11b	4Q169 frgs. 3-4 4.6-7	Mur 88 17.20
Nah 3:12a	4Q169 frgs. 3-4 4.8-9	Mur 88 17.20-21
Nah 3:14	4Q169 frg. 5 line 3	—
Hab 1:1-2a	1QpHab 1.1-2	—
Hab 1:2b	1QpHab 1.4	—
Hab 1:3a	1QpHab 1.5	Mur 88 18.1
Hab 1:3b	1QpHab 1.7	Mur 88 18.1
Hab 1:4a	1QpHab 1.10-11	Mur 88 18.2
Hab 1:4bα	1QpHab 1.12	Mur 88 18.2
Hab 1:4bβ	1QpHab 1.14-15	Mur 88 18.3
Hab 1:5	1QpHab 1.16-2.1	Mur 88 18.3
Hab 1:6a	1QpHab 2.10-11	Mur 88 18.4
Hab 1:6b	1QpHab 2.16-17	Mur 88 18.5
Hab 1:6bβ-7	1QpHab 3.2-3	Mur 88 18.5
Hab 1:8-9a	1QpHab 3.6-9	Mur 88 18.6-7
Hab 1:9aβ-b	1QpHab 3.14	Mur 88 18.7-8
Hab 1:10a	1QpHab 3.17-4.1	Mur 88 18.8
Hab 1:10b	1QpHab 4.3-4	Mur 88 18.9
Hab 1:11	1QpHab 4.9-10	Mur 88 18.9-10
Hab 1:11b	1QpHab 4.13	Mur 88 18.9-10
Hab 1:12-13a	1QpHab 4.16-5.2	Mur 88 18.10-11
Hab 1:13aα	1QpHab 5.6-7	Mur 88 18.11
Hab 1:13b	1QpHab 5.8-9	Mur 88 18.12
Hab 1:14-16	1QpHab 5.12-16	Mur 88 18.13
Hab 1:16a	1QpHab 6.2-3	—

Biblical Passage	Pesharim, Other Commentaries, and Related Documents	Other DSS
Hab 1:16b	1QpHab 6.5	—
Hab 1:17	1QpHab 6.8-9	—
Hab 2:1-2	1QpHab 6.12-16	Mur 88 18.18
Hab 2:2bβ	1QpHab 7.3	—
Hab 2:3a	1QpHab 7.5-6	Mur 88 18.19
Hab 2:3b	1QpHab 7.9-10	—
Hab 2:4a	1QpHab 7.14-15	—
Hab 2:4b	1QpHab 7.17	—
Hab 2:5-6	1QpHab 8.3-8	Mur 88 18.21-24
Hab 2:7-8a	1QpHab 8.13-15	Mur 88 18.25-26
Hab 2:8a	1QpHab 9.3-4	Mur 88 18.26
Hab 2:8b	1QpHab 9.8	—
Hab 2:9-11	1QpHab 9.12-15	Mur 88 18.29-30
Hab 2:10b	1QpHab 10.2	—
Hab 2:12-13	1QpHab 10.5-8	—
Hab 2:14	1QpHab 10.14-15	—
Hab 2:15	1QpHab 11.2-3	—
Hab 2:16	1QpHab 11.8-11	—
Hab 2:17	1QpHab 11.17-12.1	—
Hab 2:17b	1QpHab 12.6-7	—
Hab 2:18	1QpHab 12.10-12	Mur 88 19.1-2
Hab 2:19-20	1QpHab 12.14-13.1	Mur 88 19.2-3
Zeph 1:12c-13a	4Q170 frgs. 1-2 line 1	Mur 88 20.3-4
Zeph 1:13aα	4Q170 frgs. 1-2 line 3	—
Zeph 1:13b	4Q170 frgs. 1-2 line 4	Mur 88 20.4
Zeph 1:18b–2:2	1Q15 lines 1-4	Mur 88 20.10-13
Zeph 3:9a-b	4Q464 frg. 3 1.8	—
Zech 3:9a,b	4Q177 frgs. 7,9-11,20,26 line 2	4Q78 frgs. 7-10 line 10
Zech 13:9a-b	4Q176 frg. 15 lines 2-4	—
Mal 1:14a	5Q10 frg. 1 line 1	—
Mal 1:14b	5Q10 frg. 1 line 3	—
Mal 3:16-18	4Q253a 1.1-5	4Q76 4.2-7

Text-critical Variants in the Pesharim, Other Commentaries, and Related Documents

compiled by

LIDIJA NOVAKOVIC

The following pages contain lists of the most significant text-critical variants of biblical passages which appear in the pesharim, other commentaries, and related documents. Column 1 specifies the citation, and columns 2 and 3 the Qumran variant. Column 4 indicates the form preserved in the Masoretic Text (BHS). Columns 5 and 6 list variants and citations for other Dead Sea Scroll texts. Variants in the pesharim, other commentaries, and related documents are given with the restorations suggested in vol. 6B of the *Dead Sea Scrolls: Hebrew, Aramaic, and Greek Texts,* ed. James H. Charlesworth, et al. (Tübingen: Mohr [Siebeck], 2002). No attempt has been made to separate orthographic peculiarities from more substantive textual variants.

Biblical Passage	Pesharim, Other Commentaries, and Related Documents	MT	Other DSS
Gen 6:3	4Q252 frgs. 1-2 1.2	ואמר	אמר
Gen 6:3	4Q252 frgs. 1-2 1.2	ידון	יזור
Gen 6:3	4Q252 frgs. 1-2 1.2	לעלם	לעולם
Gen 6:3	4Q252 frgs. 1-2 1.2	בימי	בימי
Gen 6:15	4Q254a frgs. 1-2 line 2	המבה	המ]בול [שׁ ם]
Gen 6:15	4Q254a frgs. 1-2 line 3	התבה	התבה
Gen 7:10	4Q252 frgs. 1-2 1.3	המבול	וירדה
Gen 8:4	4Q252 frgs. 1-2 1.10	מעל	ולא
Gen 8:9	4Q252 frgs. 1-2 1.14	לא	ולא
Gen 8:10	4Q252 frgs. 1-2 1.16	שלח	לשׁלוח
Gen 8:11	4Q252 frgs. 1-2 1.16	ותבא	והבאה
Gen 8:12	4Q252 frgs. 1-2 1.19	שוב	לשׁוב
Gen 8:12	4Q252 frgs. 1-2 1.20	ולא	לוא
Gen 8:18	4Q252 frgs. 1 and 3 2.2	וירב	יצא
Gen 9:1	4Q252 frgs. 1 and 3 2.7	וירד	בנה
Gen 9:1	4Q252 frgs. 1 and 3 2.7	אלהים	אל
Gen 9:24	4Q252 frgs. 1 and 3 2.5	וייקץ	ויקץ
Gen 9:25	4Q252 frgs. 1 and 3 2.6	ויאמר	ויור
Gen 9:25	4Q252 frgs. 1 and 3 2.6	יהוה	יהיה
Gen 9:27	4Q252 frgs. 1 and 3 2.7	אלהיו	וֹאֱרדֹי
Gen 9:27	4Q252 frgs. 1 and 3 2.7	וישם	ישׁמו
Gen 22:11	4Q252 frgs. 1,3-5 3.8	ויאמר	וֹמׁאֹיׁ

Biblical Passage	Pesharim, Other Commentaries, and Related Documents		MT	Other DSS	
Gen 28:3	4Q252 frgs. 1,3-5 3.12	אל	ואל	—	—
Gen 36:12	4Q252 frg. 5 line 1	התמנה	ותמנע	—	—
Gen 36:12	4Q252 frg. 5 line 1	עשו	עשו	עשו	4Q1 frg. 5 line 20
Gen 49:3	4Q252 frg. 5 line 4	מ[ראשי]ת	מראשית	—	—
Gen 49:4	4Q252 frg. 5 line 4	פחתה	פחז	—	—
Gen 49:4	4Q252 frg. 5 line 4	יצועה	יצועי	—	—
Gen 49:4	4Q252 frg. 5 line 5	עלית	עלה	—	—
Gen 49:10	4Q252 frg. 6 line 1	מבמנו	עד	—	—
Gen 49:15	4Q254 frgs. 5-6 line 1	לעבד	עבד	—	—
Gen 49:17	4Q254 frgs. 5-6 line 4	ייי	ידן	—	—
Gen 49:17	4Q254 frgs. 5-6 line 4	יש[פיפ]	שפיפן	—	—
Gen 49:17	4Q254 frgs. 5-6 line 4	[דר]ך	ארח	—	—
Gen 49:25	4Q254 frg. 7 line 4	מבן[ע]ל	מעל	—	—
Exod 15:17	4Q174 frgs. 1-2,21 1.3	יהוה	אדני	יהוה	4Q14 frgs. 32-34 line 41
Exod 15:17	4Q174 frgs. 1-2,21 1.3	ידכה	ידיך	ידי	4Q14 frgs. 32-34 line 41
Exod 15:18	4Q174 frgs. 1-2,21 1.3	ימלך	ימלך	למקדֹשׁ	4Q14 frgs. 32-34 line 41
Exod 15:18	4Q174 frgs. 1-2,21 1.3	עלום	עולם	שלום	4Q14 frgs. 32-34 line 41
Lev 25:9	11Q13 2.25	והעברתמה	והעברת	—	—
Lev 25:9	11Q13 2.25	בכ[ל]	בכל	—	—
Lev 25:9	11Q13 2.25	א[רצ]כ	ארצכם	—	—
Num 24:15	4Q175 line 9	ונאם	נאם	—	—
Num 24:15	4Q175 line 9	בבלעם	בנו בער	—	—

Biblical Passage	Pesharim, Other Commentaries, and Related Documents		MT	Other DSS	
Num 24:15	4Q175 line 10	שותם	שתם	—	
Num 24:16	4Q175 line 10	נאם	נאם	—	
Num 24:16	4Q175 line 10	שומע	שמע	—	
Num 24:16	4Q175 line 11	הכל	הכל	—	
Num 24:16	4Q175 line 11	ויגל	ויגל	—	
Num 24:16	4Q175 line 11	עי	עיני	—	
Num 24:17	4Q175 line 11	ורא	ורא	—	
Num 24:17	4Q175 line 11	אודנה	אודנה	—	
Num 24:17	4Q175 line 12	ורא	ורא	—	
Num 24:17	4Q175 line 12	מדרכיקו	מדרכק	—	
Num 24:17	4Q175 line 12a	דרקום	דרקו	—	
Num 24:17	4Q175 line 13	כו	כל	—	
Num 24:17	4Q175 line 13	ויררד	ויחד	—	
Num 24:17	4Q175 line 13	שוע	שע	—	
Deut 5:28	4Q175 line 1	שמעתה	שמעתי	מ̊עה[ ]	4Q37 3.13
Deut 5:28	4Q175 line 2	אליאה	אליך	—	
Deut 5:28	4Q175 line 2	כול	כל	כול	4Q37 3.14
Deut 5:29	4Q175 line 3	יתנ	יתן	—	
Deut 5:29	4Q175 line 3	והיה	והיה	—	
Deut 5:29	4Q175 line 3	ליראו	ליראה	ליראי[ ]	4Q37 4.1
				ל̊ר̊[ ]	4Q38 frg. 1 line 2
Deut 5:29	4Q175 line 3	אלי	אלי	[הת]אות	4Q37 4.1

Biblical Passage	Pesharim, Other Commentaries, and Related Documents	MT	Other DSS	
Deut 5:29	4Q175 line 3	ולשמרה	ולשמעה	[ ]לֹשׁמ[ ]	4Q37 4.1
Deut 5:29	4Q175 line 3	כול	כל	—	—
Deut 5:29	4Q175 line 4	כול	כל	—	—
Deut 5:29	4Q175 line 4	הימים	הימים	ם[ ]ֹ	4Q37 4.2
Deut 5:29	4Q175 line 4	לבניאן	לבניך	ולבנ	4Q37 4.2
Deut 5:29	4Q175 line 4	יטב	ייטב	ייט	4Q37 4.2
Deut 5:29	4Q175 line 4	לכיהם	לכם	לבניךֹ	4Q38 1.3
Deut 7:15	4Q177 frgs. 1-4,14,24,31 line 2	מֹמֹמֹם	בכם	בכם	5Q1 frg. 1 1.1
Deut 15:2	11Q13 2.3	כול	כל	לֹכֹ	4Q30 frgs. 26-27 line 3
Deut 15:2	11Q13 2.3	יד	יד	ידֹ	4Q30 frgs. 26-27 line 3
Deut 15:2	11Q13 2.4	[ל]אֹ[ל]	יהוה	—	—
Deut 18:18	4Q175 line 5	בני	נביא	—	—
Deut 18:18	4Q175 line 5	לאחיהם	להם	—	—
Deut 18:18	4Q175 line 5	אחריהם	אחיהם	—	—
Deut 18:18	4Q175 line 5	מבאתם	בקרב	—	4Q33 frgs. 10-12 line 1
Deut 18:18	4Q175 line 6	יוקם	יקם	[ ]לֹ	4Q33 frgs. 10-12 line 1
Deut 18:18	4Q175 line 6	ודבר	ודבר	ודבר	4Q33 frgs. 10-12 line 1
Deut 18:18	4Q175 line 6	אליהיא	אליהם	אליהם	4Q33 frgs. 10-12 line 1
Deut 18:18	4Q175 line 6	כול	כל	—	—
Deut 18:19	4Q175 line 7	לוא	לא	—	—
Deut 18:19	4Q175 line 7	אנכי	אנכי	[אֹנֹ	4Q33 frgs. 10-12 line 2
Deut 18:19	4Q175 line 7	אדרוש	אדרש	—	—

133

Biblical Passage	Pesharim, Other Commentaries, and Related Documents		MT	Other DSS	
Deut 33:8	4Q175 line 14	ואורי	ואוריך	—	—
Deut 33:8	4Q174 frgs. 6-7 line 3	ותל֯[י]תה	תלכדו	חו֯י֯ן[ ]	4Q45 frgs. 42-43 line 7
Deut 33:9	4Q175 line 15	התורה	האמרה		
Deut 33:9	4Q174 frgs. 6-7 line 3	[מכ]ר֯א֯	ראמכה		—
Deut 33:9	4Q175 line 15	ראו֯/ה			
Deut 33:9	4Q175 line 16	לו֯א֯תה/ר֯י֯ה֯	לא ראיתיו	ל א֯א֯ין [ ]	4Q35 frgs. 11-15 line 2
Deut 33:9	4Q175 line 16	א֯ל֯ו	א֯ל	א֯ל	4Q35 frgs. 11-15 line 3
Deut 33:9	4Q174 frgs. 6-7 line 4	כ֯י	כ	כי	4Q35 frgs. 11-15 line 3
Deut 33:9	4Q175 line 17	׳	׳		
Deut 33:9	4Q175 line 17	שמר	שמרו	שמר	4Q35 frgs. 11-15 line 3
Deut 33:9	4Q174 frgs. 6-7 line 4	[כמ]ת֯ה[אמ]ר	אמרתך	א֯מרתה	4Q35 frgs. 11-15 line 3
Deut 33:9	4Q175 line 17	ותורה אמר			
Deut 33:9	4Q174 frgs. 6-7 line 4	[ות]ה֯ל֯ל֯ו֯ה֯	הלכד֯ו	הלכד֯ו	4Q35 frgs. 11-15 line 3
Deut 33:9	4Q175 line 17	ותירה/ל֯ו			
Deut 33:9	4Q175 line 17	יצר֯ו	ינצרו	[ ]ל֯ו֯	4Q35 frgs. 11-15 line 3
Deut 33:10	4Q175 line 17a	וירא֯י	יורו	וירו	4Q35 frgs. 11-15 line 3
Deut 33:10	4Q175 line 18	וההורה	התורה		—
Deut 33:10	4Q175 line 18	ובלו֯/ש֯י	ישי֯מ֯ו	שמ[ ]	4Q35 frgs. 11-15 line 3
Deut 33:10	4Q174 frgs. 6-7 line 5	ובאמכ֯	באמכ	באמכ֯	4Q35 frgs. 11-15 line 3
Deut 33:10	4Q175 line 18	באמ			
Deut 33:10	4Q174 frgs. 6-7 line 5	וכליל֯	וכליל	ו֯כל֯י֯ל	4Q35 frgs. 11-15 line 4
Deut 33:10	4Q175 line 18	ע֗ל/כלי֗ל			

Biblical Passage	Pesharim, Other Commentaries, and Related Documents	MT	Other DSS	
Deut 33:10	4Q174 frgs. 6-7 line 5	מורתכה	מורתך	[מו]ר֯ת	4Q35 frgs. 11-15 line 4
Deut 33:11	4Q175 line 18	מורתכה			
Deut 33:11	4Q175 line 19	יפעל	ויפעל	ויפעל	4Q35 frgs. 11-15 line 4
Deut 33:11	4Q175 line 19	ידי	ידו	—	—
Deut 33:11	4Q175 line 19a	מבנים	מתנים	מ֯ן ו֯ק̇	4Q35 frgs. 11-15 line 4
Deut 33:11	4Q175 line 19	קמו	יקמו	—	—
Deut 33:11	4Q175 line 19	ומשנאיו	ומשנאיו	—	—
Deut 33:11	4Q175 line 20	בן	מן	]ק[	4Q35 frgs. 11-15 line 4
Deut 33:11	4Q174 frgs. 6-7 line 6	יקומ[ון]	יקומון	[יקומ]ן	4Q35 frgs. 11-15 line 4
Deut 33:11	4Q175 line 20	יקומי			
2Sam 7:10	4Q174 frgs. 1-2,21 1.1	י֯[סים]	יסים	—	—
2Sam 7:10	4Q174 frgs. 1-2,21 1.1	ל֯ע֯וד ח֯	רשע עוד	—	—
2Sam 7:10	4Q174 frgs. 1-2,21 1.1	כבאישונה	כבאשונה	—	—
2Sam 7:11	4Q174 frgs. 1-2,21 1.7	לכה	לך	—	—
2Sam 7:11	4Q174 frgs. 1-2,21 1.7	מכל	מכל	—	—
2Sam 7:11	4Q174 frgs. 1-2,21 1.7	והגיד לכה	והגיד לך	—	—
2Sam 7:11	4Q174 frgs. 1-2,21 1.10	לכה	לך	—	—
2Sam 7:11	4Q174 frgs. 1-2,21 1.10	בא	כבא	—	—
2Sam 7:11	4Q174 frgs. 1-2,21 1.10	לכה	לך	—	—
2Sam 7:11	4Q174 frgs. 1-2,21 1.10	לכה	יעשה	—	—
2Sam 7:12	4Q174 frgs. 1-2,21 1.10	והקימותי	והקימתי	—	—
2Sam 7:12	4Q174 frgs. 1-2,21 1.10	זרעך	זרעך	—	—

Biblical Passage	Pesharim, Other Commentaries, and Related Documents	MT	Other DSS
2Sam 7:12	4Q174 frgs. 1-2,21 1.10	אחריכה	אחריך	—
2Sam 7:13	4Q174 frgs. 1-2,21 1.10	והכינותי	וכננתי	—
2Sam 7:14	4Q174 frgs. 1-2,21 1.11	לוא	לו	—
Ps 1:1	4Q174 frgs. 1-2,21 1.14	מאשרי	אשרי	—
Ps 1:1	4Q174 frgs. 1-2,21 1.14	לוא	לא	—
Ps 2:1	4Q174 frgs. 1-2,21 1.18	גויֿם	גוים	—
Ps 2:1	4Q174 frgs. 1-2,21 1.18	ולאומֿים	ולאמים	—
Ps 2:2	4Q174 frgs. 1-2,21 1.18	יﾟחﾟ	יחד	—
Ps 6:2	4Q177 frgs. 12-13 1.4	באפֿכה	באפך	—
Ps 6:4	4Q177 frgs. 12-13 1.5	מאדה	מאד	—
Ps 6:4	4Q177 frgs. 12-13 1.5	ועתה	ואת	—
Ps 7:9	11Q13 2.11	אל	יהוה	—
Ps 11:1	4Q177 frgs. 5-6 line 7	לדויד	ליהוה	—
Ps 11:2	4Q177 frgs. 5-6 line 8	הﾟדﾟריֿ	כוננו	—
Ps 11:2	4Q177 frgs. 5-6 line 8	החם	חזק	—
Ps 13:2	4Q177 frgs. 7,9-11,20,26 line 8	פניכה	פניך	—
Ps 13:3	4Q177 frgs. 7,9-11,20,26 line 8	אלוהי	אלהיﾟ	—
Ps 13:5	4Q177 frgs. 7,9-11,20,26 line 11	אוי﾿ב	אי﾿	—
Ps 16:3	4Q177 frgs. 1-4,14,24,31 line 2	כול	כל	—
Ps 17:1	4Q177 frgs. 1-4,14,24,31 line 4	לֿ[תﾟפﾟלֿה]	תפלה	—
Ps 37:7	4Q171 frgs. 1-10 1.25	ודאל	אל	—
Ps 37:7	4Q171 frgs. 1-10 1.25	וﾟהﾟתﾟ	תתחר	—

Biblical Passage	Pesharim, Other Commentaries, and Related Documents	MT	Other DSS	
Ps 37:8	4Q171 frgs. 1-10 2.1	ויעזוב	ועזוב	— —
Ps 37:8	4Q171 frgs. 1-10 2.1	ואל	אל	— —
Ps 37:8	4Q171 frgs. 1-10 2.2	חרה	תתחר	— —
Ps 37:9	4Q171 frgs. 1-10 2.2	יכרתו	יכרתון	— —
Ps 37:9	4Q171 frgs. 1-10 2.4	וקוא]	וקוי	— —
Ps 37:9	4Q171 frgs. 1-10 2.4	ירשו	יירשו	— —
Ps 37:10	4Q171 frgs. 1-10 2.7	ואתבוננתה	והתבוננת	— —
Ps 37:11	4Q171 frgs. 1-10 2.9	ירש	יירשו	— —
Ps 37:11	4Q171 frgs. 1-10 2.9	חן	ח	— —
Ps 37:12	4Q171 frgs. 1-10 2.13	זומם	זמם	— —
Ps 37:12	4Q171 frgs. 1-10 2.13	חורק	חרק	— —
Ps 37:13	4Q171 frgs. 1-10 2.13	[אל] יושׁׁ	אדני	— —
Ps 37:13	4Q171 frgs. 1-10 2.14	כא	כי	— —
Ps 37:14	4Q171 frgs. 1-10 2.16	דרכו	דרכם	— —
Ps 37:14	4Q171 frgs. 1-10 2.16	ללו	להפיל	— —
Ps 37:14	4Q171 frgs. 1-10 2.17	טבוח	טבוח	— —
Ps 37:15	4Q171 frgs. 1-10 2.17	תשחתרין	מחיריהם	— —
Ps 37:17	4Q171 frgs. 1-10 2.24	[ה]בורד	וסומך	— —
Ps 37:19	4Q171 frgs. 1-10 2.27	יבש	יבשו	— —
Ps 37:19	4Q171 frgs. 1-10 3.2	עב	ושבעו	— —
Ps 37:20	4Q171 frgs. 1-10 3.3	יבדו	יאבדו	— —
Ps 37:20	4Q171 frgs. 1-10 3.5a	ואודבי	כאיב	— —

137

Biblical Passage	Pesharim, Other Commentaries, and Related Documents	MT	Other DSS
Ps 37:20	4Q171 frgs. 1-10 3.5a	מ̇ריב̇	כלים
Ps 37:20	4Q171 frgs. 1-10 3.7	מעשן	מעשן
Ps 37:20	4Q171 frgs. 1-10 3.7	כלו	כלו
Ps 37:21	4Q171 frgs. 1-10 3.8	ולוא	ולא
Ps 37:22	4Q171 frgs. 1-10 3.9	כמ[בׄ]רב[ו]	מברכיו
Ps 37:22	4Q171 frgs. 1-10 3.9	ומקללי̇ן	ומקלליו
Ps 37:22	4Q171 frgs. 1-10 3.11	ומ[קוללי]ו̇	ומקלליו
Ps 37:25	4Q171 frgs. 1-10 3.17	גם	גם
Ps 37:25	4Q171 frgs. 1-10 3.17	ולוא	ולא
Ps 37:30	4Q171 frgs. 1-10 4.3	החכ̇מ̊[ה]	החכמה
Ps 37:34	4Q171 frgs. 1-10 4.10	וישמ̇ר	ישמר
Ps 37:34	4Q171 frgs. 1-10 4.10	ומרומ̇מ̇כׄ[ה]	וירוממך
Ps 37:36	4Q171 frgs. 1-10 4.13	ואמ̇א̇[ל]	ואבקשהו
Ps 37:36	4Q171 frgs. 1-10 4.13	ולוא	ולא
Ps 37:38	4Q171 frgs. 1-10 4.17	פ̇ישׄעים	פשעים
Ps 37:38	4Q171 frgs. 1-10 4.18	יח̇ד	יחדו
Ps 37:38	4Q171 frgs. 1-10 4.18	וא̇[ח]ר̇יאׄת	אחרית
Ps 37:40	4Q171 frgs. 1-10 4.20	מלרׄעים	מרשעים
Ps 37:40	4Q171 frgs. 1-10 4.20	מ̊לׄעים̊	מרשעים
Ps 45:2	4Q171 frgs. 1-10 4.25	א[לו]מ̊	אמר
Ps 45:2	4Q171 frgs. 1-10 4.26	לש̇וני	לשוני
Ps 60:8	4Q171 frg. 13 line 4	אמדדה	אמדד

Biblical Passage	Pesharim, Other Commentaries, and Related Documents		MT	Other DSS	
Ps 68:13	1Q16 frg. 3 line 3	[ידו]דֿיֿ֯	ידדון	—	—
Ps 68:27	1Q16 frg. 8 line 2	א[לה]ים	אלהים	—	—
Ps 68:31	1Q16 frg. 9 line 2	בֿעֿרת	געׂר	—	—
Ps 82:1	11Q13 2.10	אלוהים	אלהים	אלוׄהים	Masle 2.4
Ps 82:1	11Q13 2.10	בקרב	בקרב	בקרב	Masle 2.4
Ps 82:1	11Q13 2.10	אלוהים	אלהים	אלוהים	Masle 2.4
Ps 82:1	11Q13 2.10	ישפט	ישפט	ישפוט	Masle 2.4
Ps 82:2	11Q13 2.11	תֿשׁפֿטֿו[ן]	תשפטו	תמשפט	Masle 2.5
Ps 82:2	11Q13 2.11	עולה	עול	עולה	Masle 2.5
Ps 129:8	4Q173 frg. 4 line 1	[ולוׄ]א	ולׄא	שלוׁאׄ	11Q5 5.8
Ps 129:8	4Q173 frg. 4 line 2	א[לי]כֿםׄ	אליכם	כמליׄא	11Q5 5.9
Isa 1:1	3Q4 line 1	ישעיה	ישעיהו	ישׁעׄיׄה/שׁ	1QIsa[a] 1.1
Isa 1:1	3Q4 line 1	[י]רׄושׄל[ים]	ירושלים	ירושׁלים	1QIsa[a] 1.1
Isa 1:1	3Q4 line 1	[בי]מי	בימי	בׄ/יׄמׄ/יׄ	1QIsa[a] 1.1
Isa 1:1	3Q4 line 1	[עוׄזי]	עזיהו	עוזיה	1QIsa[a] 1.1
Isa 1:1	3Q4 line 2	יֿותׄם	יותם	יותם	1QIsa[a] 1.2
Isa 1:1	3Q4 line 2	[חזׄקיה]יֿ֯	יחזקיהו	יחזקיהוׄ/	1QIsa[a] 1.2
Isa 1:2	3Q4 line 4	[אׄר]ץׄ	ארץ	הארץׄ	1QIsa[a] 1.2
Isa 5:5	4Q162 1.1	[הסׄר]	הסר	אׄסׄיׄר	1QIsa[a] 4.17
Isa 5:5	4Q162 1.1	[ויׄיׄ]	והיה	ויׄיׄה	1QIsa[a] 4.17
Isa 5:5	4Q162 1.1	[לׄבׄעׄר]	לבער	לבער	1QIsa[a] 4.17
Isa 5:5	4Q162 1.1	וׄהׄיׄ	והיה	ויׄהׄיׄה	1QIsa[a] 4.18

139

Biblical Passage	Pesharim, Other Commentaries, and Related Documents	MT	Other DSS
Isa 5:6	4Q162 1.2	[לוא]	לא	ולוא	1QIsa^a 4.18
Isa 5:11	4Q162 2.2	בבקר	בבקר	בקר	1QIsa^a 4.26
Isa 5:11	4Q162 2.2		מאחרי	מאחרי	1QIsa^a 4.26
Isa 5:11	4Q162 2.3	ידליקם	ידליקם	ידליקם	1QIsa^a 4.26
Isa 5:12	4Q162 2.3	והן	הן	—	—
Isa 5:12	4Q162 2.3	יין	ייי	ין[ ]	1QIsa^a 4.27
Isa 5:12	4Q162 2.3	כעל	כעל	כעלו	1QIsa^a 4.27
Isa 5:12	4Q162 2.4	יביטו	יביט	הביטו	1QIsa^a 4.27
Isa 5:12	4Q162 2.4	מעשיהו	מעשהו	ומעשיהו	1QIsa^a 4.27
Isa 5:12	4Q162 2.4	ידיו	ידיו	—	—
Isa 5:13	4Q162 2.5	הדמון	המונו	הדמונו	1QIsa^a 4.28
Isa 5:13	4Q162 2.5	אצי	אצה	—	—
Isa 5:14	4Q162 2.5	פיה	פה	פיה	1QIsa^a 4.29
Isa 5:14	4Q162 2.6	הדמונה	המונה	הדמונה	1QIsa^a 5.1
Isa 5:14	4Q162 2.6	ושאונה	ושאונו	ושאונה	1QIsa^a 5.1
Isa 5:14	4Q162 2.6	עליז	עלז	[עו]	1QIsa^a 5.1
Isa 5:14	4Q162 2.6	בה	בה	בה	1QIsa^a 5.1
Isa 5:24	4Q162 2.7	יהוה	יהוה צבאות	יהוה צבאות	1QIsa^a 5.11
Isa 5:25	4Q162 2.8	ידי	ידו	ידי	1QIsa^a 5.12
Isa 5:25	4Q162 2.9	בתחב	בחמתו	בחמתה	1QIsa^a 5.13
Isa 5:25	4Q162 2.9	בחצות	בחצות	בחצות	1QIsa^a 5.13
Isa 5:25	4Q162 2.9	בכל	בכל	בכל	1QIsa^a 5.13

Biblical Passage	Pesharim, Other Commentaries, and Related Documents	MT	Other DSS
Isa 5:25	4Q162 2.9	ואת	ואת	1QIsaᵃ 5.13
Isa 5:25	4Q162 2.9	לוא	לא	1QIsaᵃ 5.14
Isa 5:25	4Q162 2.10	[ידי]	ידי	1QIsaᵃ 5.14
Isa 8:7	4Q163 frg. 2 line 3	אליק	אליק	4Q59 frgs. 4-10 line 5
Isa 8:7	4Q163 frg. 2 line 3	[גו]יֿות	גדודיו	1QIsaᵃ 7.29
Isa 8:8	4Q163 frg. 2 line 4	יה[יה]	ויהי	1QIsaᵃ 8.1
Isa 8:8	4Q163 frg. 2 line 4	כבד	כבד	1QIsaᵃ 8.1
Isa 8:8	4Q163 frg. 2 line 4	אל[ד]רך	אלדרך	1QIsaᵃ 8.1
Isa 8:11	4Q174 frgs. 1-2,21 1.15	[הֿה]	הֿה	1QIsaᵃ 8.4
Isa 8:11	4Q174 frgs. 1-2,21 1.15	[הוֿ־ם]	למוקש	1QIsaᵃ 8.4
Isa 9:11	4Q163 frgs. 4,6-7 1.7	[נב]ל	נבל	1QIsaᵃ 8.30
Isa 9:11	4Q163 frgs. 4,6-7 1.8	[נב]ל	נבל	1QIsaᵃ 9.1
Isa 9:11	4Q163 frgs. 4,6-7 1.8	[את]	ואת	1QIsaᵃ 9.1; 4Q56 frg. 4 line 2
Isa 9:11	4Q163 frgs. 4,6-7 1.8	[לוא]	לא	1QIsaᵃ 9.1
Isa 9:13	4Q163 frgs. 4,6-7 1.9	ב[ואג]בה	ואגבה	1QIsaᵃ 9.3
Isa 9:13	4Q163 frgs. 4,6-7 1.9	םוֿי	יום	1QIsaᵃ 9.3
Isa 9:14	4Q163 frgs. 4,6-7 1.10	[ונשכ]ר	ונשכר	1QIsaᵃ 9.3
Isa 9:14	4Q163 frgs. 4,6-7 1.10	הֿוא	הוא	1QIsaᵃ 9.4
Isa 9:16	4Q163 frgs. 4,6-7 1.12	[ישמ]ח	ישמח	1QIsaᵃ 9.5
Isa 9:16	4Q163 frgs. 4,6-7 1.12	[ימר]	ירחם	1QIsaᵃ 9.6
Isa 9:16	4Q163 frgs. 4,6-7 1.12	אלמנ[תיו]	אלמנתיו	1QIsaᵃ 9.6

Biblical Passage	Pesharim, Other Commentaries, and Related Documents		MT	Other DSS	
Isa 9:16	4Q163 frgs. 4,6-7 1.12	לוא	לֹא	לוא	1QIsaᵃ 9.6
Isa 9:16	4Q163 frgs. 4,6-7 1.13	[כיל]ו	כלו	כלו	1QIsaᵃ 9.6
Isa 9:16	4Q163 frgs. 4,6-7 1.13	[יד]ו	ידו	ידי	1QIsaᵃ 9.7
Isa 9:16	4Q163 frgs. 4,6-7 1.13	[כימ]ו	כמו	כמה	1QIsaᵃ 9.7
Isa 9:16	4Q163 frgs. 4,6-7 1.13	ז̇א[ות]	זאת	זאות	1QIsaᵃ 9.7
Isa 9:16	4Q163 frgs. 4,6-7 1.14	[ידו]	ידו	יד׳	1QIsaᵃ 9.7
Isa 9:17	4Q163 frgs. 4,6-7 1.17	נ̇צׁהת	נצרה	וחזה	1QIsaᵃ 9.8
Isa 9:17	4Q163 frgs. 4,6-7 1.18	[גאו]ת	גאות	גיאות	1QIsaᵃ 9.9
Isa 9:18	4Q163 frgs. 4,6-7 1.18	עמ[ה]	עתם	עתם	1QIsaᵃ 9.9
Isa 9:18	4Q163 frgs. 4,6-7 1.19	[איש]	איש	איש	1QIsaᵃ 9.9
Isa 9:18	4Q163 frgs. 4,6-7 1.19	[ידיו]	אליו	ידיו	1QIsaᵃ 9.9
Isa 9:19	4Q163 frgs. 4,6-7 1.20	[על]	על	יעו	1QIsaᵃ 9.11
Isa 9:19	4Q163 frgs. 4,6-7 1.21	[ישמא]ו[ל]	שמאל	שמאול	1QIsaᵃ 9.11
Isa 9:20	4Q163 frgs. 4,6-7 1.22	י̇חד	יחדו	יחדיו	1QIsaᵃ 9.12
Isa 9:20	4Q163 frgs. 4,6-7 1.22	[יהוד]ה	יהודה	יהודה	1QIsaᵃ 9.12
Isa 10:12	4Q163 frgs. 6-7 2.1	כ̇יא	כי	כיא	1QIsaᵃ 9.25
Isa 10:12	4Q163 frgs. 6-7 2.1	[ומעשהו]	מעשהו	מעשיהו	1QIsaᵃ 9.26
Isa 10:13	4Q163 frgs. 6-7 2.2	[אמר]	אמר	יאמר	1QIsaᵃ 9.27
Isa 10:20	4Q163 frgs. 6-7 2.11	אהרה	ההוא	ההיא	1QIsaᵃ 10.7
Isa 10:20	4Q163 frgs. 6-7 2.12	[ע]ל	על	אל	1QIsaᵃ 10.8
Isa 10:22	4Q163 frgs. 6-7 2.14	מ	כי	כם	1QIsaᵃ 10.8
Isa 10:22	4Q161 frgs. 2-6 2.6	ה̇י[ה]	יהיה	יהיה	1QIsaᵃ 10.9

Biblical Passage	Pesharim, Other Commentaries, and Related Documents	MT	Other DSS	
Isa 10:22	4Q163 frgs. 6-7 2.14	צבה	צבא	צבה	1QIsa^a 10.9
Isa 10:22	4Q161 frgs. 2-6 2.7	שוטף	שוטף	שוטף	1QIsa^a 10.9
Isa 10:24	4Q161 frgs. 2-6 2.11	במ[שב]ב	במבמ	מכשבה	1QIsa^a 10.11
Isa 10:24	4Q161 frgs. 2-6 2.11	[ובמטה]	ובמטה	ובמה	1QIsa^a 10.11
				[ובמ]ה[ ]	4Q57 frgs. 3-5, 50 line 3
Isa 10:26	4Q161 frgs. 2-6 2.13	[ר]ע[י]ו	רעיהו	רעיו	1QIsa^a 10.12
Isa 10:28	4Q161 frgs. 2-6 2.21	אל	על	על	1QIsa^a 10.15
				אל	4Q57 frgs. 3-5, 50 line 6
Isa 10:28	4Q161 frgs. 2-6 2.21	עיתה	עית	עיה/עיו	1QIsa^a 10.15
				עיוה	4Q57 frgs. 3-5, 50 line 6
Isa 10:29	4Q161 frgs. 2-6 2.22	[עבר]	עברו	עבר	1QIsa^a 10.15
Isa 10:29	4Q161 frgs. 2-6 2.22	מעברתה	מעברה	מעברתה	1QIsa^a 10.15
Isa 10:29	4Q161 frgs. 2-6 2.22	לנו	לו	לו	1QIsa^a 10.15
Isa 10:29	4Q161 frgs. 2-6 2.22	ה[חת]ה	חתתה	חתתה	1QIsa^a 10.15
Isa 10:30	4Q161 frgs. 2-6 2.23	הקליבי	הקליב	הקיב	1QIsa^a 10.16
Isa 10:30	4Q161 frgs. 2-6 2.23	[ש]י[ל]	לישה	ליש	1QIsa^a 10.16
Isa 10:32	4Q161 frgs. 2-6 2.25	[היקמ]	הקם	היה	1QIsa^a 10.17
Isa 10:32	4Q161 frgs. 2-6 2.25	יד	יד	ידו	1QIsa^a 10.17
Isa 10:32	4Q161 frgs. 2-6 2.25	בה	בת	בה	1QIsa^a 10.17
Isa 10:32	4Q161 frgs. 2-6 2.25	שרירים	םלשוריי	שרירים	1QIsa^a 10.17
Isa 10:34	4Q161 frgs. 8-10 3.6	כ[ב]וב	כבב	כבב	1QIsa^a 10.19
Isa 10:34	4Q161 frgs. 8-10 3.6	והלבנון	והלבנון	והלבנון	1QIsa^a 10.19

Biblical Passage	Pesharim, Other Commentaries, and Related Documents	MT	Other DSS
Isa 10:34	4Q161 frgs. 8-10 3.10	ו/ויקב]	ויקב	ויקף	1QIsaᵃ 10.19
Isa 10:34	4Q161 frgs. 8-10 3.10	סוכב	סובכ	סבכי	1QIsaᵃ 10.19
Isa 10:34	4Q161 frgs. 8-10 3.11	הלבנ	הלבנון	הלבנון	1QIsaᵃ 10.19
Isa 11:1	4Q161 frgs. 8-10 3.15	[ואצ]א ל[...]	מישרשיו	מישרשיו	1QIsaᵃ 10.20
Isa 11:2	4Q161 frgs. 8-10 3.15	עלו	עליו	עלי[ ]	1QIsaᵃ 10.20
Isa 11:2	4Q161 frgs. 8-10 3.16	החכמה	החכמה	החכמה	1QIsaᵃ 10.20
Isa 11:3	4Q161 frgs. 8-10 3.17	[וי]רֶ[יא	עיניו	עניו	1QIsaᵃ 10.21
Isa 11:3	4Q161 frgs. 8-10 3.18	[יורא]	אזניו	אזנו	1QIsaᵃ 10.22
Isa 11:4	4Q161 frgs. 8-10 3.19	[ארץ]	ארץ	הארץ	1QIsaᵃ 10.22
Isa 11:4	4Q161 frgs. 8-10 3.19	[ארץ]	ארץ	הארץ	1QIsaᵃ 10.23
Isa 11:4	4Q161 frgs. 8-10 3.20	[יביה]	יביה	הכבי	1QIsaᵃ 10.23
Isa 11:5	4Q161 frgs. 8-10 3.20	[מותנ]אֶ֯יֶ	מותניאתו	האמותני	1QIsaᵃ 10.23
Isa 11:11	4Q165 frg. 11 line 3	ישאָ	שׁעיו	שעור	1QIsaᵃ 10.29
Isa 11:12	4Q165 frg. 11 line 5	[לגוי]ם]	לגוים	לגואים	1QIsaᵃ 11.1
Isa 14:8	4Q163 frgs. 8-10 line 2	לכב[?]	לך	לו	1QIsaᵃ 12.9
Isa 14:8	4Q163 frgs. 8-10 line 2	לכבו	לכבוה	הלכבוה	1QIsaᵃ 12.9
Isa 14:8	4Q163 frgs. 8-10 line 2	[שכבת]	שכבת	שחתה	1QIsaᵃ 12.9
Isa 14:8	4Q163 frgs. 8-10 line 3	[לוא]	לא	הלוא	1QIsaᵃ 12.10
Isa 14:8	4Q163 frgs. 8-10 line 3	יכ'לע	עליכה	הליכה	1QIsaᵃ 12.10
Isa 14:26	4Q163 frgs. 8-10 line 5	הארת	הזאת	החוה	1QIsaᵃ 12.28
Isa 14:27	4Q163 frgs. 8-10 line 6	[יי''ז]	ידיו	ידיהו	1QIsaᵃ 12.29
Isa 14:29	4Q163 frgs. 8-10 line 12	כ'ה	כי	כ	1QIsaᵃ 13.1

144

Biblical Passage	Pesharim, Other Commentaries, and Related Documents	MT	Other DSS	
Isa 14:29	[מכה]	מכך	מכבה	1QIsaᵃ 13.1
Isa 14:30	ה֯רי֯ג֯	יהרג	אהריג	1QIsaᵃ 13.3
Isa 15:4	[וחלצי]	חלצי	חלצו	1QIsaᵃ 13.11
Isa 15:4	[חצרי]	חצרי	צרי	1QIsaᵃ 13.11
Isa 15:5	[חללי]	חללו	חללה	1QIsaᵃ 13.11
Isa 15:5	[אצעד]	אצר	אצרו	1QIsaᵃ 13.11
Isa 15:5	[היליל]	יחליה	חיהליה	1QIsaᵃ 13.12
Isa 15:5	[שבר]	שבר	שבכי	1QIsaᵃ 13.12
Isa 19:9	ם֯ראואי	ואראים	םיראואי	1QIsaᵃ 15.13
Isa 19:9	[חיה]	חיה	חיח	1QIsaᵃ 15.13
Isa 19:10	[שחתותש]	שחתות	ה֯תחתוש	1QIsaᵃ 15.13
Isa 19:11	[מבי]	מבי	מבעה	1QIsaᵃ 15.14
Isa 19:11	[מכבכם]	מכבכם	מכבכם	1QIsaᵃ 15.15
Isa 19:11	בני	בן	בן	4Q56 frgs. 10-13 line 17
Isa 19:12	[הכמיהם]	החכמי	הן	1QIsaᵃ 15.15
Isa 19:12	ה֯לך	לך	המבי	1QIsaᵃ 15.16
Isa 21:10	[גברג]	גברג	לך	1QIsaᵃ 15.16
Isa 21:10	ה[לכב]	להב	גברי	1QIsaᵃ 16.26
Isa 21:11	[מלכיך]2	מלכיך	לכם	1QIsaᵃ 16.27
Isa 21:12	[מבערה]	מבערה	מכיכ	1QIsaᵃ 16.28
Isa 21:12	[בעיר]	בעיר	מבעה	1QIsaᵃ 16.29
Isa 21:12	[בעיר]	בעיר	בעיר	1QIsaᵃ 16.29

Biblical Passage	Pesharim, Other Commentaries, and Related Documents	MT	Other DSS
Isa 21:13	[דודים]	דודים	דודים	1QIsaᵃ 16.30
Isa 21:14	[התיו]	התיו	האתיו	1QIsaᵃ 16.31
Isa 21:14	[קדמהו]	קדמהו	קדמו	1QIsaᵃ 16.31
Isa 21:15	חרבות	חרבה	חרבוה/	1QIsaᵃ 16.32
Isa 21:15	נדד	נדדו	נדד	1QIsaᵃ 16.32
Isa 21:15	נטשה	נטשה	נטשה/	1QIsaᵃ 16.32
Isa 21:15	[כבד]	כבד	כבד	1QIsaᵃ 17.1
Isa 22:13	הנה̊	הנה	הנה	1QIsaᵃ 17.18
				1Q8 frg. 5 line 3
Isa 22:13	ששומ	ששון	ששומ	1QIsaᵃ 17.18
Isa 22:13	צאן	צאן	צאן	1QIsaᵃ 17.18
Isa 29:10	כל[עינ]ם	כליכם	כלעינם	1QIsaᵃ 23.18
Isa 29:10	כנבי̊אמ[ה]	כנביאם	כנביאמה	1QIsaᵃ 23.18
Isa 29:11	היה	היה	היתה	1QIsaᵃ 23.19
Isa 29:11	לכמה	לכם	לכמ	1QIsaᵃ 23.19
Isa 29:11	הסתר	הספר	הספר/	1QIsaᵃ 23.20
Isa 29:11	[אמר]	אמר	יאמרו	1QIsaᵃ 23.20
Isa 29:11	כ̊י̊[א]	כי	כי	1QIsaᵃ 23.20
Isa 29:12	הני̊	הנה	הנה	1QIsaᵃ 23.20
Isa 29:15	[ויהיו]	ויהיו	ויהיו	1QIsaᵃ 23.26
Isa 29:16	[הפככמה]	הפככם	כמ וכן	1QIsaᵃ 23.26
Isa 29:16	[כמו]	כמו	כמו	1QIsaᵃ 23.26

Biblical Passage	Pesharim, Other Commentaries, and Related Documents	MT	Other DSS
Isa 29:18	לֹ֯אֿל֯יֹ	וֹאָל֯יֿ	וֹלאליהֿ֯	1QIsaᵃ 23.29
Isa 29:20	[לץ]	לץ	ליץ	1QIsaᵃ 23.31
Isa 29:23	[ו]קדיש[ו]°	ויקדישו	יקידשו	1QIsaᵃ 24.4
Isa 30:1	[נאם]	נאם	נואם	1QIsaᵃ 24.6
Isa 30:1	[מני]	מני	ממני	1QIsaᵃ 24.6
Isa 30:3	[לכלמה]	לכלמה	לכלמה	1QIsaᵃ 24.9
Isa 30:4	[היו]	היו	היו	1QIsaᵃ 24.9
Isa 30:5	[כ]ל	כל	כל	1QIsaᵃ 24.9
Isa 30:5	[הב]אֿ֯ש	הבאיש	באש	1QIsaᵃ 24.10
Isa 30:5	[לעז]יֿ֯ר	לעזיר	לעזיר	1QIsaᵃ 24.10
Isa 30:5	[להועי]ל	להועיל	להועיל	1QIsaᵃ 24.10
Isa 30:5	קדוש	קדוש	קדוש	1QIsaᵃ 24.10
Isa 30:15	נואנו	המנוחה	ובהנחת	1QIsaᵃ 24.25
Isa 30:15	לכה	אבית	תאבו	1QIsaᵃ 24.25
Isa 30:15	בסוסים	סום	בהכם	1QIsaᵃ 24.26
Isa 30:16	לכן	על	ועל	1QIsaᵃ 24.26
Isa 30:16	רדפיכמה	רדפיכם	רדפיכמ	1QIsaᵃ 24.27
Isa 30:17	מגער	מגערת	מגערת	1QIsaᵃ 24.27
Isa 30:17	ותן	תנוסו	תנוסו	1QIsaᵃ 24.28
Isa 30:17	תנבה	תנבאת	תנבאת	1QIsaᵃ 24.28
Isa 30:18	לכן	ולכן	ולכן	1QIsaᵃ 24.28

Biblical Passage	Pesharim, Other Commentaries, and Related Documents		MT	Other DSS	
Isa 30:18	4Q163 frg. 23 2.8	אדור	יהוה	יהוה	1QIsaᵃ 24.29
Isa 30:18	4Q163 frg. 23 2.8	להֿ[כנ]מֿה	לחככם	לחככם	1QIsaᵃ 24.29
Isa 30:18	4Q163 frg. 23 2.9	לרחמכמה	לרחמכם	לרחמכם	1QIsaᵃ 24.29
Isa 30:19	4Q163 frg. 23 2.15	[ים]לשור[...]	בירושלים	לירושלי[ב]	1QIsaᵃ 24.30
Isa 30:19	4Q163 frg. 23 2.15	[תבכה]	תבכה	תבכה	1QIsaᵃ 24.31
Isa 30:19	4Q163 frg. 23 2.15	[יחנך]	יחן	יחנך	1QIsaᵃ 24.31
Isa 30:19	4Q163 frg. 23 2.16	יעקדֿ	כעתו	יעקד	1QIsaᵃ 24.31
Isa 30:20	4Q163 frg. 23 2.16	[לכם]	לכם	לכבד	1QIsaᵃ 25.1
Isa 30:20	4Q163 frg. 23 2.17	יכבה	יכבה	יכבה	1QIsaᵃ 25.1
Isa 30:20	4Q163 frg. 23 2.17	[מו]רֿיכֿה	מוריך	מוראיך	1QIsaᵃ 25.1
Isa 30:21	4Q163 frg. 23 2.18	ואזנכה	ואזניך	ואזניכה	1QIsaᵃ 25.2
Isa 30:21	4Q163 frg. 23 2.19	מימ[ינ]	תאמינו	תחאמינו	1QIsaᵃ 25.3
Isa 30:23	4Q163 frg. 22 line 4	לחם	לחם	לחמ	1QIsaᵃ 25.5
Isa 31:1	4Q163 frg. 25 line 5	[רכב]	רכב	רכב	1QIsaᵃ 25.24
Isa 31:1	4Q163 frg. 25 line 6	[מאד]	מאד	מאדה	1QIsaᵃ 25.24
Isa 31:1	4Q163 frg. 25 line 6	[על]	על	אל	1QIsaᵃ 25.24
Isa 32:5	4Q165 frg. 6 line 2	[יקר]א	יקרא	יקראי	1QIsaᵃ 26.13
Isa 32:5	4Q165 frg. 6 line 3	יאמר	יאמר	יאמרו	1QIsaᵃ 26.14
Isa 32:6	4Q165 frg. 6 line 3	[ישע]ה	יעשה	נעשה	1QIsaᵃ 26.14
Isa 32:6	4Q165 frg. 6 line 4	[הו]נ̊חל̊	לחניף	לחניף	1QIsaᵃ 26.15
Isa 32:7	4Q165 frg. 6 line 5	[וכלי]	וכלי	וכלי	1QIsaᵃ 26.16
Isa 32:7	4Q177 frgs. 5-6 line 6	[וֿהוֿא]	הוא	אוהי	1QIsaᵃ 26.16

148

Biblical Passage	Pesharim, Other Commentaries, and Related Documents	MT	Other DSS
Isa 32:7	4Q165 frg. 6 line 6	[אכי]ר	אכיר	אכירים	1QIsaᵃ 26.17
Isa 37:30	4Q177 frgs. 5-6 line 2	אכול	אכול	אכלי	1QIsaᵃ 31.8
Isa 37:30	4Q177 frgs. 5-6 line 2	[מ]פש	מפס	מפס	1QIsaᵃ 31.9
Isa 40:1	4Q176 frgs. 1-2 1.5	יאמר	אמר	יאמר	1QIsaᵃ 32.29
Isa 40:1	4Q176 frgs. 1-2 1.5	אלהיכם	אלהיכם	אלהיכמה	1QIsaᵃ 32.29
Isa 40:2	4Q176 frgs. 1-2 1.5	ירושלים	ירושלם	ירושלים	1QIsaᵃ 32.29
			מלאה	מלאתה	4Q56 frgs. 24-25 line 14
Isa 40:2	4Q176 frgs. 1-2 1.6	קרא	קראו	קרא	1QIsaᵃ 33.2
Isa 40:3	4Q176 frgs. 1-2 1.6	קרה	קרא	קרא	1QIsaᵃ 33.2
Isa 40:3	4Q176 frgs. 1-2 1.7	שיר	שיר	ישר	1QIsaᵃ 33.2
			שיר	שיר	4Q56 frgs. 24-25 line 16a
Isa 40:12	4Q165 frgs. 1-2 line 3	[מי]	מי	מי	1QIsaᵃ 33.12
Isa 40:12	4Q165 frgs. 1-2 line 3	[מים]	מים	מים	1QIsaᵃ 33.12
Isa 40:12	4Q165 frgs. 1-2 line 4	[בזר]ת	בזרת	בזרת	1QIsaᵃ 33.12
Isa 40:12	4Q165 frgs. 1-2 line 4	שלש	שלש	בשליש	1QIsaᵃ 33.12
Isa 40:12	4Q165 frgs. 1-2 line 4	[ושק]ל	ושקל	ושקל	1QIsaᵃ 33.12
Isa 40:12	4Q165 frgs. 1-2 line 4	[במאז]נים	במאזנים	במאזנים	1QIsaᵃ 33.13
Isa 41:9	4Q176 frgs. 1-2 1.10	[מקצות]יה	מקצותיה	מקצותיכה	1QIsaᵃ 34.12
Isa 41:9	4Q176 frgs. 1-2 1.11	[מאצי]ליה	מאציליה	מאציליכה	1QIsaᵃ 34.13
Isa 43:1	4Q176 frg. 3 line 1	כ[ה]	כה	כוה	1QIsaᵃ 36.9
Isa 43:4	4Q176 frgs. 4-5 line 1	אדם	אדם	אדם/	1QIsaᵃ 36.13
Isa 49:13	4Q176 frgs. 1-2 2.2	ופצחו	ופצחו	יפצחו	1QIsaᵃ 41.12

Biblical Passage	Pesharim, Other Commentaries, and Related Documents	MT	Other DSS
Isa 49:13	4Q176 frgs. 1-2 2.2 — נהם	נחם	מנחם — 1QIsaª 41.12
Isa 49:13	4Q176 frgs. 1-2 2.2 — אלֹ[ה]ים	יהוה	יהוה — 1QIsaª 41.12
			יהוה — 4Q58 frgs. 6-10 line 23
Isa 49:16	4Q176 frgs. 1-2 2.5 — חֹוֹמֹתֹיֹכֹי	חומתיך	חומותיך — 1QIsaª 41.15
Isa 52:1	4Q176 frgs. 8-11 line 2 — מלבושי[כי]	בגדיך	מלבושיך — 1QIsaª 43.15
Isa 52:2	4Q176 frgs. 8-11 line 3 — שֹבֹי	שבי	שבי — 1QIsaª 43.16
Isa 52:2	4Q176 frgs. 8-11 line 3 — יושבי	יושבי	יושבי — 1QIsaª 43.16
Isa 52:2	4Q176 frgs. 8-11 line 3 — התפתחה	התפתחה	התפתחה — 1QIsaª 43.16
Isa 52:7	11Q13 2.16 — יהוה	יהוה	יהוה — 1QIsaª 43.22
Isa 52:7	11Q13 2.16 — אל[א]	אל	אלוא — 1QIsaª 43.23
Isa 52:7	11Q13 2.16 — אלוהי	אלהיך	אלוהיך — 1QIsaª 43.23
Isa 54:4	4Q176 frgs. 8-11 line 6 — ת[עלוב]י	תעלובי	תעלובי — 1QIsaª 44.28
Isa 54:4	4Q176 frgs. 8-11 line 6 — אלכלמה	תכלמי	אלכלמה — 1QIsaª 44.28
Isa 54:5	4Q176 frgs. 8-11 line 6 — לבעלכה	לבעלך	לבעלכי — 1QIsaª 45.1
Isa 54:5	4Q176 frgs. 8-11 line 7 — כי גאלכי	כי גאלך	כיא באלה — 1QIsaª 45.1
Isa 54:7	4Q176 frgs. 8-11 line 9 — קנמכה	קטן	גואלכי — 1QIsaª 45.4
Isa 54:8		קטן	קֹטֹן — 4Q57 frgs. 41-42 line 1
Isa 54:8	4Q176 frgs. 8-11 line 10 — נחמתי	הסתרתי	נחמתי — 1QIsaª 45.5
Isa 54:8			נחמתי — 4Q57 frgs. 41-42 line 2
Isa 54:9	4Q176 frgs. 8-11 line 10 — גאלי	גאל	גואלכי — 1QIsaª 45.5
Isa 54:9	4Q176 frgs. 8-11 line 10 — כמי	כי מי	מבלי — 1QIsaª 45.6
Isa 54:9	4Q176 frgs. 8-11 line 11 — על אלה	על הארץ	על הארץ — 1QIsaª 45.6-7

Biblical Passage	Pesharim, Other Commentaries, and Related Documents	MT	Other DSS	
Isa 54:10	4Q176 frgs. 8-11 line 12	החמתבמתה	מהבמתתה	החמתבמתה	1QIsaᵃ 45.8
Isa 54:10	4Q176 frgs. 8-11 line 12	מבאתי׳	מבאתך	מבאתי׳	1QIsaᵃ 45.8
Isa 54:11	4Q164 frg. 1 line 1	יסוֹדתיך	יסודתיך	איסודתי/החד׳	1QIsaᵃ 45.10
Isa 54:12	4Q164 frg. 1 line 6	[אקדח]	אקדח	אקדוח	1QIsaᵃ 45.11
Isa 65:22	4Q174 frg. 15 line 2	[ועץ]	עץ	עץ	1QIsaᵃ 53.5
Isa 65:22	4Q174 frg. 15 line 2	עמי	עמי	עמיא	1QIsaᵃ 53.5
Isa 65:22	4Q174 frg. 15 line 2	[ידיהם]	ידיהם	ידיהם׳	1QIsaᵃ 53.5
Isa 65:23	4Q174 frg. 15 line 3	[יגיעו]	יגיעו	גדה	1QIsaᵃ 53.6
Jer 5:7	4Q182 frg. 1 line 5	אَלָֹ[כَ]ה	לכבה	—	—
Ezek 25:8	4Q177 frgs. 7,9-11,20,26 line 14	מ[ו]אב	מואב	—	—
Ezek 25:8	4Q177 frgs. 7,9-11,20,26 line 14	[א]לוֹ	הלוא	—	—
Ezek 37:23	4Q174 frgs. 1-2,21 1.16	בכל[ו]לֶ[ותיהם]	בכל מושבותיהם	—	—
Ezek 37:23	4Q174 frgs. 1-2,21 1.17	יושיעי	יושיע	—	—
Dan 11:32	4Q174 frgs. 1 and 3 2.4a	אלוה	אלהי	—	—
Dan 11:32	4Q174 frgs. 1 and 3 2.4a	יחזקו	יחזק	—	—
Dan 11:32	4Q174 frgs. 1 and 4 2.4a	וֹ[עשו]	ועשו	—	—
Hos 2:8	4Q166 1.7	[גדרה]	גדרה	—	—
Hos 2:9	4Q166 1.15	[ואחר]	ואחר	—	—
Hos 2:10	4Q166 2.1	אנכי	אנכי	—	—
Hos 2:11	4Q166 2.9	עשיתי	עשיתי	—	—
Hos 2:11	4Q166 2.9	כלמכסה	להכסות	—	—
Hos 2:12	4Q166 2.10	נגליתי	נגליתה	—	—

Biblical Passage	Pesharim, Other Commentaries, and Related Documents	MT	Other DSS
Hos 2:13	מועדה	מועדה	—
Hos 2:14	ושמתיה	ושמתי	—
Hos 2:14	אתנם	אתנה	—
Hos 2:14	הם	המה	—
Hos 5:14	אׄני	אני	—
Hos 6:9	כמהם	כמחכי	—
Hos 8:6	שׄ[בב]יׄם	שבבים	—
Hos 8:6	היה	יהי	—
Hos 8:7	סותמׄ	סותם	—
Hos 8:7	[ו]גׄערתיׄ	וגערתה	—
Amos 9:11	יׄקׄיׄמׄהׄ	אקים	אקים · Mur 88 8.26
Amos 9:11	סוכה	סכה	—
Amos 9:11	הברכה	הברכה	—
Mic 1:3	[א]ׄרׄ[ץ]	ארץ	אׄריׄ · Mur 88 11.38
Mic 1:5	שד	בני	כׄלׄ · Mur 88 12.1
Mic 1:6	שדה	השדה	השדה · Mur 88 12.2
Mic 4:8	סׄ[ל]ׄ[שׄ]יׄרׄי	לשעיר	—
Mic 4:9	הקרׄ[ח]ׄ[ה]	תקרחי	—
Mic 6:16	במׄצׄריהׄבם	במצרימה	—
Nah 1:4	לׄגׄבׄר	לגבר	לׄגׄבׄר]ו[· Mur 88 16.12
Nah 1:5	[ה]ׄרׄיׄם	הרים	הׄהׄרים · Mur 88 16.12
Nah 1:5	[ו]ׄהבׄקׄ[ע]ׄו	תבקע	—

152

Biblical Passage	Pesharim, Other Commentaries, and Related Documents	MT	Other DSS	
Nah 2:11	4Q177 frgs. 1-4,14,24,31 line 3	ופק	ופק	[ ]ֿבֿק	Mur 88 16.37
Nah 2:11	4Q177 frgs. 1-4,14,24,31 line 3	בכל	בכל	—	
Nah 2:12	4Q169 frgs. 3-4 1.1	איה	איה	אריה	Mur 88 16.39
Nah 2:12	4Q169 frgs. 3-4 1.1	לביא	לבא	לבא[ ] לֿ	Mur 88 16.39
Nah 2:13	4Q169 frgs. 3-4 1.4	אי	אריה	אריה	Mur 88 17.1
Nah 2:13	4Q169 frgs. 3-4 1.4	גורה	גורה	גורותיו	Mur 88 17.1
Nah 2:13	4Q169 frgs. 3-4 1.4	ללביאיו	ללבאתיו	ללבאתיו	Mur 88 17.1
Nah 2:13	4Q169 frgs. 3-4 1.6	חורה	חורה	חוֿרֿ	Mur 88 17.1
Nah 2:13	4Q169 frgs. 3-4 1.6	מענתו	מענתו	מענתו	Mur 88 17.2
Nah 2:14	4Q169 frgs. 3-4 1.9	רכבכה	רכבה	רכבה	Mur 88 17.3
Nah 2:14	4Q169 frgs. 3-4 1.9	וכפי[ר]	וכפירי	וֿכֿ[ ]ֿבֿי	Mur 88 17.3
Nah 3:1	4Q169 frgs. 3-4 2.1	טרפ[ה]	טרף	טרף	Mur 88 17.6
Nah 3:1	4Q169 frgs. 3-4 2.3	ימיש	ימיש	ימיש	Mur 88 17.6
Nah 3:2	4Q169 frgs. 3-4 2.3	וקול	קול	—	
Nah 3:3	4Q169 frgs. 3-4 2.3	ולהב	להב	[ ]ֿלֿ	Mur 88 17.8
Nah 3:3	4Q169 frgs. 3-4 2.4	וכבד	וכבד	—	
Nah 3:3	4Q169 frgs. 3-4 2.4	קצ	קצה	הֿ קֿצֿ	Mur 88 17.9
Nah 3:3	4Q169 frgs. 3-4 2.4	בגויה	בגויה	—	
Nah 3:3	4Q169 frgs. 3-4 2.4	גליהם	מרב	גליהם	Mur 88 17.9
Nah 3:4	4Q169 frgs. 3-4 2.7	המכמכה	מכשפה	—	
Nah 3:4	4Q169 frgs. 3-4 2.7	ממכרת	מברות	מֿמֿכֿרֿת	Mur 88 17.10
Nah 3:5	4Q169 frgs. 3-4 2.10	וגליתי	וגליתי	וֿגֿליתי	Mur 88 17.11

153

Biblical Passage	Pesharim, Other Commentaries, and Related Documents	MT	Other DSS	
Nah 3:5	הֿ[וא]ֿרֿהֿ	והראיֿ	והראיֿ	Mur 88 17.12
Nah 3:6	כאלוֿח	אלֿכ	—	—
Nah 3:7	יֿדֿוֿדֿ	יֿדֿוֿד	—	Mur 88 17.14
Nah 3:7	ואבמֿ	ואבֿמ	שאבֿ°	Mur 88 17.14
Nah 3:7	שדֿדֿה	שֿדֿדֿה	שׁדדֿה	Mur 88 17.14
Nah 3:7	אבקשׁ	אבקׁשׁ	—	—
Nah 3:7	מבֿק°סֿ°ֿ	מבקׁסֿ	—	—
Nah 3:8	כֿיֿ אֿ[ב°][ֿן]	מבֿ אֿבֿא	[מֿ]אֿ[אֿבֿ]ֿן[ ]	Mur 88 17.15
Nah 3:8	הֿלֿה	הֿלֿ	הֿלֿ	Mur 88 17.16
Nah 3:8	ובֿים	מֿים	מֿים	Mur 88 17.16
Nah 3:8	חומֿ(ת)ֿה	חומֿתֿה	חומֿתֿה	Mur 88 17.16
Nah 3:9	מֿ°צֿרֿים	מֿצֿרֿים	—	—
Nah 3:9	[לֿיֿם°מֿ]ֿ°יֿ	ימֿ°לֿים	ימֿ°לֿים	Mur 88 17.17
Nah 3:10	הֿלֿכה	לֿלֿה	[לֿלֿ]	Mur 88 17.17
Nah 3:10	עֿ°לֿ°לֿ°יֿה	עֿלֿ°לֿיֿה	עֿלֿלֿיֿה	Mur 88 17.18
Nah 3:10	יֿדֿיֿ	יֿדֿ	—	—
Nah 3:11	הֿלֿה	הֿלֿ	הֿ°לֿ°°ֿ	Mur 88 17.19
Hab 1:4	הֿמֿשׁפֿט	משׁפֿט	—	—
Hab 1:6	הֿלֿאֿוֿמֿים	המֿרֿתֿים	םֿ°תֿ°לֿאֿוֿ	Mur 88 18.4
Hab 1:8	וֿקֿלֿו	וקֿלֿו	יֿקֿלֿו	Mur 88 18.6
Hab 1:8	סֿוֿסֿו	סֿוֿסֿו	סֿוֿסֿו	Mur 88 18.6
Hab 1:8	ופֿשׁוֿ	ופֿשׁוֿ	[שׁוֿפֿ]	Mur 88 18.6

154

Biblical Passage	Pesharim, Other Commentaries, and Related Documents	MT	Other DSS	
Hab 1:8	ופרשׁו פרשו	ופשו פרשיו	[ ] וֹשׁיֹם	Mur 88 18.6
Hab 1:9	כלוֹ	כלה	לכה	Mur 88 18.7
Hab 1:9	קדים	קדימה	ה[ ]	Mur 88 18.7
Hab 1:10	יקלס	יתקלס	מֹלֹהי	Mur 88 18.8
Hab 1:10	והוא	הוא	—	—
Hab 1:10	ויתלולֹ	יתלוֹלֹ	הֹהוֹיֹ	Mur 88 18.9
Hab 1:10	זו שׂם זו	זו ואשׂם	[אׂו]	Mur 88 18.9
Hab 1:11	למוֹכיחוֹ	להוכיח	הֹוֹהֹתֹ	Mur 88 18.11
Hab 1:12	נגלא	לא	—	—
Hab 1:13	סבוֹט	מבוֹט	—	—
Hab 1:13	והחרשׁ	תחרישׁ	—	—
Hab 1:13	ובבלע	כבלע	—	—
Hab 1:14	כרמשׂ	לא כרמשׂ	—	—
Hab 1:14	יהיב	יהיה	—	—
Hab 1:15	ויהוֹה	יהוה	—	—
Hab 1:15	ויאספֹה	ויאספהו	—	—
Hab 1:15	בחם	נחמה	—	—
Hab 1:16	לֹע	לאכל	—	—
Hab 1:16	הדגה	דגה	—	—
Hab 1:17	תמיד	תמיד	—	—
Hab 1:17	נגלא	לא	—	—

155

Biblical Passage	Pesharim, Other Commentaries, and Related Documents		MT	Other DSS	
Hab 2:1	1QpHab 6.13	מצפי	מצור	—	
Hab 2:2	1QpHab 7.3	הלוקרא	קורא	—	
Hab 2:3	1QpHab 7.6	יפח	יפח	נפ̇ח̇	Mur 88 18.19
Hab 2:3	1QpHab 7.9	ולוא	לוא	—	
Hab 2:5	1QpHab 8.3	הון	ייין	—	
Hab 2:5	1QpHab 8.3	בגבר	גבר	—	
Hab 2:5	1QpHab 8.4	ולא	ולא	—	
Hab 2:5	1QpHab 8.5	יאסוף	יאסף	—	
Hab 2:5	1QpHab 8.5	ויקבוץ	יקבץ	—	
Hab 2:6	1QpHab 8.6	וילילמו	כל־אלה	—	
Hab 2:6	1QpHab 8.7	ולידו	וליד	—	
Hab 2:6	1QpHab 8.7	ולוא	לא	—	
Hab 2:6	1QpHab 8.7	יכבד	מכבד	—	
Hab 2:7	1QpHab 8.13	פתע[ ]אום	מתעתעים	—	
Hab 2:7	1QpHab 8.13	ויקום	יקום	—	
Hab 2:8	1QpHab 9.3	השליתה	שלות	[ ]שלו̇	Mur 88 18.26
Hab 2:9	1QpHab 9.12	הבוצע	בצע	—	
Hab 2:9	1QpHab 9.13	לצב	להציל	—	
Hab 2:10	1QpHab 9.14	קצות	קצות	—	
Hab 2:10	1QpHab 9.14 and 10.2	וחמס	חטוא	—	
Hab 2:12	1QpHab 10.6	וכונן	וכונן	—	
Hab 2:13	1QpHab 10.7	מעם	מאת	—	

Biblical Passage	Pesharim, Other Commentaries, and Related Documents		MT	Other DSS	
Hab 2:13	1QpHab 10.7	יגֿע	ייגֿעו	—	
Hab 2:14	1QpHab 10.15	הֿים	ים	—	
Hab 2:15	1QpHab 11.2	והֿבֿיט	והֿבֿיט	—	
Hab 2:15	1QpHab 11.3	מֿחֿתֿה	מֿחֿתֿה	—	
Hab 2:15	1QpHab 11.3	אֿף	ואֿף	—	
Hab 2:15	1QpHab 11.3	מֿעֿוריֿהֿם	מֿעֿוריֿהֿם	—	
Hab 2:16	1QpHab 11.9	מֿכֿבֿד	מֿכֿבֿד	—	
Hab 2:16	1QpHab 11.9	הֿעֿרֿל	הֿעֿרֿל	—	
Hab 2:17	1QpHab 12.1	יֿחֿתֿה	יֿחֿתֿן	—	
Hab 2:17	1QpHab 12.7	קֿיֿר	קֿיֿר	—	
Hab 2:18	1QpHab 12.10	פֿסֿל	פֿסֿל	פֿסֿלֿו	Mur 88 19.1
Hab 2:18	1QpHab 12.11	מֿסֿכֿה	מֿסֿכֿה	מֿ[ ]סֿכֿה	Mur 88 19.1
Hab 2:18	1QpHab 12.11	וֿמֿ	וֿמֿרֿה	הֿ[ ]	Mur 88 19.1
Hab 2:18	1QpHab 12.11	יֿצֿר	יֿצֿר	[ ]צֿ[ ]	Mur 88 19.1
Hab 2:18	1QpHab 12.11	עֿלֿיֿוֿ	עֿלֿיֿ	[יֿ]	Mur 88 19.1
Hab 2:20	1QpHab 13.1	וֿמֿבֿלֿו	וֿמֿבֿמֿה	וֿיֿ[ ]לֿ	Mur 88 19.3
Hab 2:20	1QpHab 13.1	הֿרֿ	הֿאֿרֿץ	הֿאֿרֿץ	Mur 88 19.3
Zeph 1:13	4Q170 frgs. 1-2 line 3	וֿשֿ[סֿה]	וֿמֿשֿסֿה	—	
Zeph 2:1	1Q15 line 2	הֿתֿקֿוֿשֿשֿ[וֿ]	הֿתֿקֿושֿשֿוֿ	וֿהֿתֿקֿושֿשֿוֿ	Mur 88 20.11
Zeph 2:1	1Q15 line 2	[וֿשֿ]וֿקֿ[וֿ]	וֿשֿוֿקֿוֿ	וֿקֿוֿ	Mur 88 20.11
Zeph 2:2	1Q15 line 3a	בֿטֿרֿם	בֿטֿרֿם	בֿטֿרֿם	Mur 88 20.12
Zech 3:9	4Q177 frgs. 7,9-11,20,26 line 2	[וֿשֿמֿתֿיֿ]	וֿשֿמֿתֿיֿ	וֿשֿמֿתֿיֿ	4Q78 frgs. 7-11 line 10

Biblical Passage	Pesharim, Other Commentaries, and Related Documents	MT		Other DSS
Zech 3:9	4Q177 frgs. 7,9-11,20,26 line 2	מחֿהֿ[וברה]	מחצב	חחה[ ]	4Q78 frgs. 7-10 line 10
Zech 3:9	4Q177 frgs. 7,9-11,20,26 line 2	פתחה	פתחה	—	—
Zech 3:9	4Q177 frgs. 7,9-11,20,26 line 2	ונאם	נאם	—	—
Mal 1:14	5Q10 frg. 1 line 1	מלושחה	מלושחה	—	—
Mal 3:16	4Q253a 1.1	[את]	את	על	4Q76 4.3
Mal 3:17	4Q253a 1.2	ויר	ויר	ויריו	4Q76 4.4

Bibliography

Pesharim, Other Commentaries, and Related Documents	Charlesworth, James H., et al., eds. *The Dead Sea Scrolls: The Pesharim, Other Commentaries, and Related Documents*. PTSDSSP 6B. Tübingen: Mohr (Siebeck); Louisville: Westminster John Knox, 2002.
1QIsa[a]	Burrows, Millar, with John C. Trever and William H. Brownlee, eds. *The Dead Sea Scrolls of St. Mark's Monastery*. New Haven: American Schools of Oriental Research, 1950-51.
	Trevor, John C. *Scrolls from Qumrân Cave I*. Jerusalem: Albright Institute of Archaeological Research and Shrine of the Book, 1972.
1QS	Charlesworth, James H., et al., eds. *The Dead Sea Scrolls: Rule of the Community and Related Documents*. PTSDSSP 1. Tübingen: Mohr (Siebeck); Louisville: Westminster John Knox, 1994.
1Q2 (1QExod)	Barthélemy, Dominique, and J. T. Milik, eds. *Qumran Cave I*. DJD 1. Oxford: Clarendon, 1955.
1Q5 (1QDeut[b])	DJD 1
1Q8 (1QIsa[b])	DJD 1
	Sukenik, Eleazar L., ed. *The Dead Sea Scrolls of the Hebrew University*. Jerusalem: Magnes, 1955.
4Q1 (4QGen-Exod[a])	Ulrich, Eugene C., and Frank M. Cross et al., eds. *Qumran Cave 4.VII: Genesis to Numbers*. DJD 12. Oxford: Clarendon, 1994.
4Q11 (4QpaleoGen-Exod[l])	Skehan, Patrick W., Eugene C. Ulrich, and Judith E. Sanderson, eds. *Qumran Cave 4.IV: Palaeo-Hebrew and Greek Biblical Manuscripts*. DJD 9. Oxford: Clarendon, 1992.

4Q14 (4QExod^c)	DJD 12
4Q22 (4QpaleoExod^m)	DJD 9
4Q30 (4QDeut^c)	Ulrich, Eugene C., and Frank M. Cross, eds. *Qumran Cave 4.IX: Deuteronomy, Joshua, Judges, Kings.* DJD 14. Oxford: Clarendon, 1995.
4Q33 (4QDeut^f)	DJD 14
4Q34 (4QDeut^g)	DJD 14
4Q35 (4QDeut^h)	DJD 14
4Q37 (4QDeut^j)	DJD 14
4Q38 (4QDeut^{k1})	DJD 14
4Q45 (4QpaleoDeut^r)	DJD 9
4Q55 (4QIsa^a)	Ulrich, Eugene C., et al., eds. *Qumran Cave 4.X: The Prophets.* DJD 15. Oxford: Clarendon, 1997.
4Q56 (4QIsa^b)	DJD 15
4Q57 (4QIsa^c)	DJD 15
4Q58 (4QIsa^d)	DJD 15
4Q59 (4QIsa^e)	DJD 15
4Q60 (4QIsa^f)	DJD 15
4Q61 (4QIsa^g)	DJD 15
4Q63 (4QIsa^j)	DJD 15
4Q68 (4QIsa^o)	DJD 15
4Q69 (4QpapIsa^p)	DJD 15
4Q69a (4QIsa^q)	DJD 15
4Q70 (4QJer^a)	DJD 15
4Q72 (4QJer^c)	DJD 15
4Q76 (4QXII^a)	DJD 15
4Q78 (4QXII^c)	DJD 15
5Q1 (5QDeut)	Baillet, Maurice, J. T. Milik, Roland de Vaux, and H. Wright Baker, eds. *Les 'Petites Grottes' de Qumrân.* DJD 3. Oxford: Clarendon, 1962.
11Q5 (11QPs^a)	Sanders, James A., ed. *The Psalms Scroll of Qumrân Cave 11 (11QPs^a).* DJD 4. Oxford: Clarendon, 1965.
Mur 2 (Deut)	Benoit, Pierre, J. T. Milik, and Roland de Vaux, eds. *Les Grottes de Murabb'at.* DJD 2. Oxford: Clarendon, 1961.
Mur 88 (XII)	DJD 2
Mas1e (MasPs^a)	Talmon, Shemaryahu, and Yigael Yadin, eds. *Masada VI: The Yigael Yadin Excavations 1963-1965, Final Reports.* Jerusalem: Israel Exploration Society, 1999.

Index of Biblical Texts

Index of Dead Sea Scrolls

Index of Other Ancient Writings

Index of Modern Authors

Index of Subjects

Alcimus, 34
Alexander Jannaeus, 20, 47, 92, 99-106, 114-15
Alexandra Salome, 20
AMS C-14, 49
anonymity, 12
Antiochus IV *(Epiphanes)*, 114, 117
archaeology, 19

calendar, 13, 27, 57
celibacy, 62-65

Demetrius III *(Eukerus)*, 112-17

Eleazar the Pharisee, 33
Ephraim, 4, 106-9

Formulae, of pesharim, 4, 80-81
fulfillment hermeneutics, 6, 14-16, 116

Gilead, 4

Hebrew language, 18-19
Herod the Great, 51-52
House of Absalom, 8
House of Judah, 4
House of Peleg, 107-8
Hyrcanus II, 92, 110

James the Just, 33
Jesus of Nazareth, 33, 35
John Hyrcanus, 33, 44, 66, 98
John the Baptist, 33
Jonathan, 34, 36-37, 44, 91-92
Judas Maccabeus, 32
Judah, 106-9
Judah the Essene, 33

Kittim, 2, 73, 103, 109-12, 117

Man of the Lie(s), 36, 65, 67, 89, 94-97, 117
Manasseh, 4, 106-9, 117
Mattathias, 32
Menahem (son of Judas), 33
miqva'oth and cisterns, 42, 45-46, 58

neutron activation analysis, 59-60, 75
numismatics (coins), 44, 47, 52, 58-59

Onias III, 32, 92
Onias the Righteous, 33

Paleo-Hebrew, 7
Parthian invasion of 40 B.C.E., 50-51
Pharisees, 20, 47-49, 97-98, 101, 108